12791

The Last Exquisite

The Last Exquisite

A PORTRAIT OF
FREDERIC MANNING

Verna Coleman

MELBOURNE UNIVERSITY PRESS

1990

First published in 1990
Printed in Australia by
Brown Prior Anderson Pty Ltd, Burwood, Victoria, for
Melbourne University Press, Carlton, Victoria 3053
U.S.A. and Canada: International Specialized Book Services, Inc.,
5602 N.E. Hassalo Street, Portland, Oregon 97213-3640

National Library of Australia Cataloguing-in-Publication entry

Coleman, Verna.
   The last exquisite: a portrait of Frederic Manning.
   Bibliography.
   Includes index.
   ISBN 0 522 84370 0.
   1. Manning, Frederic, 1882-1935—Biography. 2. Authors,
   Australian—Biography. I. Title.
A828.209

To Peter

Contents

Illustrations

Acknowledgements

Manuscript material is reproduced by permission of the following individuals and libraries. My thanks are due to them all, but especially to Mrs Patricia Dickson, daughter of Sir Henry Manning and niece of Frederic Manning, for her interest and the information she provided in discussions about the Manning family. My special thanks also to Alister Kershaw for his help and encouragement.

For permission to quote from manuscripts I would like to thank: Mrs Patricia Dickson for Manning manuscripts and other documents; Alister Kershaw, literary executor of Richard Aldington, for permission to quote from Richard Aldington manuscripts and printed works; T. E. Lawrence Trust, for the letters of T. E. Lawrence; Omar S. Pound, for permission to use photographs; Mary de Rachewiltz for the Pound papers.

Quotations from manuscripts are also by permission of the following institutions and my thanks are due to them all. For the Fairfax papers, Australian Collections and Services, the National Library of Australia, Canberra. For the Manning papers and other manuscripts as noted, Australian Research Collections and Mitchell Library, State Library of New South Wales, Sydney. For the Houtin correspondence, Department of Manuscripts, Bibliothèque Nationale, Paris. For the Harriet Monroe *Poetry* correspondence, Manuscripts and Archives Special Collection, Joseph Regenstein Library, University of Chicago. For the Pound papers and the Newbolt collection, Collection of American Literature, Beinecke Rare Book and Manuscript Library, Yale University. New Haven, Connecticut. For the Rothenstein collection, The Houghton Library, Harvard University, Cambridge, Massachusetts. For letters in the Derek Patmore collection, Harry Ransom Humanities Research Center, The University of Texas at Austin.

My thanks are due to the staffs of the above libraries, and also to those of the Australian War Museum, Canberra, The Imperial War Museum, London, the Archives Authority of New South Wales, the Australian Biographical Centre, the Australian National University, Canberra, the State Library of New South Wales and the British Library.

For permission to quote from printed material acknowledgements are due to the following publishers: Edward Arnold Ltd for E. M. Forster's *The Longest Journey* and *Howard's End*; Methuen and Co. for *The Letters of Wyndham Lewis*, ed. W. K. Rose; William Heinemann Ltd for Henry Handel Richardson's *Myself When Young* and *The Getting of Wisdom* and Max Beerbohm's *Zuleika Dobson*; John Murray Ltd for James Griffyth Fairfax's *The Fifth Element*; Macmillans Ltd for John Maynard Keynes's *Two Memoirs*; Hamish Hamilton for Albert Camus's *The Plague*, trans. Stuart Gilbert; Jonathan Cape Ltd for *The Letters of T. E. Lawrence*, ed. David Garnett; Faber and Faber for Patricia Hutchins's *Ezra Pound's Kensington*, Ezra Pound's *Guide to Kulchur, Literary Essays*, ed. T. S. Eliot, *A Lume Spento, Ezra Pound and Dorothy Shakespear. Their letters 1909-1914*, ed. Omar Pound and A. Walton Litz, *Letters of Ezra Pound*, ed. D. D. Paige, *Pound-Joyce. The Letters of Ezra Pound to James Joyce*, ed. Forrest Reid, *Pound-Lewis. The Letters of Ezra Pound and Wyndham Lewis*, ed. Timothy Materer and *Some Letters of Ezra Pound*, ed. Louis Dudek; Cornell University Press for William Murphy's *Prodigal Father*; Collins for Stephen Spender's *Eliot*; Weidenfeld and Nicolson Ltd for Mary McCarthy's *Occasional Prose*; New York Public Library for *A Passionate Prodigality: Letters to Alan Bird from Richard Aldington*, ed. M. J. Benkovitz; Viking for *Literary Lifelines. Richard Aldington–Lawrence Durrell Correspondence*, ed. Ian MacNiven and Harry T. Moore; University of Southern Illinois for Richard Aldington's *Selected Critical Writing*, ed. Alister Kershaw; Hogarth Press for Lyn Macdonald's Introduction to *Her Privates We*.

My thanks are also due to the following individuals for permission to quote: Rupert Hart-Davis for Max Beerbohm's *Seven Men*; Guy Boyd for Martin Boyd's *A Difficult Young Man, Retrospect, A Single Flame* and *When Blackbirds Sing*; Sir John Rothenstein for *Summer's Lease*, and (with Michael Rothenstein) for permission to reproduce Sir William Rothenstein drawings.

For their kind help in various matters I am indebted to Charles Seaton of the *Spectator*, Sam Harris, Professor Norman Gates, W. C. Wentworth, the Librarians at Sydney Grammar School and St Ignatius College, Riverview, Sydney, the Historic Houses Trust of New South Wales, Owen Harries, Ivan Katz and Tanya Costello.

Introduction:
The Man in Question

AT A PARTY in Venice in the 1960s,
given by Australian expatriate scholar and writer Bernard Hickey for the
young Australian writer, Desmond O'Grady, there was much pleasure at
the arrival of a very distinguished guest, Ezra Pound. The old poet, living
in seclusion after the storm resulting from his treason in World War II, and
the trauma of the years spent in an American asylum, rarely made such
appearances. He had withdrawn into silence, and if he spoke in public the
effect was almost startling.

O'Grady was talking about his homeland to Pound's companion of so
many years, Olga Rudge, and she shouted across the room to where Pound
stood, sunk in his customary silence: 'Why don't we go to Australia,
Ezra?' Back across the room came a quavering reply: 'Is . . . Frederic . . .
Manning . . . still . . . there . . . ?'[1] The guests standing around may well
have muttered to themselves: 'Frederic who?' Who was this person whose
name could break into Pound's isolation? He was not well known in most
literary circles.

Pound, his memories stirred, was reaching back into the past, crossing
five decades to his own youthful years in London, before the Great War of
1914. A somewhat controversial figure even then, young, cranky and
ablaze with energy and determined ambition, he had admired and become
quite friendly with a delicate scholar and versifier, Fred Manning, 'very
much of the *Spectator*',[2] a typical English Edwardian man-of-letters, it
might seem. The content of Pound's cry across the room indicated another
aspect of this exquisite person and writer, one of the paradoxes associated
with his elusive figure; for Fred Manning, 'the last of the aesthetes'[3] was
born and raised in the distant cultural wilderness of New South Wales in
the Victorian age.

This was the Manning Ezra Pound knew, before the aesthete
metamorphosed, for a few years, into the man of action and became Private
19022 in the British Army and fought on the Somme. The soldier in turn,

1

a decade after the war, became the novelist, the author of one of the great books of that unbelievable war and one of the great books on war in general, best known in England and Australia as *Her Privates We*, and in the United States as *The Middle Parts of Fortune*. (The latter name seems to be gaining the ascendancy today.) That his finest work should have two names is a fitting symbol of the double-nature of this scholar-soldier with a double nationality, who faced both ways on the Edwardian literary cusp, looking back to the 1890s in his verses, looking forward to modern theories of existentialism in his prose. A Catholic who was an Epicurean philosopher, a sceptic who was a believer, a Tory who was a democrat, loving the ordinary man but hating the mob, a recluse who had a gift for friendship, a soldier in the worst of modern battles who was terrified of crossing Piccadilly Circus before the war,[4] a bachelor with affectionate relationships with both men and women, Frederic Manning was a complex, puzzling and intriguing personality as well as a fine writer.

Why then 'forgotten Fred'; called by one critic, a little extravagantly, 'perhaps the most elusive figure in modern literature',[5] the unknown Australian writer, neglected as far as most Australians are concerned? How many recognize the name of one of the few Australian writers who has won some overseas fame? Despite the scholarly research that has been done by Professor Laurence Hergenhan on Manning's life and work,[6] and the stimulating articles by John Douglas Pringle, Stephen Murray-Smith and Leonard Mann, among others, Frederic Manning still has little recognition in Australia, except among students of literature. Why this state of affairs when there is such broad interest today among Australians in the writings of Australians?

Fundamentally it must be due to the fact that he lived so long abroad and belonged to the class of expatriates. It also has much to do with the fact that he published his most successful book under a pseudonym. Katherine Mansfield, of course, did much the same and is certainly not unknown in her native New Zealand. But Frederic Manning, shy and retiring and nervous, avoided the publicity associated with using his own name in his best known book. Dogged by bronchial asthma all his life he was forced to live quietly, away from the literary centre in London, sequestered in the English countryside. In consequence he had little to do with the circles and cliques of the English literary world, preferring to devote himself to his art; and he was such a perfectionist that his output was slight. He was contemptuous too of the influential, middlebrow literary establishment in England in the 1920s, represented by J. C. Squire and his friends. On the other hand he was not a member of the literary avant-garde. Consequently his name even then, when he was living and working, was little known. The *Spectator* on which he was leading reviewer for some years did not use bylines.

The lack of knowledge of his work in his homeland has much to do also with the inturned nationalism of Australia in the 1930s, the period of the first great success of *Her Privates We*. Struggling to encourage an indigenous, typically Australian literature, local critics looked for local subjects and local flavour. Manning's work was international. Nettie Palmer declined to claim him, regretfully, in the 1930s;[7] H. M. Green left him out of his *Outline of Australian Literature* (1930) and his *Australian Literature 1900 to 1950* (1951) but included him in *A History of Australian Literature, Pure and Applied* ten years later. Cecil Hadgraft also omitted Manning from his *Australian Literature: a critical account to 1955*, which was published in 1960, although Morris Miller's *Bibliography of Australian Literature*, extended by F. T. Macartney in 1956, noticed him in a few lines.

The mood began to change in the 1960s, however, with a revival of interest in war literature overseas and the work begun by J. T. Laird on Australian literature of World War I. Today the *Oxford Companion to Australian Literature* (1985) and Leonie Kramer's selection of prose and verse over two hundred years, *My Country*, of the same year, both accept Manning without question as an Australian writer. As Australian society has become more confident, less insular and less isolated, the international complexity of Frederic Manning has been recognized, as in Robin Gerster's *Big-Noting: The Heroic Theme in Australian War Writing* (1987). Manning can belong both to Australia and the world.

Manning's war novel was acclaimed overseas on first publication, 1929–30, by such famous names as Arnold Bennett and E. M. Forster, as well as by fellow expatriate and ex-A.I.F. soldier, Eric Partridge, who called the work 'a perdurable masterpiece'.[8] Since then Frederic Manning's war writings, both prose and poetry, have aroused interest in a number of literary critics abroad, as well as among the historians John Terraine, Lyn Macdonald and, most notably, Michael Howard, who wrote of Manning, in the introduction to the English edition of 1977, which carried the title *The Middle Parts of Fortune*:

> an unlikely figure to be responsible for what is without doubt one of the greatest books about soldiers in the whole of western literature . . .
> For this is a book not so much about war as about men. The war itself is background and environment: as in all great tragedy, the theme is human destiny and suffering as experienced by a small group of individuals. That is what sets it apart from, and indeed above the work of such better known writers as Edmund Blunden, Robert Graves and Siegfried Sassoon . . . [It is] as timeless as Aeschylus.

Manning has figured in the major studies on war literature by Cyril Falls, Bernard Bergonzi, H. M. Klein, Andrew Rutherford and C. N. Smith. Bergonzi asserts that he 'treats war with a Shakespearian inclusiveness, concretely, presenting the humour as well as the horror and pathos' and he praises his war poem, 'The Face', saying 'Manning writes about death with a delicacy that shows up the comparative crudeness of Aldington's treatment';[9] while Andrew Rutherford calls *Her Privates We*: 'one of the masterpieces of war literature in English'.[10]

Leading American critics have been as warm in their acclaim as English, among them Paul Fussell, and Mary McCarthy, who wrote of the Great War: 'Out of that war, the English, as far as I remember, produced only a single novel, though that was a masterpiece, first published, in expurgated form, as *Her Privates We* and written in fact by an Australian, Frederic Manning'.[11] The *aficionado* of courage, Ernest Hemingway, included a part of Manning's novel in his collection *Men at War: The Best War Stories of All Time*, first published in 1942 in the midst of another great struggle. He placed it in the section headed 'War demands resolution, firmness and staunchness'; and he wrote in his introduction: 'It is the finest and noblest book of men in war that I have ever read. I read it over each year to remember how things were so that I will never lie to myself nor to anyone else about them' (p. xi).

It may be that the neglect of Manning stems from his subject, war. It is not a happy topic and his attitude is a daunting one. There should be no war, we may say; and Manning replies: But there is. It exists. 'It is in the nature of things'.[12] He does not say this as a militarist; he has no love for blood and battle. He observes the world and sees that war is part of it. Several critics have noted the existentialist strain in his reflections on war, and the attitude of existentialist novelist Albert Camus in *The Plague*, seen in part as an allegory for war, has much in common with Manning's view: 'there have been as many plagues as wars in history', writes Camus

> yet always plagues and wars take people take people equally by surprise . . . When a war breaks out people say, 'It's too stupid; it can't last long'. But though a war may well be 'too stupid', that doesn't prevent it lasting. Stupidity has a knack of getting its way; as we should see if we were not always so much wrapped up in ourselves.
>
> In this respect our townsfolk were like everybody else, wrapped up in themselves; in other words they were humanists; they disbelieved in pestilences. A pestilence isn't a thing made to man's measure; therefore we tell ourselves that pestilence is a mere bogey of the mind, a bad dream that will pass away. But it doesn't always pass away and, from one bad dream to another, it is men who pass away, and humanists first of all, because they haven't taken their precautions.[13]

Manning's is a pessimistic view and the history of this century seems to have borne it out; from the Russo–Japanese War of 1904 to the recent bitter conflict between Iran and Iraq, and the other bloody and passionate struggles in which modern man is engaged. It is the great fact of our century. Manning does not engage in controversy over the causes of war, or argue rights and wrongs. As Mary McCarthy writes in her article:

> A curious aspect of this pure and beautiful work . . . is the absence of politics from it, as remarkable in its way as the same absence in *The Iliad*, and I mean

politics of any kind–there is neither glorification nor condemnation of war, still less of 'our' side in contrast to the enemy beyond the barbed wire, and, most unusual of all, no idealisation of the class of privates as opposed to the officer class that made up the basic politics of of American war fiction. We will not find that neutrality in our war literature, which has a strong accusatory ring; none of our soldier authors could have written these two sentences (from the prefatory note to *Her Privates We*, 1929): 'War is waged by men, not by beasts, or by gods. To call it a crime against mankind is to miss at least half of its significance; it is also a punishment for a crime'.

In Manning's view individuals, or groups of individuals, nations, will always seek power, revenge, glory, wealth. This is the crime which brings the punishment not only to those like Hitler and Stalin, the evil-doers, but to the innocent as well, their victims; and the innocent may have to oppose them. Manning was not happy with this conclusion. His favourite saint and one of his favourite characters was sweet and gentle Francis of Assisi, a 'fool for Christ's sake',[14] who loved the beauty of the world and God's creatures and was incapable of doing harm to any living thing. He saw, however, that many others are as evil and cruel and stupid as Francis was loving.

It is an austere, stark view, little in tune with the happy-go-lucky optimism, the 'she'll be right, mate' position of most Australians today, or with the attitude that there is a solution for every problem. Manning was too aware of the unreason of man to expect that war would disappear magically after century upon century of strife. His sympathy with humanity in its sufferings made him hope, however, that that some answer to the moral problem of war might be found one day. His Preface ends: 'Perhaps some future attempt to provide a solution for it may prove to be even more astonishing than the last'. He may well have been astonished at how the uneasy peace is sustained between the great powers today. As his terrible war had been hailed as the war to end war, his pessimism is not surprising. But Manning, always two-faceted, was pessimist-optimist. Against the great fact of war he sets the comradeship of human beings, the theme of perhaps the most typical of Australian writers, Henry Lawson. War is an allegory of human suffering, to be overcome by tenderness, endeavour and endurance. Manning asserts a belief in life and in the nobility of ordinary people.

The solemnity of his subject and his philosophical reflections are lightened by some humorous scenes and characters; but the basic concept is deeply serious. The theme of *Her Privates We* is universal, as relevant to Australians as to the English or the people of any nation which has suffered in war. In like manner his earlier prose work, the set of stories known as *Scenes and Portraits* (1909), deals with general ideas about the place of religion in human affairs and the question of the existence of God in the face of human suffering. These two thoughtful, small classics are not works likely to be popular, though in its day, the war novel was a best seller and it is still in print. As the products of an artistic and intellectual talent of high level, however, they are contributions to the world of the spirit and art. In that sense Frederic Manning is an Australian who has left his country a legacy. He has earned his 'well-upholstered niche in our literature'[15] as T. E. Lawrence expressed it, both as prose writer and as poet.

The Australian interest in his life extends beyond his work, into his background and the circumstances which formed him. That arch-expatriate, T. S. Eliot, who transformed himself during his years in England into an Englishman, as far as possible, maintained that a writer's art must be 'racial', based on the sensations of the first twenty-one years.[16] Manning's friend, Ezra Pound, so long an expatriate, so centred on Europe, could not cease to be an American. And Patrick White, who spent a number of years abroad, has stressed the importance to the artist of earliest experience, 'the purest well from which the creative artist draws'.[17] Although Frederic Manning did not write about the country of his birth, he spent the first fifteen years of his life in Sydney, followed by another three years between eighteen and twenty-one and then two years in long visits after the war. In all he spent rather more time in his birthplace than that other great expatriate writer, Henry Handel Richardson, who left Melbourne at the age of eighteen and returned only once, for a visit of a few weeks. Frederic Manning was an odd and unusual Australian, but as far as he possessed a nationality that was it; and his life bore the marks of its origins. It was in the interaction of his family with the Australian society of the late nineteenth century that the basis of his nature was laid.

Unfortunately, that early life is not well documented and the material of the later years is patchy, so that some important friendships, especially that with Eva Fowler, cannot be given the space they may deserve. Perhaps at some future date caches of letters and writings may be discovered which will make possible the traditional definitive biography of this elusive man.[18] At the moment, however, sufficient material survives in his works and letters to present a portrait of the writer, his character, his views, his friendships and his achievements, against an impressionistic background of his times and places, in a life span linking the Victorian age in Australia to the modern age in England.

1

Young Fred and Family

IN FEBRUARY 1930 Lawrence of Arabia wrote to his confidant, Charlotte Shaw, wife of George Bernard Shaw, about a new friend: 'Manning is a very exquisite person: so queer'.[1] Himself a rather strange man, Lawrence was underlining the touch of mystery, of puzzlement that surrounded the personality of Frederic Manning: on the one hand an Edwardian scholar and poet, an aesthete of aesthetes, a friend of the young Ezra Pound and of other poets; on the other, Private 19022 in the British Army on the Somme and the chronicler of the experience of the British Tommy in that terrible battle. Both scholar and soldier, he exemplified in his life the double-natured quality which he admired in others.

The oddness of Manning extends further; this exquisite person, this 'intellectual of intellectuals',[2] this English soldier, had emerged from a most unlikely background. His ancestry was Irish Catholic, his upbringing was colonial and his birthplace was the remote and provincial town of Sydney, New South Wales, then only two generations removed from its convict past.

His family roots lay in Ireland. His paternal grandfather, John Manning, a baker from County Cork, arrived in Sydney as a free settler on the *Moffatt* in 1841, with his future wife, Mary Hourigan.[3] The early 1840s were not an easy time for newcomers, with hundreds of emigrants starving in the streets, according to one of the number who survived, future Premier, Henry Parkes.[4] And Sydney was still a raw town, very close to its unhappy origins. Old lags from Van Diemen's Land hung about the streets and bushranging ex-convicts still terrorized remote farms. The Mannings, however, survived, with many others like them; and the fine Government House, into which Governor Gipps moved in 1845, symbolized the solidity and respectability that such free settlers sought. Some big landholders continued to fume over the loss of cheap labour with the abandonment of the transportation of convicts to New South Wales but most citizens of

Sydney, particularly investors, merchants and professional men wanted to wipe out the old stain and to build a society based on the purchasing power of a free and prosperous population. In the rise of the colonial bourgeoisie, to use Professor Manning Clark's term, John Manning's son, William, born in the working-class suburb of Chippendale in November 1845, was to play a vigorous part.

John Manning later moved to the eastern edge of the town, to Norton Street, Darlinghurst, a street of small tradesmen: carpenters, tailors, millers, builders. It was a suburb of fine houses as well as of workmen's cottages; in nearby Pott's Point the splendid mansions of the rich looked down over the harbour from their lush gardens. Young William Manning could observe, as he grew, that not everybody lived in little houses in the shabby streets shadowed by Darlinghurst Gaol. A bright boy, however hampered by being one of the Irish Catholic underdogs, could learn his letters and figures at St Mary's Cathedral School and plan to move up in this open, if rough, society. His parents had not made a fortune, but he might; many of the great names in early colonial history rested on simple beginnings.

William Manning did not follow his father's trade. At sixteen he took a step up the social ladder, becoming a junior clerk in the counting house of the Sydney Foundry and Engineering Works. This firm, headed by a Scottish-born engineer, Peter Nicol Russell, had prospered during the gold rushes, selling tools and machinery to the miners, and had moved on into government contracts for railways and steam dredges. Young William showed such financial skills that he eventually became chief accountant and Peter Nicol Russell, who left the colony a very rich man to settle in England, entrusted his bright employee with the control of his Australian investments.

On 8 August 1868, at St Mary's Cathedral, William Manning, aged twenty-two, married a twenty-year-old woman of similar background, Irish-born Catholic, Honora (Nora) Torpy, daughter of a dressmaker, Honora Mihill and an Irish farmer, John Torpy (or Torphy). The rise in the world of this energetic and talented pair can be charted from their changes of address. In 1869 they were living in crowded Darlinghurst, at 323 Bourke Street. Their first child, Felicia (Dot), was born in 1871. Their first son, William Ernest (Will), arrived in 1873, followed by another daughter, Edith, in 1875. As Sydney grew, and railways developed and the hinterland opened up, the trade of this busy port increased. William Manning, building up a reputation as a shrewd adviser on investments, prospered. The firm of Peter Nicol Russell closed in 1874 after an industrial dispute. By 1875 Manning was in practice as an accountant at 294 Victoria Street, Darlinghurst.

The second son, Henry (Harry), was born in 1877, and the third, John (Jack), in 1879. By this time the family had moved to developing Paddington—to Glenview Street—with its pleasant, spacious terraces decorated with iron lace and Italian tiles, built for middle-class occupation by clerks, shopkeepers and small business men, each house enjoying its own small garden. The expanding eastern suburbs were pleasant places to live. Edged by the city on the west, by the long, white, lagoon-fringed beach of Bondi on the east, by the harbour to the north and by the open ground of the future Centennial Park to the south, they were full of space and sunshine. Wildflowers still bloomed on Bellevue Hill and the Chinese market gardens on the site of the future Royal Sydney Golf Club spread a green blanket around Rose Bay. Jacarandas and frangipanni, wistaria and magnolias bloomed in the gardens of the village-like suburbs.

The city itself, however, was a different story: fine public buildings were surrounded by slums and crowded, dirty, narrow streets, choked with steam trams, horse omnibuses, delivery drays and hansom cabs. Livery stables and markets added to the refuse and the smells, and on nearly every corner there was a public house, open from 6 a.m. to 11 p.m. Drunks and larrikins infested the streets and the sanitary arrangements were 'almost invariably objectionable and disgusting'.[5] An English journalist, Francis Adams, who spent from 1884 to 1889 in the colonies, thought that no European manufacturing city boasted more hideous suburbs than those of working-class inner Sydney.[6] To the English eye matters were not all that much better among the wealthy. Their clothes lacked style, their houses and furniture were ugly, and gambling, drinking and swearing were as rife among the rich as among the poor. Not only visitors were critical. One native son described the Sydney of the 1880s as 'a crude community living mostly on beer and bread', with 'the old lawlessness . . . still there'.[7] It was small wonder that the English visitor often preferred 'marvellous' Melbourne, which boasted elegant mansions and a more cultured ambience. Most Sydneysiders, the beauty of the harbour shining in their eyes, seemed blind to man-made ugliness. It was a most unlikely environment to nourish a subtle and delicate mind, to produce an aesthete like Frederic Manning.

For even worse than the squalor and the slums, to a radical intellectual and disciple of Matthew Arnold like Francis Adams, were the boring provincial hedonism, the third-rate nature of the literary society and the sleaziness of the politics of New South Wales. He acknowledged, however, one great virtue. He found the emerging Australian type remarkably free from cant. And the bush life, with its sad, sweet charm, its pessimism and despair, was another world.

The fortunes of William Manning, the boy who had played marbles at school to win the textbooks he could not afford, continued to improve. As the city grew, older estates were carved up and fortunes were to be made in suburban and city land development. Manning was prominent in the affairs of the largest building society, the Sydney Permanent Freehold Building and Investment Society, and he represented the interests of large British investors like Billyard and Co. and Lords Rosebery and Sherbrooke. By 1882 he had opened a city office at 34 Castlereagh Street and moved his

family into a substantial house, Orvieto (later demolished), at 29 Upper
William Street South, which became with street rearrangements 35
Bayswater Road, Kings Cross. The shops of busy William Street were
close by, but at the top of the hill the old road had divided to skirt large
estates like Goderich Lodge, one of architect John Verge's fine contributions to early Sydney.

Near where the cars now charge down to Rushcutters Bay out of the
Kings Cross tunnel, the Manning children played.

> We played in this garden, long ago,
> Long ago! Wind stirs the young grasses;
> Petals drift from the apple-boughs
> Like snow, that covers up everything,
> Everything![8]

And they might watch, entranced, the flying objects sent soaring over
Rushcutters Bay Park from the back veranda of 40 Roslyn Gardens by
aeronautics pioneer, Lawrence Hargrave, who later became a 'close friend'
of young Frederic.[9]

Frederic Manning, as noted in the births column of the *Sydney Morning
Herald* (1 August 1882) was born at Orvieto on 22 July 1882, the same
year that welcomed to the world that quartet of modernists, Virginia
Woolf, James Joyce, Igor Stravinsky and Georges Braque, a year that could
be called a hidden turning point in the high tide of Victorianism. Fred, as
he was known to family and friends, was baptized a month later, on 22
August, in the little Church of the Sacred Heart, (now a school) near
Taylor Square, Darlinghurst. His reign as baby lasted until 1885 when he
was supplanted by Charles (Charlie); and the last child in the family,
Beatrice (Trix), was born in 1888, the year the colony of New South Wales
celebrated its centenary.

Manning's childhood was spent in comfortable enough surroundings,
but the children of the colonial middle class were raised usually amid the
typically ugly cretonne and cedar furnishings of the late Victorian age,
with a badly trained cook in the kitchen to ruin the plentiful food and a
good-natured but ignorant nursemaid as a model in manners. In this rough
and ready society there was little emphasis on the social graces and the
'good form' encouraged in prosperous English nurseries. Here broad
accents and free and easy ways prevailed.

But Australian children had one special factor in their upbringing which
softened the often graceless ambience. Mother was an ever present figure.
The children were not banished to a special region of their own, except in
a few very English style households. Babies lived in the family circle from
the time of their birth, lashed into a chair beside their mothers at meal
times, accompanying them on their household duties, being present when
visitors called. To an English eye Mother devoted herself too much to her
children, at the expense of her husband and her social life. But, for Frederic

Manning, this maternal solicitude may have laid the basis of his own concerned and gentle nature, and it led to a strong and life-long bond with his mother. Emotional Nora Manning was fiercely protective of her brood. When she heard that her eldest son, Will (later a crack jockey), was to ride in a steeplechase, she went out to the stables at Randwick to put a stop to it.

With William Manning so busy providing for his family and realizing his ambitions, the day-to-day dealings with the children fell heavily on Nora. Australian children were on the whole energetic physically, full of animal spirits, but Fred was an exception. From early years he was a semi-invalid, suffering so badly from chronic asthma that he was unable to go to school except for a brief period. The protective, loving mother became a key figure in a number of his later poems, reflecting the mother who had watched over him in his illnesses. Danäe weeps over the danger to her son Perseus; Demeter, the sorrowing mother, seeks her lost child, Persephone; a mother sings a lullaby over her frail son:

> Hush ye, hush! he is weak and ailing
> Send his mother his share of weeping:
> Hush ye, winds, from your endless wailing:
> Hush ye, hush ye, my babe is sleeping.[10]

The closeness to his mother led perhaps to his special relationships with older women in later life, and to a sensitive understanding of the joys and restraints of the maternal role, given expression in his poem, 'The Mother'. A woman sits in an orchard with her young son. The child is enchanted by the beauty of the blossom, and watching him

> . . . in her there stirs
> A dream, a delight, a wonder, her being knew not,
> Yet now remembers, wistfully, as a thing long lost.

The sense of loss mingles with her love for the child, and she 'Stoops over him quickly, with sudden, hot, passionate kisses'.

Small Fred, cosseted, perhaps over-protected, nevertheless had his special place in the hurly-burly of sibling relationships in a large, boisterous Irish-Australian family. The comradeship of these years lasted into adulthood and the children, grown, kept in touch over vast distances. Membership of such a company was a safeguard against self-centredness, though it may have meant that a tendency to bow to stronger wills and personalities developed too. Harry, however, was always ready to champion Fred, particularly against critical Will, and in later years he championed Fred's writings.

There was little, however, in this lively Sydney household to nurture deeply intellectual interests. There were intelligence, energy and ambition but nothing of the support for scholarly thought that existed in the great interbred scientific and literary families of nineteenth century England: the

Huxleys, Stracheys, Stephens, Trevelyans, Arnolds, Darwins, Haldanes, Macauleys, Gaskells, Wedgewoods, Priestleys, Russells and others. Sydney, it is true, could boast of a few cultured families in the British mould, centring mainly around the law and the university: Windeyers, Wises, McCallums and Badhams, as well as another Manning family, led by the English-born Chancellor of Sydney University, Sir William Montagu Manning. Such Anglo-Australian families, to use the term broadly, looked back to British traditions: to public schools and universities, to the Inns of Court, to Canterbury Cathedral or the great dissenting tradition, to London and Edinburgh and to British landscapes. Old loyalties held firm, and the motto of Sydney University, *sidere mens eadem mutato*, the same mind under a different star, summed up that wish to keep the essence of the old world alive in this distant land. Self-made William Manning, however brilliant and intelligent, was outside that inheritance with his Irish forebears and his Catholic faith. So young Fred carried, as further handicaps to his eventual emergence as a scholarly intellectual, his supposedly ignorant and feckless Irish ancestry, and his membership of that state within a state, that careful guardian of faith and thought, the Catholic Church in Australia.

By the time of his birth Australian Catholics had ridden out the storm of sectarianism which followed the attempted assassination of H.R.H. Prince Alfred, son of Queen Victoria, at Clontarf in Sydney in 1868, but much prejudice remained. The Church was embroiled in a running battle with the government over state aid for its schools. As well, Irish nationalism had become interwoven with the faith, so that Australian-born children in parish schools could sing fervently of a land they had never seen, that mournful hymn of the Irish exile, 'Hail Glorious Saint Patrick'. Although Fred's grandparents were Irish and his own mother was Irish born, his invalidism saved him from much of the double patriotism of Catholic schools and the anti-British bitterness often found there. He also escaped their educational methods, which, according to one pupil of those days, future surgeon and writer, Herbert Moran, were very bad, aiming at orthodoxy rather than scholarship. Moran formed the opinion that most of the Irish priests, who predominated in the church, disliked the ambitious members of their flock, preferring ignorant piety to dangerous learning, although many talented Irish-Australian Catholics longed to escape from the 'bleak moorland of perpetual resentment'.[11]

Native-born William Manning, however, managed to dwell fairly comfortably in a half-way house between countries being both Irish-Catholic and British-Australian. He was not much troubled by what the clergy might think. He had survived his parish schooling and prospered, balancing his religious inheritance against his business and political interests. Confident and talented, he took his religion as his birthright without too much fuss about theological points. As Fred later wrote: 'My father does not care two straws for orthodoxy, but has a vague notion that orthodoxy

is what he thinks himself'.[12] Strong-minded, self-willed William was prepared to send his sons to a non-Catholic school, if it suited him, or to
attend, with his wife, a Church of England wedding, both serious matters
in those days for lesser men.[13]

Despite his Irish background he was as loyal an imperialist and monar-
chist in this high tide of British imperialism as any member of the Protestant establishment, so much so that he earned the contempt of the
radical *Bulletin* for 'an historic grovel'[14] before the English aristocracy.
But in the growing swell of Australian nationalism that accompanied the
Centennial celebrations of 1888 his patriotic feelings for his native land
surfaced and he took up with his customary vigour the cause of the federation of the Australian colonies into one nation. The Centennial year was
one of much patriotic emotion and, no doubt, the highlight of little Fred's
life was the excitement of the great celebrations held then in Sydney. His
father, as a leading Catholic, was prominent in organizing the picnic held
by the Catholic community at Cabarita, on the Parramatta river, in honour
of Cardinal Moran and the bishops. As well, William Manning, in full evening dress, was one of the selected guests at the great Centennial Banquet,
to which tickets were a social honour. And the Town Hall, where William
Manning was an alderman, was seen by the *Sydney Morning Herald* as
perhaps the most beautiful sight in the decorated city, a fairy palace bright
with coloured lights and flags. The grand finale of the celebrations, with
the ships in the harbour lit up and fireworks exploding over the water, created an occasion to linger in the memory of a small child. An occasion, too,
to fire the nationalism of William, who began to turn his attention towards
Parliament.

In the early 1890s he was at the peak of his abilities. Irish-born Cardinal
Moran, who was determined Catholics should have an influence pro-
portional to their numbers, could be proud indeed of this influential and
prominent Catholic, especially when, in 1891, William Manning was
elected first citizen of his native city, Mayor of Sydney. He was Mayor again
in 1892 and in 1893, when he also became the member for South Sydney
in the Legislative Assembly. Small Fred, observing his father's adroit balancing act between his simple Irish ancestry and his membership of the
Anglo-Saxon establishment may have begun to speculate then on the
peculiar double-nature of great men; and he must have learnt from this
dynamo of a man lessons of perseverance and courage. On the other hand,
with his energy and drive and will, and his great practical gifts, William
Manning may well have been a somewhat overwhelming father to a delicate, impractical, young son. But young Fred, the odd one out among his
robust siblings, had the sensitivity and intelligence to see, no doubt, that
his brilliant father was also something of an oddity. Whatever their differences, he seems to have respected his father deeply, to have admired his
strength and individuality and to have appreciated his sense of justice.

The ambivalent position of the Mannings in Sydney society contrasts with the secure family standing of another Australian aesthete, novelist and soldier, Martin Boyd, who, set firmly in Melbourne's upper class, could trace his ancestry from Irish Protestant army officers, and from a line of Wiltshire squires, said to be kinsmen of St Thomas à Becket. In 'marvellous' Melbourne Boyd enjoyed the idyllic childhood of the prosperous Anglo-Australian gentry and grew up with its values, manners and snobberies, so that he remembered from his childhood 'nasal patriotic demonstrations by state school children, presided over by mayors, who, I had been led to believe, were not gentlemen'.[15] His family mixed easily with the very English viceregal set and looked to England as 'home', although 'for four generations . . . used to the sun'[16] the Boyds might have claimed to be as Australian as anyone. Both parents were talented artists, backed by a family tradition of a civilized life style in which art, beauty, pleasure and wit held an important place. And in Melbourne before the Great War, Boyd felt 'culture was thick in the air'.[17] Boyd's development as a writer and an aesthete was therefore not so surprising.

Young Fred lacked such cultural advantages. On the other hand his parents were by no means commonplace. They too had an eye for beauty and a sense of style. William was something of a dandy. Tall and handsome he always presented a distinguished appearance, whether in top hat and boutonniere for the races, or in the full court dress which later won him the nickname of 'the knight with the beautiful London Journal legs'.[18] Nora, too, though short and plump, dressed with flair and a sense of colour which showed off her splendid jewellery. William demonstrated as well a taste for fine houses and an interest in music. He was for many years President of the New South Wales Royal Royal Philharmonic Society, which in 1891 gave a performance in the Town Hall of an oratorio by a local composer. Philistine Sydney was not totally indifferent to the arts.

Francis Adams admitted that music was 'the saving clause' in this uncouth society. Music shops like Palings and Nicholsons flourished, every middle-class mother longed to have a pianist in the family and musical evenings abounded. Unhappily, as one acid-tongued visitor observed, there was no part of the world where you heard so much bad music.[19] The city also took a lively, if personality-centred, interest in the theatre. Hundreds waited outside Redfern Railway Station in 1891 to see Sarah Bernhardt arrive for a Sydney season, which included *La Dame aux Camélias*, and Mayor Manning hosted a Town Hall reception for her. Local actresses Nellie Stewart and Maggie Moore were idolized. It was, however, very much a broad-brush culture for the easy-going, middlebrow middle class. Fine discriminations, elitist interests had no place. That 'art, science and literature' were 'entirely without status'[20] in Australia meant nothing to the good-humoured masses crowding the streets of a Saturday night in search of enjoyment; nor did it matter much to parvenus wangling invitations to Government House.

And for any Sydney child there were delights enough: a trip to Manly

Beach, on a ferry bucketing the Pacific rollers as it crossed the Heads, with the thrill of waves plashing the decks; paddling in the ocean, clutching hands in delicious panic at the thought of the sharks lurking further out; feeding the ducks in the lily ponds of the Botanic Gardens, while on the rotunda the brass band blared; sandcastles and spades, space and sunshine for endless play in the summer Christmas, when the crowded city arcades were decorated with ferns and flowers, the pantomime took over the Theatre Royal and Handel's *Messiah* was performed in the Great Hall of the University by the Philharmonic Society. And in the winter, while for some children there was a ride on the steam merry-go-round at Belmore Markets, for the Manning clan, there were real horses when the family holidayed at Bowral in the southern tablelands. For the robust child it was an idyllic physical world.

What future lay ahead, however, for a delicate boy, 'ever gentle and retiring'[21] and 'precociously intelligent'[22] in such a materialist city with little interest in the things of the mind? It was a lonely place for those few individualists who found their happiness in scholarship, books and high culture. David Scott Mitchell, the great bibliophile and benefactor of the Mitchell Library, had turned into a reclusive eccentric; and the greatest poet of the day, Christopher Brennan, who preferred the French symbolists to bush balladists, was suffering from the pressures of a philistine puritanism which had no understanding of his brilliance.

In 1893, when Frederic was still only ten years old, the problem of his place in life lay, it seemed, some years in the future. He still belonged to childhood, that time which he described later as 'unsuspicious of the future, and forgetful of the past, but living always with a vivid intensity, in that little, shut-in pleasure house of the senses, the moment'.[23] But in May that year, an odd, middle-aged gentleman, arrived in Sydney, as Private Secretary to the newly appointed Governor, Sir Robert Duff. He came fortuitously, with no special interest in the colony or its people. He was to become in time, however, the major influence in Frederic Manning's life. His name was Arthur Howard Galton.

2

Mr Galton

O N 29 MAY 1893 the P. & O. liner, the
R.M.S. *Parramatta*, entered Sydney Harbour, and anchored in Neutral Bay
at 7.30 a.m.[1] It was not a typical blue and gold Sydney autumn morning;
the skies were grey and cloudy, the waters pewter-coloured. The few local
notabilities, however, were not to be put off by the weather and were determined to make the most of the arrival of a new English Governor. The
ships in the harbour ran up bunting and some flags flew on public buildings. At 8 a.m. Premier George Dibbs, that one-time republican, hastened
out by launch to greet His Excellency. Then the viceregal party proceeded
by the steamship, *Premier*, to the Man o' War steps and strolled to Government House. By grand English standards the house was small but Lady
Duff and her companions, who included Private Secretary Arthur Galton,
could admire the view and the gardens running down to the harbourside.
So far, so good, this late refugee from Grub Street might well have
thought. Four hundred pounds a year, a charming residence in the city, a
country house at Sutton Forest, servants galore and the use of a private
steam launch mitigated the pains of exile in this strange country.[2] But
first local pomp and ceremony had to be endured.

At 2 p.m. the viceregal party made its official first appearance in the
city to be welcomed again. As several bands struck up the national anthem
and the guns fired a salute, the *Premier* approached Circular Quay. Waiting to greet the Governor were the Premier, and beside him, some petty
point of precedence having been settled, the handsome Mayor of Sydney,
William Manning, decked in his official robes. The good-humoured crowd,
swollen to a few thousand or so by the grant of a half-holiday, let out some
hearty cheers. Banks might be crashing all around them, following the
disastrous droughts of the late 1880s and the consequent depression, but
citizens of this hedonistic town were always in a mood to celebrate, to
enjoy a parade and to show their loyalty to the old Queen. William
Manning, in his role as M.L.A. for South Sydney, had spoken frankly in

Parliament only a few weeks before about the deficiencies of colonial banking. This day, however, was for celebration of the tie with the Crown. The worthies made some speeches. Then the long procession set out for Government House: the mounted police, the Mayor and the Councillors, an escort of Lancers and a band, the handsome new Governor and his party in open carriages and the Premier, in a showy uniform that earned him some jeers from the crowd, bringing up the rear. It may well have been the high point of Arthur Galton's colonial service. No doubt the Manning children, including Fred, were present on this historic occasion to watch Papa in all his civic glory and to cheer the imposing bearded Governor and his entourage, including the dapper figure of the Private Secretary, so noticeably clean-shaven in that hirsute Victorian age.

'A little thing is sufficient to divert the whole course of our progress; it has even been said, by our philosophers, that the world itself is an accident, and that God is chance.'[3] Mr Galton, riding through the streets of Sydney, was scarcely godlike, but he was certainly Chance so far as Frederic Manning was concerned, for Galton's past and the boy's future were to become so linked that any account of the life of Frederic Manning must start with an investigation of the life and character of Arthur Galton.

He was born on 14 December 1852, the younger son of Herman Galton, a captain in the 60th Rifles and a member of the noted Midlands family of Howard Galtons centring around Hadzor House, Droitwich, Worcestershire.[4] The Galtons, along with the Priestleys, the Daltons, the Schimmelpennicks and the Huttons, had made the Old Lecture Theatre in Birmingham a great centre of scientific learning in the nineteenth century. Arthur Howard Galton was a cousin of eugenics pioneer, Sir Francis Galton, and of the noted military engineer, Sir Douglas Galton, and a connection of Erasmus and Charles Darwin. It was a family which included bishops, priests, barristers and soldiers as well as men of science. Galton also claimed links, through his Scottish-born mother, Mary Duff, with the aristocracy, as the second cousin of James Duff, the Duke of Fife, and as a connection of the Earl of Northumberland. (Manning accepted these claims.)[5] He was born, then, into a secure position in the English country gentry and had contacts with the British intellectual elite.

As a child growing up in the quiet and beautiful Worcestershire countryside, largely in the care of his grandmother, Isabella Galton, Galton's interests and pleasures were rural. He loved the outdoors, exercise, dogs and horses. And he loved his birthplace. 'As I was not born to be the squire I looked forward to being rector of my old home.'[6] The Galtons, originally Quakers, showed a tendency to conversions; and, Herman Galton having joined the Church of England in his youth, his son Arthur was raised in a hazy Anglicanism. After primary school at Leamington, preparatory school at Wimbledon and public school at Empire-oriented Cheltenham (Patrick White's later prison) he went up to Clare College, Cambridge, at the age of twenty, to read for the

Church. The quiet future he had looked forward to seemed fully assured.

But a refractory streak ran through the outwardly dutiful son. It was a difficult time for religious belief, with the Bible and tenets of faith challenged by science in general and Darwinism in particular, and with the Church of England still stunned by the conversion of one of its brightest stars, John Henry Newman, to Catholicism. Young Galton hungered after certainty. In the autumn of 1874, while staying overnight at the house of a Galton uncle who had been converted to Catholicism, he read one of his cousin's prayerbooks, *A Garden of the Soul*. He was converted on the spot by the text: 'Thou art Peter and upon this Rock I will build my church'. Here were the strength and conviction that his masterful nature demanded.

Previously Galton had been attracted by the solidity and nationalism of the Jewish faith and by the power of imperial Rome; now he responded to the clear-cut Papal theory. Impulsive and wilful, he was given to strong opinions and hasty decisions. His conversion had nothing of the anguished, 'one step enough for me', through a glass darkly, personal belief of Newman, nor was he drawn by the ritual that attracted a number of undergraduates in the late 1870s, including Oscar Wilde, nor by new theological arguments. Although he knew of Newman, 'As far as I was concerned the Oxford Movement might never have been started'.[7]

Six months later, without bothering to discuss the matter with his family, this head-strong youth was received into the Catholic Church at the fashionable Jesuit church at Farm Street in London. Outraged, his father offered this black sheep the choice of the colonies or a West Indian regiment. When the boy stood firm he was banished from home and his living allowance was cut off. Feeling injured and martyred, young Galton, who had hoped to finish his degree at Cambridge, took refuge with the community at the Brompton Oratory. Here he made another decision. Instead of being an Anglican clergyman he would become a Catholic priest.

His hard-to-please nature was disenchanted within two years, by the poor food, the lack of exercise, the foggy London climate and the little reading done at the Oratory. He transferred to the great Catholic college at Oscott, Birmingham, where Newman had also studied. Again, despite the pleasures of the country—walking, riding and sculling, which he loved—he was soon unhappy. Even before he took his final vows in 1880 he had begun to doubt, through his linguistic and Biblical studies, the authenticity of the text which had initially won him over. And when he began teaching English and History at Oscott, late in 1880, he found much more to criticize, from the standards of scholarship in the school to its methods of discipline.

Irascible and opinionated, he was bound to strike sparks from his superiors. He also took a very cool-headed view, for a Catholic priest of the Victorian age, of one of the major concerns of a religious boarding school for boys between the ages of eight and eighteen: homosexual behaviour. He disagreed strongly with the Catholic school's methods of supervision.

'A boy is never trusted and knows he is not' was his view and he thought neither the confessional nor the carrying of tales, which he branded as a spy system, could stamp out 'that particular form of weakness which seemed to be inseparable from school life or from the isolation of the sexes'.[8] Given the behaviour at some of the great public schools in the nineteenth century—'the animal lust in the dormitories at Harrow',[9] the 'hotbed of vice'[10] at Charterhouse. and the scandals at Harrow and Eton which led to the resignations of such famous masters as Charles Vaughan, William Johnson Cory and Oscar Browning—it is not surprising that the Catholic clergy kept a close watch on their charges. But Galton, product of an English public school, was convinced of the superiority of the English public schools in every area from morals to scholarship and manners. Whereas at Oscott he thought: 'The whole system develops cunning, distrust and a moral irresponsibility'.[11]

Englishness was replacing Roman Catholicism as his religion; he began to regret bitterly that he had cut himself off from English traditions and from the great Anglican divines. At this stage, in 1882, when he was just beginning to doubt, in his unhappiness, not only Catholicism but Christianity itself, he began reading and rereading that great Englishman, Matthew Arnold. It was another conversion. Arnold's gentle influence, his ability to accept both the findings of science and the figure of Christ, earned Galton's hero worship and kept him a Christian. 'He taught me how to think and how to write.'[12] And Arnold's hatred of dreary materialism and philistinism, his broad sweep of thought, his moral strength, carried the young man away into another burst of enthusiasm. He spent three holidays in the Lakes District where Arnold might be found sometimes at his old family home, Fox How; and at the end of 1884 he volunteered for the Italian mission at Windermere, much as he had come to hate Romanism. Predictably he found the parish duties petty and soon begged to be released. His amiable bishop agreed and, leaving the priesthood behind, Galton set out for a three months holiday in Italy.

Having turned his back on Romanism he was welcomed back into the bosom of his family and to its support. His enchantment with Arnold had shown him his new course; he would be a scholar, a writer and a thinker. In 1885 he published his first book, *Urbana Scripta*, a study of five living poets: Tennyson, Swinburne, Browning, Arnold and Mark Pattison. He decided to return to university, this time to Oxford, and in 1886 became a rather mature undergraduate of New College, studying Classics and English. At thirty-three, and already an author, he must have appeared exceedingly ancient to eighteen- and nineteen-year-olds. Never daunted, he soon found a group which respected his opposition to the materialism of the modern world; some rather prissy, genteel aesthetes. Talented, if a trifle anaemic, they produced the elegant highbrow quarterly, the *Hobby Horse*. Galton brought to literature and aesthetics a similar enthusiasm to that he had shown in the religious field. 'Art is our queen, for whom stern war we wage',[13] he trumpeted. And he lashed out at the wishy-washy state of modern writing. 'The age needs a writer', he asserted, 'who shall proclaim that man cannot subsist upon landscapes and vague sentiment'.[14] William Sharp, who wrote under the name Fiona McLeod, earned his special contempt for mysticism and romanticism.

The *Hobby Horse* set, though languid, was able. But, heirs of the Pre-Raphaelites and devotees of William Morris, they were more interested in physical beauty than in morality. The undergraduate editor, Herbert Horne, 'one of the most ladylike gentlemen in the world',[15] was the author of some pallid verses, *Diversi Colori*, and a one-time acquaintance of Oscar Wilde. He was to become the architect of the Church of the Redeemer in Bayswater Road and an esteemed expert on Italian art. An older member of the group was Horne's intimate friend at this time, Selwyn Image, poet, clergyman and designer, who was also a friend of Wilde and who later became Slade Professor of Fine Art at Oxford. Image had the distinction later of writing the last letter Wilde received before the prison gates closed on him, and of welcoming him with the first letter when he came out of gaol. The founder and one-time co-editor of the *Hobby Horse*, Arthur Heygate Mackmurdo, an architect who was still active in the group, was an early proponent of art nouveau and the designer of the Savoy Hotel. Contributors to the journal included Ernest Dowson, John Addington Symonds, Christina Rossetti, Lionel Johnson, Laurence Binyon and Oscar Wilde.

These devotees of the beautiful lacked, however, the moral fervour which was necessary to Galton. He had been in correspondence with Matthew Arnold since spring 1887 and when his hero died suddenly in 1888 Galton mourned him in some lame lines, which expressed the sombre side of his own nature:

> Nor worth, nor piety averts the doom;
> The common doom that solemn Clotho brings.
> For thee, for thee, the cypress and the tomb,
> For me 'the sense of tears in mortal things'.[16]

But he had found already a new idol, half-way between aestheticism and the moral sense, in the bald-headed, hump-backed don of Brasenose, Walter Pater. Pater's *Studies in the History of the Renaissance* (1873), Wilde's golden book, had brought a new creed to replace the undermined religious faith and a new invocation for the aesthetic movement, 'to burn always with this hard, gemlike flame'. For Paterians the meaning of life lay in perfect moments of aesthetic experience, in art and life.

Such a creed slid too easily into decadence for Galton. He found more inspiration in Pater, the teacher and scholar, than in Pater the writer. Studying the classics under this guidance Galton found much solace and joy, almost a new religion. The thought of the Greek philosophers gave a new, broader basis to his life after his unhappiness in the Catholic church, convincing him that he was an intellectual and a scholar rather than a priest. In remote Australia he was to recall the ambience of Pater's room with much affection:

> the small room at Brasenose, an old panelled room with a few delicate paintings, a cabinet of Grecian medals, some casts and statues, a tall clock, a curious ancient screen of embossed and gilded leather, a small shelf of choice books, a comfortable window seat for sunny meditations, or a wintry chair and table near the firelight.The bow window looks down upon the Radcliffe Library, with its domes and pillars; and the music of Saint Mary's chime comes floating in.[17]

It was a perfect setting for a scholar-aesthete, with the lawns and crumbling walls 'dreamy with the sound of bees', and 'with the bright movement of the place, but especially in the summer term, when the streets are thronged with youths in all the glow of athletic health and beauty, like the Parthenon frieze come to life as he (Pater) would say; or certain of the Platonic dialogues in action'.[18] With the sanction of such dialogues 'Greek love' was being acknowledged more openly in Oxford and Cambridge in the late nineteenth century. Pater, fastidiously in love with young male beauty, enjoyed the company of picturesque and athletic undergraduates between nineteen and twenty-three. But Galton was well beyond the magic age, and oppressively serious. He was tart about Pater's infatuation with the twenty-three-year-old symbolist poet, Arthur Symons. 'I had to listen the other day to all his excellences: how he is as deep and great as Browning, without Browning's obscurity; he is like Meredith, without Meredith's faults; he is a great poet, of immense powers, with a real message, whatever a "message" may be.'[19]

There were, however, compensations in maturity. At his own college he made a young disciple who became his close friend, a nineteen-year-old poet, Lionel Johnson, who, like Galton, was a son of the gentry, came of a military family and had been educated at a private school, 'Mother mine, loved Winchester',[20] where one of his friends was his cousin, Lord Alfred Douglas, Wilde's future votary. Johnson was very small, precocious and seemingly an obvious target for public-school bullying. Yet he was happy there, crowning a brilliant school career with many honours and a scholarship to New College. And, according to critic Iain Fletcher, he was also the leader of a homosexual circle. 'The wonderful child',[21] with his frail physique, his charm and his amazingly youthful appearance had dazzled his school friends, including Francis, Earl Russell, elder brother of Bertrand.

Johnson won Oxford, too, with his sunny charm. A golden boy, it seemed. Yet already he was tending to melancholy and lost causes. It may be that Galton's obsession with 'the sense of tears in things', emphasized the shadows that hung around Johnson. The irascible ex-priest, severe and grave, was rather an odd companion for a boy, seemingly with the world at his feet. But the older man was learned, masterful—even bullying—experienced, determined and dedicated to literature, art and thought. Obvi-

ously Galton had his own charm; and Johnson shared his devotion to
Arnold, was an admirer of Pater and a member of the *Hobby Horse* set.
Some of his best poems appeared first in their little magazine.

The friendship lasted through their happy undergraduate days and
Johnson dedicated his farewell to Oxford in 1890 to this older friend:

> Over the four long years. And unknown powers
> Call to us going forth upon our way:
> Ah! Turn we and look back upon the towers
> That rose above our lives and cheered the day.[22]

The days had been cheered by a number of visitors too, including the
future art connoisseur, Bernard Berenson, twenty-three years old and
fresh from Harvard, who was delighted with both Galton and Johnson.[23]
Oscar Wilde also visited Johnson, who wrote lightheartedly to Galton: 'I
am in love with him'.[24] John Addington Symonds, man-of-letters, scholar
in Renaissance art, who chose to live abroad for health reasons and to
pursue a homosexual life style, also took an interest in the pair on a visit
in 1888. He observed young Lionel Johnson with special interest, for he
was a great tracker of any homosexual essence, saying that if they came to
know one another better he thought they would discover a great many
tastes in common.[25] His interest in brilliant, youthful Johnson is
understandable, while the continued attention he showed Galton is testimony that the older undergraduate had his own particular appeal and
intelligence. Indeed, Symonds appeared quite struck with Galton's charm
and his possible future as a writer. Galton had reviewed Symonds's *History
of the Renaissance in Italy* favourably in the *Hobby Horse* in January
1887. A correspondence between them began then.

After returning to the continent Symonds kept in touch with Galton,
encouraged him in his writing with some extravagant praise for his light-
ness of erudition, mental force, urbanity, irony and modernity of thought
and judgement. He urged several times that the pair should visit him and
lamented when they did not come, saying that they had both forgotten to
come to see him at Davos in the winter, but would they come to Venice in
the autumn. Symonds wrote a number of long letters to Galton, and felt
free to write to him in October 1890 on what he called sexual aberration,
(homosexuality) pointing out that in Italy what were called charges of
unnatural offences had been totally abolished. He professed himself deeply
and affectionately interested in Galton and repeated his wish for a visit.[26]
But his two new friends do not seem to have taken up the invitations,
though Galton sent copies of his edition of Tacitus's *The Reign of Tiberius*
to both Symonds and Wilde that year.

Galton and Johnson left Oxford in 1890. Neither had done well enough
to take up the life of the don; Galton took a second class honour in History, Johnson did better with a first class degree in Literature but won
only a poor second class in Moderations. In any case both were determined

on a literary life. They settled at the *Hobby Horse* headquarters at 20 Fitzroy Street, London, a centre of much artistic activity, where 'evenings' drew many young artists, poets and writers. Augustus John, who had a studio there for a time, described it as 'a nest of decayed pre-Raphaelites',[27] but from a distance it could look exciting and most attractive. Symonds, writing in July 1890, longed to see them all together at Fitzroy Street. Meanwhile he was doing his best to promote Galton in a journalistic career. But by October 1890 he was beginning to wonder whether literary journalism was really Galton's forte. He suggested instead a volume of essays in the Pater style. Yet he retained his faith in the ex-priest, wondering how far Galton and his school would go.[28]

Flattering as it was to be praised by this prominent man-of-letters, little resulted from it. And contending with the world beyond the Oxford towers was testing. The friends began to drift apart. Even at Oxford Johnson had shown a marked tendency to melancholy, a leaning towards religion and a taste for the bottle. Now he began drinking more heavily, and turned towards Catholicism as a remedy for his despair. On 22 June 1891 Galton's great friend was received into the church which Galton had fled; and, according to Iain Fletcher, he then ceased being an active homosexual. His friends now were other Catholic poets, especially Ernest Dowson and Victor Plarr. The romantic pessimism of these 1890s poets, of Dowson's 'they are not long, the the days of wine and roses' was no creed for earnest, austere, still ambitious Arthur Galton. As Manning later said of him, Galton was a prophet.[29] He had messages to spread, ideas to promulgate, truths to pass on. Evangelism was his field.

He wrote a number of articles for the solemn journal, *The Academy*, but London was full of struggling writers. Galton, a Victorian gentleman from a comfortable background, was no fit inhabitant of Grub Street. By March 1891 he was in the Lakes district again. At this crucial time, no doubt as a result of family concern, there came the offer of the post in New South Wales with his uncle, the newly knighted Sir Robert Duff of Felteresso. Duff was a former Gladstonian Liberal M.P., a member of the Scottish Duff family and a connection of the Earls of Fife, being descended from Robert Duff, Rear-Admiral of the Red in 1781, a cousin of the first Earl who had married that Earl's daughter. In the tangled relationships of gentry and aristocracy, Galton's claim to be the second cousin of a Duke had some basis, though an attenuated one. And when the first Duke of Fife married the Princess Royal, Louise Victoria, in 1889, Galton could have made his boasts even grander.

So Arthur Galton, forty-one-year-old fussy bachelor, ex-student of Cambridge, graduate of Oxford, ex-Catholic priest and prophet of Anglicanism, scholar and man-of-letters, disciple and friend of Arnold and Pater, rode through the streets of Sydney in May 1893 in what passed there for state. He carried with him a baggage of emotions, prejudices, beliefs, experiences, ambitions. Given his energy and ambition he was planning, no doubt, to use the contents of this baggage in making some mark among these colonial savages. At the very least the time in the colony should be an interesting interlude, something to reminisce about at home. How unlikely it would have seemed to this arrogant and very English gentleman that among the rough and boisterous crowd greeting the procession there should be a prospective soul-mate, a mind and spirit he could respect and nurture, in the person of a ten-year-old colonial boy.

3

Philistia

Government house, the centre of Arthur Galton's new career, was, in his English opinion, a very comfortable, 'second or third rate country house'.[1] While the outlook over the Botanic Gardens and the harbour was delightful the new duties, for someone of his severe nature, were a trifle frivolous; dinners, dances, garden and tea parties, banquets and levees now formed the setting of his life, as, attired in the meticulous dress suited to each occasion, he attended to the myriad guests of the Governor. These, by English standards, were very much a mixed lot. 'The man who sells you a dozen of wine in the morning sits by your side at Government House or Bishop's Court in the evening',[2] wrote one astonished visitor. Galton maintained that many of the better people kept away, for fear of whom they might meet at the Governor's table. The grand ball supper, he said, was a dangerous and indecent scramble. Pushing women, 'dubious in age as in other qualities'[3] enraged him most, for some tried to force themselves into Government House to lay siege to the staff. With no royalty, no aristocracy, no squirearchy, no real landed gentry, no leisured class, this egalitarian society, free and easy in dress as in manners with few social graces, few recognizable marks of social distinctions and with Jack sure that he was quite as good as his master, was a shock to a snobbish English gentleman.

There were, however, some aspects of his new world which might remind new chum Galton of home: from the Georgian style architecture of Macquarie Street and the neo-Gothic of the University buildings, down to the bowler hats of the cabbies and the huge hats and large baskets of the flower sellers. The Parliament was run (supposedly) on Westminster lines; the law courts, the clubs, the private schools and many of the churches followed British models. The people played the same sports: rugby, tennis, golf and that English institution, cricket. The race course held the same sacred position as in English society and the cooking was in the British style. Social climbers admired English clothes and accents, and the population spoke English—if of a somewhat odd kind.

The dully respectable *Sydney Morning Herald* was not *The Times*, however, and the servants were mostly untrained Irish girls. Real 'culture' and 'society' did not exist for someone like Galton, and he found viceregal life 'a weary round of banquets, balls, bazaars, public meetings, of visits to cattle shows, town halls, schools, convents, races and regattas'.[4] The harbour city, all the same, had its own special charm. Its golden sandstone buildings shone in the sun, athletic young men sculled and sailed on the blue-green waters, ferries chugged along carrying picnic parties to pleasure grounds and the air smelt both salty and aromatic. Such were its pleasures that some talented native-born, English-educated men, who might have made a career abroad, had chosen to come home. Such a one was brilliant lawyer and politician Bernhard Wise. In seeking new friends in this small city, Galton soon looked up this Sydney-born product of Rugby and Oxford. For a colonial, Wise had achieved a dazzling career as a student. A disciple of economist Arnold Toynbee, he carried off the Cobden prize in 1878, was *proxime* for the Lothian Historical Essay in 1880 and President of the Union in Michaelmas term that year, succeeding his friend, George Curzon. He also took a first in Law that year. 'Handsome as the radiant ever young Apollo'[5] he may well have been one of those young gods who delighted Pater's eye, for he was President of the Oxford Athletic club, mile champion of Great Britain 1879–81 and founder of the Amateur Athletic Association. Elegant, cultured, cosmopolitan, a friend of Wilde and Robert Louis Stevenson, he was one citizen of Sydney who could share those of Galton's literary tastes that were a little *risqué* for the stuffy provinces.

Galton wrote to him from Government House on 26 November 1893, about a review he had written on a writer they both enjoyed:

> My dear Wise,
> I send you my Rabelais, as a most inadequate expression of my thanks for introducing me to Urquhart's fine version ... My review is not, of course, what one would say of Rabelais if one were speaking intimately but it's about as much as the public will swallow ... The *Herald* funked it, after its manner, or want of manners ...[6]

Wise, 'with manners, accent, phraseology, all of the most approved Oxford type' according to Beatrice Webb,[7] was nevertheless a true son of his hedonistic native city, and consequently a disappointment to rigid Galton. A bon viveur, a yachtsman, a clubman, a lover of pretty women and frivolous pleasures, restless Bernhard Wise failed finally to discipline his talents in the interests of ambition. Far too English in his style for most Australians, yet too radical in his economic theories for the Anglo-Saxon establishment, he fell between two stools.[8] Even his patron and mentor, Sir Henry Parkes, at last lost faith in his protégé, describing him as a butterfly of society.

The Governor's Private Secretary found, perhaps to his own surprise, that he had more in common with the vulgar, aitchless, but demonically energetic ex-Premier, Parkes, who had left school at eight, and arrived in Australia in 1839 burdened with a wife, a baby and only three shillings in his pocket, than with the brilliant Oxford graduate. The *Bulletin* might call the uxorious, champagne-swilling octogenarian 'that awful old man', but Parkes, Premier five times, bankrupt as often, 'the Ned Kelly of Australian politics' in Francis Adams's phrase, exuded the qualities Galton most admired, force and will. The two also shared a detestation of the Catholic Church and English-born Parkes, who still loved a lord, was infatuated with any member of the English gentry. Galton corresponded with the old man, mainly on politics, visited him in his final illness, negotiated with an English publisher about an edition of his poems[9] and wrote an introduction to the English edition of *An Emigrant's Home Letters*, published in 1897, calling Parkes's extraordinary life 'a romance of the 19th century'.

It was a lonely city, however, for this severely scholarly visitor. Like the historian J. A. Froude, he probably dismissed the bulk of the Sydney population as dedicated to comfort and ease, with no liking for real intellectual interests. But generous-natured Froude had paid tribute to this new society's easy-going ways in his well-known dictum about Australians: 'It is hard to quarrel with men who only wish to be innocently happy'.[10] This would not do for Galton. Materialism and philistinism must be combated with lectures on such martial subjects as 'The Military Art of the Romans, as illustrated by the wars of Caesar' (in 1894) and 'The Life and Times of the Duke of Marlborough' (in 1895 at the United Services Institution). This evangelist of the arts was determined to spread the message of scholarship and culture, however unreceptive the local ear.

This happy-go-lucky society had a further defect for a refugee from Rome: the strength and growing influence of Catholics in the population. Although there was still much bigotry (Herbert Moran remembered seeing, as a boy in the 1890s, 'No Catholic Need Apply' signs), by 1891 the largely Catholic new Labor Party held the balance of power in the Legislative Assembly. Catholics were coming forward, too, in the professions of law and medicine and in business. It was perhaps with some shock that Galton discovered that the leading citizen of his new city, the Mayor, William Manning, was a Catholic; he could take some comfort, though, in the fact that the clergy were largely Irish, not the Italians he so detested.

Yet the main source of irritation in his new life was not the Church but the Fourth Estate, particularly that irrepressible, cheeky advocate of Australian nationalism and republicanism, the *Bulletin*, which was obsessed with the pretensions of the Government House set. Its witty social columnist, Sappho Smith (otherwise twenty-five-year-old Alexina Wildman), while professing to despise viceregal goings-on, delighted her readers with her weekly inside stories and gossip. It was lively reading, and as the *Bulletin* reached into many homes, young Fred may have smiled over the pictures Sappho sketched. There was unfashionable Lady Duff, speechless on important public occasions, do-gooding in private with her Sunday School classes at Government House for factory girls and her boxes of scraps from viceregal dinners donated to the soup kitchens. Poor Lady Duff, conscientiously attending every flower show and bazaar in her unexciting clothes and dull bonnets, had no understanding of, or liking for, the frivolity of Sydney 'sassiety', which sneered when she planted a bed of Australian wildflowers at Government House or sent her children by public transport to some small engagements. At last even that good democrat, Sappho, began to sigh for the return of the previous Governor's wife, flighty Lady Jersey of the suspiciously golden hair and ever rattling tongue. Then there was Sir Robert Duff himself, cultured and able but aloof; hating all social engagements except the races and avoiding as many as he could. As a consequence he offended everybody from the Scots on New Year's Day to the yachting fraternity on Regatta Day. The popularity of 'His Ex.' and his good lady plummeted to such an extent that Sappho speculated about a demand for his recall.

But the special target for her sharp pen was the fussy, vain, humourless Private Secretary. She implied a certain effeminacy in his appearance, and ridiculed his dandyish dress and highbrow tastes.[11] Judging from a photograph of this time Arthur Galton, in his early forties, was reasonably good-looking, and curiously youthful and modern in appearance with his slim build, clean-shaven face and short brush of prematurely grey hair in an age of Victorian beards and beefiness.[12] These boyish looks, combined with his English elegance of dress, had aroused at first certain hopes in the hearts of some daughters of the *nouveaux riches*. What were these sprigs of the English gentry doing at Government House, if not looking for a wealthy colonial wife? At the very least, they were expected to dance and flirt. Dapper Mr Galton was most ill at ease in such pastimes, preferring to give lectures. Sappho had some fun with one such effort: 'A large audience', she reported, 'attended the recent funeral service conducted by Mr Galton at the Sydney Women's Literary Society'; she prescribed a course of Galton for insomnia.[13]

The disenchantment with this supercilious gentleman was complete when some bulky object in his breast-pocket was seen to spoil the line of his dress-coat as he waltzed dutifully around a ballroom. There was much speculation, until a straying guest chanced on the Private Secretary, sheltered by a potted palm, deep in a volume of Homer in the original Greek. From then on he was the Homeric Mr Galton to Sappho, and the subject of some *Bulletin* doggerel and a Hop cartoon (13 January 1894).

> Galton, hero of the life romantic,
> Dancers in a ballroom once drove frantic,
> Not with airs, or intellectual 'jam',
> But with a swelling neath his diaphra[g]m

Doggedly intellectual in this materialist society and hopelessly English and arrogant in a time of booming, touchy nationalism, he was worse than useless to his employer, he was damaging. The condescending speeches he wrote for the Governor, especially one delivered at the Art Gallery, enraged the citizenry, and matters became so tense between the two men that by April 1894 Duff refused to have Galton in attendance. The official Private Secretary was demoted to trailing around dejectedly after Lady Duff on her engagements.

In his career of balls and levees and dinners, Galton had met often both the Premier and the Mayor. Now, impressed perhaps by his pedigree and lordly ways, they came to his assistance. Premier Dibbs was himself at odds with Governor Duff, over the question of appointments to the Legislative Council. In one of his last official acts, before being defeated at the polls in July 1894, Dibbs appointed the true-blue English gentleman, Arthur Galton, as historiographer for New South Wales, charged with the task of editing the official historical records of the colony.

The *Bulletin* of 18 August 1894 was outraged at what it termed an insult to Australians.

> This more or less young gentleman has now graced Australia with his presence for something over a year . . . Dibbs gives the power of meddling with our historical documents into the hands of a literary wayfarer from Britain, and with it the power of selection of documents for publication in the official history . . . In general he has observed Australia from the deck of an ocean liner, the window of a first-class carriage and the towers of Government House.

It scoffed at the literary record of this 'Imperial straggler', claimed he would never have got the appointment but for his gubernatorial background and suggested that certain records might be suppressed in the interests of the wealthy, 'the drapers of Potts Point'. (At a time when a convict ancestor could be social death, some citizens were extremely sensitive about official records.) It also sneered that at least he was cheap, having accepted £500 a year instead of the previous rate of £1200.

Such criticisms might be passed off with a superior sniff. But Dibbs's defeat was devastating to Galton. The incoming Premier, wily, jovial, unpretentious George Reid, was pledged to balance the budget and reduce government expenditure. As the *Bulletin* reported (4 May 1895) the Civil Service Commission had pointed out that a quarter of a million pounds a year could be saved simply by abolishing officers who got their appointments through political influence. Such sinecures were under attack and retrenchment. Galton's period as historiographer was brief. It was the historian F. W. Bladen who edited the volumes of *Historical Records* published in 1895, 1896 and 1897. And Galton was extremely bitter about Reid, in his letters to Parkes in the first half of 1895. The intemperate language he used ('despicable', 'low rascal') reveals a rage that was more than his usual testiness or political disagreement and which extended to another perceived enemy: 'As for the Press it's past praying for: but one can say nothing worse of it than that it matches the Premier and the government'.[14]

It was a wretched time in other ways as well. The news from England was disturbing with the Wilde scandal shaking the literary world. That the darling of society, London's favourite playwright, having been found guilty of charges of gross indecency, should have been sentenced to two years gaol was almost too shocking for the Sydney press, which was so guarded in reporting the case that an unworldly reader might have been mystified as to what Wilde had done. The *Bulletin* satirized this delicate approach by using the term 'galvanised iron' as a synonym for homosexuality. 'Is "galvanised iron" an anti-social act?', it asked (20 July 1895) and came to the conclusion that Wilde had indeed transgressed community standards and was rightly convicted. The *Bulletin's* radical politics did not mean radical social views. It scolded at times on 'moral' questions including homosexuality. Homosexual scandals were not unknown in the colonies. At Vance Palmer's school, Ipswich Grammar, there was a notorious case a few years later, involving an Oxford graduate master and a murder.[15] Miles Franklin's novel, *Cockatoos*, set in this period (though written much later) featured as a minor character a curate with Wildean tendencies. The life of isolated shepherds and stockmen of that day is thought to have contained a homosexual element. But such matters were not discussed openly in the prudish colonial society of the Victorian age.

The Wilde affair, however, must have caused Galton some concern. So many of his friends were also friends of Wilde, and his former bosom companion, Lionel Johnson, had introduced an old school-friend, Lord Alfred Douglas, to the now disgraced and notorious playwright. Many of Wilde's former admirers, terrified of scandal, were distancing themselves from this gaol-bird and all the nasty vulgarity of court cases and lurid publicity. Galton's health seems to have come under a strain around this time, as he excused himself from visiting Parkes in May on the grounds that he was living in baths, one day Turkish, the next electric, and he had to be careful about what he ate and drank. It was a period of reappraisal perhaps. Should he return to England, having lost two posts in the colonies, or should he wait for a better moment? In later life he clouded over these years with the incorrect statement that he had been Private Secretary to the Governor of New South Wales from 1893 to 1898.[16] But according to the Post Office Directory of 1895, William Pennington was Private Secretary that year. As it happened, the term of Sir Robert Duff ended prematurely, when that unfortunate Governor died suddenly on 15 March 1895 of septicaemia contracted while on holiday in Tasmania. His successor, Viscount Hampden, brought with him his own Private Secretary, Mr Gathorne Hardy, when he arrived in Sydney in November. Yet Galton chose to remain in the colony, although it was a predicament. He had lost two places already. What was there fit for a man of his breeding, education and vanity to do in this narrow and plebian town? One influential citizen who appeared to appreciate the talents of the stranded scholar, as well perhaps as the Galton coat of arms, the entry in Burke's *Landed Gentry* and the

Oxford–Cambridge ambience came to the rescue. According to Frederic Manning's friend of later years, the writer Richard Aldington, Sir William Manning, who had been knighted in 1894, employed Galton as a kind of private secretary and as a tutor for his invalid son.[17] Galton could appreciate Sir William, so energetic, so able and successful; the son, though totally different in character, was certainly intriguing and full of promise, and surprisingly well read already. After all his difficulties and much disappointment, to be entrusted with the training of this sensitive, intelligent boy was in the nature of an unexpected opportunity. Now all that Oxford–Cambridge scholarship, all that literary severity, all that unfulfilled ambition and determination were to be focused on a frail thirteen-year-old. Galton's task would be to save this unusual young mind from the philistines of his society. 'To treat of Culture and Society in Australia . . . would be like treating of the snakes in Ireland',[18] said Francis Adams. But Galton in 1894 had an ideal in mind: 'What we desire now is not a romantic Wordsworth but an austere and rigorous classic; an author to create fine models, to be a terror to our modern Grub-street, to chastise and restrain the *"Canaille écrivante"'*.[19] Possibly he might form his protégé in that mould.

4

When London Calls

THE SNOBBISH, utterly English Arthur Galton with his prejudices against Romanism, the Jesuits and the dull colonies settled to the task of moulding his young pupil. That he was employed by an Irish Catholic family of humble origins with sons at the Jesuit college, Riverview, did not disturb him. He could separate his personal views from his polemics. 'Some of my dearest friends are Catholic',[1] he could write in the midst of his fulminations. This was especially so if the friends were men of standing, like Sir William and Cardinal Moran. As for Sir William, having the reputed cousin of a duke as his son's tutor could not be matched in Sydney's narrow society, and Galton was undoubtedly a true scholar, a former teacher at a great Catholic school, who would bring out Fred's talents. Busy as ever, although no longer Mayor, Sir William could pursue his ambitions, confident that young Fred was in good hands.

Sir William had steered the city through the years of crisis in the depression of the early 1890s. When the run on the State Bank in 1892 was followed by other bank failures, many small investors were ruined and confidence crumbled. The departure of the *Royal Tar* from Sydney in March 1893, with a boatload of socialists and fiery trade unionists bent on founding a New Australia in Patagonia, could be seen as one expression of a loss of belief in the Australian Utopia which had been expected to emerge.

Coping with the city's difficulties and restoring confidence, Sir William reached new heights in status and prosperity. According to the *Sydney Morning Herald* (21 April 1915) his work at this time stamped him as one of Sydney's most able financial men. He spoke in the Legislative Assembly in May 1893 on the deficiencies of colonial banking and assisted Premier Dibbs in drafting the Bank Issue Act of 1893. In later years he was credited with reconstructing, almost single-handed, the failed Australian Joint Stock Bank into the Australian Bank of Commerce between 1911 and 1915. He chaired a Royal Commission on Chinese gambling, involving charges against the police in 1891–92, and was a member of the Royal Commission into military service in New South Wales in 1892.[2] In 1894–95 he won some nationalistic kudos when he championed the Australian captain of a foreign ship seized by the Dutch government.

During his city council service he remodelled Belmore markets, and showed vision and enterprise in his efforts to apply the American betterment principle, under which improvements in replanning Sydney would be financed in part by the ratepayers affected. The Upper House drastically amended the bill, so that it applied only to Moore Street, the first stage of the Martin Place development. 'Thus failed the most serious attempt before 1900 to come to grips with the fundamental problems of economic, comprehensive and integrated city replanning in Sydney.'[3] In these difficult years he supported as well the scheme for the building of the grand Queen Victoria Building, a statement of belief in the great future of the city.

He was a director of the Citizens Life Assurance Co. from 1894–1908, chairman of the local office of the Insurance Office of London 1894–1915, director of a number of building societies and administered the grants made by his old employer, Peter Nicol Russell, to found an engineering school at the University of Sydney. He found time to serve as a Fellow of Saint John's College within the University of Sydney from 1893 to 1915; assisted in the building of St Mary's Cathedral; and was, in general, so prominent in Catholic circles that he was appointed Papal Chamberlain by Leo XIII in 1903. At the same time he was financial adviser to such grand British investors as the Earl of Carnarvon and the Duke of Manchester. All he had behind him in his successful career were his own talents. Totally self-made, rising in his life time from near poverty to financial eminence he may well have been a somewhat overwhelming father. His boundless energy, his ability to handle people, his confidence, his daring, were all hard to emulate. But he appears to have been a loving father to all his children and proud, at first, of his literary son.

Successful as he was, some tensions remained, for a certain supercilious bigotry lingered in top circles. It was rumoured after Governor Duff's death that a lady in the highest position had set it down in black and white that she could not possibly have anything to do with Catholic functions.[4] Lady Manning and her daughters were noted for their work for Catholic charities. The rumour was denied but it was surely unfortunate that, according to the *Bulletin* (22 June 1895), neither the acting Governor nor his wife could be present, in their ex-officio positions as patrons, at Lady Manning's Catholic Charity Ball at the Paddington Town Hall that month.

Sir William was not likely to be bothered by such matters. With his remarkable financial ability, representing such powerful British interests, he was not to be overlooked by even the most crusty Anglo-Saxons in Sydney's ruling class. And by 1897 this self-made man was living in perhaps the most beautiful and most stylish house in the city, Elizabeth Bay House, Onslow Avenue.[5] This fine, Palladian style villa with its stunning oval saloon, its elegant, cantilevered staircase and unusual, soaring, domed roof had been designed by John Verge in the 1830s for the leader of the colony's aristocratic set in those days, the Treasurer and Speaker of the Legislative Council, Alexander McLeay. In the 1890s the lessee was Lady McLeay, a connection of the original owner. She, in turn, appears to have sublet it to the Mannings for a couple of years, though she died there in 1903.

Elizabeth Bay House, very grand by Sydney standards, with its spacious rooms, library lined with cedar bookcases and butler's room was, by any standards, beautiful, even if the furnishings of the day did not match its elegant lines. It was a house to arouse much aesthetic emotion, with its touch of the baroque. Frederic Manning, disturbed by the gaunt wrecks on the Western Front, explained that he had 'always felt the character or personality of a house'[6], surely a legacy in part from his acquaintance in his youth with several beautiful Verge-designed houses: Goderich Lodge, Elizabeth Bay House and Tusculum, Potts Point. The view from the first floor morning room, an equivalent of today's family room, out over the blue harbour waters, was one of the best in Sydney and the large garden running down to a sandy cove gave scope for imaginative play. In a rare reference to his childhood, Manning has his hero, Bourne, summon up, in the midst of battle, some of the lost sunny ambience of his childhood.

> Bourne found himself playing again a game of his childhood, though not now among rocks from which reverberated heat quivered in wavy lines but in fissures too chalky and unweathered for adequate concealment. One has not, perhaps, at thirty years the same zest in the game as one had at thirteen but the sense of danger brought into play a latent experience which had become a sort of instinct with him . . . [7]

Harry, in his last years at Riverview College, was too big for such games in 1896 but Jack and the youngest brother, Charlie, could join in, although eldest brother, William, was a grown-up student of Sydney University. Lady Manning had left behind 'the pitched battles over the buffets at Town Hall receptions'[8] but remained active in her charity work, aided by her put-upon daughters, Felicia and Edith. Sappho had accused her of not being sufficiently 'sassiety-souled' for a Mayoress. But Nora, hard-pressed mother of a large family, had done her task loyally and well, presenting an elegant public appearance (which could not be faulted by the columnist's sharp eye), whether in black and violet silks, with bonnet to match at the races, or in white silk, black lace and black velvet to set off her diamonds at a ball. It could not have been easy for Lady Manning, with two of her children still small and an invalid son. Sappho termed Sir William 'unctuous'; her only criticism of his wife was she was perhaps rather delicate. (Ironically, Sappho died aged twenty-eight in 1896 while Nora lived into her nineties.)

Fred, with a tutor accomplished in religion and French, Latin, Greek, English and history settled to his studies. Galton, maintaining his privacy, lodged quite modestly at 35 Roslyn Gardens, Elizabeth Bay,[9] within walking distance, or a short ride. There is a family story of the dignified tutor being almost thrown from a grey horse in the drive of Elizabeth Bay House. Quick-witted Fred, child of a racing family, quipped: 'I'll bet my money on the bob-tailed man, somebody bet on the grey'. But despite his pomposity this dazzling cosmopolitan figure, friend of great names like Arnold and Pater, opened new vistas of scholarship and thought to the young Catholic colonial. Yet Fred told a French friend, some years later, that he had been raised by the Jesuits and lost his faith at college.[10] The friend may well have misunderstood, or this may have been a young man's idea of the proper romantic pedigree for an intellectual. The registers of Riverview do not list Fred as a student, although his brothers appear there. His sister, Dot, was his first teacher and probably he was tutored privately by teachers from the college; possibly he counted Galton as an unorthodox kind of Jesuit.

As for the college where he lost his faith, that, with a little touching up of the few months he spent there, was Sydney Grammar School; for in October 1897 the Mannings enrolled their perplexing child at the handsome sandstone building in College Street,[11] and took sixteen-year-old Jack away from Riverview, so that he might shepherd his nervous younger brother to school and keep an eye out for possible difficulties in the playground. Galton may have suggested that his pupil needed a broader range of subjects, or it may have been a last bid by the Mannings to fit their delicate child into an ordinary boy's world.

Grammar had built up a reputation for fine scholarship under its great headmaster, Alfred Bythesea Weigall, an Oxford-educated Englishman, who had adapted some of the educational theories he had learnt from Thomas Arnold of Rugby to the far more egalitarian Australian conditions. Weigall laid emphasis on the classics, introduced a cadet corps, a prefect system and a school uniform; he also prided himself on knowing by name every boy in the school. Grammar, almost entirely a day school, had nothing of the atmosphere of a closed kingdom that prevailed in many English public schools. The conditions there were the best possible for a delicate, clever boy: a short journey from the security of a comfortable, loving home; the care of a robust elder brother; good teachers under an outstanding headmaster who encouraged scholarship; and a policy that aimed at fitness, without being obsessed by sport. The venture was not, however, a complete success. Fred, who was partly absent (ill), left Grammar in December 1897, although Jack stayed on to finish sixth form and to play for the First XV. Athletic Jack eventually captained an Australian Rugby Union team against the New Zealand All Blacks, while Charlie, at Grammar, became an outstanding schoolboy batsman.

The question now was what to do with Fred. It was clear that he showed exceptional promise. In this mix of brilliance and frailty he was reminiscent of that young, earlier friend of Galton, Lionel Johnson. Galton, a man of the great world, of wide experience in scholarship, urged that this special talent needed a wider ambit than existed in provincial Sydney. He suggested, according to Manning's niece, Eleanor Manning, that he should take Fred abroad to finish his education. She also believed that the family thought Fred was so ill that he might not live long.[12] As for the tutor himself, the Australian experience had scarred his vanity badly. He had failed twice; first as secretary and then as historian. But if he took this brilliant lad back to England with him, if he led him into the literary career that John Addington Symonds had once prophesied for Galton himself,[13] then the colonial failure would be redeemed. Galton must have overcome any misgivings felt by the Manning parents by stressing that their unusually talented son needed overseas experience to reach his full potential.

Fred, with his special nature, his distinctive gifts for literature and scholarship, his delicate health, needed extra care and encouragement, unlike his brothers. Harry, as well as being bright at his studies, was athletic and outgoing. He, like Will, had no problems at the University of Sydney. Galton spoke of further schooling and of preparation for Cambridge. Sir William could well afford such extravagances, and why should not his own brilliant boy, like Bernhard Wise, reach the scholarly and social heights, usually the preserve of the Anglo-Saxon colonials, of the sons of well-bred, professional gentlemen? It seemed a satisfactory course for all as Galton had some hopes for his own literary future, bookseller Elkin Mathews having published his *Two Essays on Matthew Arnold* (first printed in the *Hobby Horse*) that year. And with his friend John St Loe Strachey—the nephew of his former patron, John Addington Symonds—now editor and proprietor of the *Spectator*, he might try once more to gain an entrance into the literary world of London.

Sir William, busy as ever, was nursing political ambitions His vision was as impressive as ever, as he interested himself in the questions of an Eastern Suburbs Railway, a Harbour Trust and the reform of the Upper House.[14] Although his attempt to return to the Legislative Assembly in 1898 ended in failure, he also had hopes, given his strong support for Federation, of a seat in the future Federal Parliament. It must have seemed to him a very satisfactory arrangement that Frederic should have a grand educational tour before settling down like his brothers in his native land. And 'Father' Galton, as the family called him, with his scholarship, his viceregal background, his literary and aristocratic connections, his university and religious training, had impeccable standing as a guardian. Whatever doubts may have troubled the parents, especially Nora, they must have been overridden by the thought that this would be a great opportunity for clever young Fred.

Some eyebrows may have been raised in more sophisticated circles at the idea of these Catholic parents handing over their shy, fifteen-year-old son to a middle-aged bachelor, to be taken so far away from parental control and observation. It was, however, a naïve society. But the circumstantial evidence, his friendships, his contempt for women in general, his bachelor-hood, the effeminacy in manner and dress noted by that shrewd-eyed observer, Sappho, would indicate possibly repressed homosexual tendencies in Galton. Late Victorian England, however, was full of eccentrics who managed to combine a life of high seriousness with a range of non-conforming sexual attitudes. The scholar-bachelor, often a don, was an honoured member of society. And sickly young Fred, so protected, must have liked his unusual teacher, so blessed with energy and authority, to be willing to undertake the adventure.

For it was the Great Adventure for creative young Australians. London, the great imperial centre, was a magnet drawing those who felt imprisoned on the Empire's edge. A decade before, eighteen-year-old Henry Handel Richardson had escaped from the dullness of colonial Melbourne and found excitement in the music schools of Europe. Her adolescent heroine, Laura, expressed the yearnings of the questing young. 'I want to see things—yes, that most of all. Hundreds and thousands of things. People and places . . .'[15] It was not so much the cultural cringe that drew the creative abroad, as what Alistair Kershaw labelled decades later 'the cultural yawn',[16] the boredom of the inturned, isolated society. Young artists needed to experi-ence a richer, more complex and less complacent culture, to test themselves against the highest standards, against the young of other countries. Europe, in that period, was packed with such expatriates, especially painters. One might read Shakespeare in Sydney, but one could not see Rembrandt. The talented flocked overseas, to look, to study, to hear and sometimes to seek fame and fortune. Melba had succeeded, others might too.

> They leave us, artists, singers all
> When London calls aloud
> Commanding to her festival
> The gifted crowd.[17]

This was the plaint of Irish-born Victor Daley in Sydney at the turn of the century about the city he termed 'the ogress by the Thames'.

But to many young Australians, nourished on its history and literature, England was the promised land. Young Fred, under Galton's tuition, must have known from hearsay, like Richardson's Laura 'just how England looked'. As was the case with many an Australian schoolchild of the era, who 'like a destiny drank England's deeds',[18] he would have known the poetry, the legends, the battles, the kings. A present day novelist, Shirley Hazzard, writing of a childhood some forty years later, could say: 'There was nothing mythic at Sydney: momentous objects, beings and events all occcurred abroad'.[19] For her, too, 'the true hemisphere' still lay in the north. How much greater was the pull of the imperial city for the provincial young Australians of the turn of the century.

Dreams of England meant more, however, to bookish city children in comfortable circumstances than to their contemporaries in the bush, raised in the heat and isolation and poverty of a small selection. Such children might take refuge in a different dream: Paterson's chivalrous bushmen 'of the sunlit plains extended'. Or they might find their life of milking and clearing, of drudgery and drunkenness, of ignorance and poverty, of endurance and ironic humour, of comradeship and danger reflected in the writings of Henry Lawson, Joseph Furphy and Miles Franklin. Frederic Manning knew nothing of the brutalities of this life. His closest approach to the bush was on holidays in the Blue Mountains, only thirty miles from the city. His childhood was passed among the many and varied distractions protecting 'the spurious and blue-moulded civilization of the littoral'[20] from the emptiness and aridity and loneliness of the interior: shops, crowds, cabs, cafes, beaches, newspapers, theatres, lectures, entertainments. But from early childhood he had faced his own terrors, so that his life was not as secure as his pleasant surroundings might indicate. He had gasped and struggled for breath, known pain and fear, brushed close with death.

As a child in his native Darlinghurst he could see that not everybody enjoyed a comfortable home and the care of loving parents. Drunks lurched from the pubs, barefoot larrikins with tangled hair and hand-me-down clothes cheeked passers-by. The Pushes, the tough young working-class gangs, swaggered along, flashily dressed in their cheap finery, spitting, swearing, insulting the public. Occasionally a devastated Aborigine from the camp at La Perouse would be seen on a city street, and sundowners slept out in the open spaces of the Domain. Crowded tenements and filthy alleys lay around the corner from fine mansions. And Henry Lawson's 'faces in the street', drifting past 'to the beat of weary feet',[21] could haunt a sensitive child, as might Barcroft Boake's grim verses of the arid interior, 'Where the Dead Men Lie'. Only one generation removed from narrow circumstances, Frederic Manning could empathize more with the sufferings of ordinary people than Martin Boyd, who grew up cushioned from the world, in the bay-side suburb of Sandringham, in turn of the century Melbourne. Boyd recalled a sunny, aromatic world 'where real poverty was unknown excepting that of the extremely idle and feckless. There was no unemployment and there were no slums'.[22] It is unlikely that Manning's memories were so idyllic. The broad sympathy with simple people which is so marked in his work must have had its origins in the observations of a gentle, sensitive child aware of the struggles of small-farmer grandparents.

By the time Frederic Manning sailed through the heads of Sydney Harbour in March 1898,[23] he had laid down fifteen years of observations and impressions, all important in the forming of his ideas and his character. Later experience would cover over the events of his childhood but the basis of his nature had been laid; the ironic scepticism of the enduring Australian, exemplified in the bush myth, reached even into city dwellers. He could see that the energy, talent and determination of his father had brought him great success; he could see also that many others had failed.

He could contrast the robustness of his brothers with his own burden of frailty; he could set the warmth of his Irish-born mother against the English reserve of his tutor, while noting the elegant dress and style of Mr Galton, his learning, his panache, in comparison with the happy-go-lucky manners of his too egalitarian countrymen. Already half-democrat, half-Tory, half-scholar, half-observer, a child turning into a young man he faced the departure, his first great separation.

He was leaving his mother, his father, his siblings and his friends, his country and his childhood. Years later, in another country, memories of that lost childhood might flood back. His hero, Bourne says in France: 'we sit here and think of England as a lot of men might sit and think of their childhood. It is all past and irrecoverable, but we sit and think of it to forget the present'.[24] But at fifteen, with all the joys of Europe ahead, excitement must have outweighed sadness at what seemed a temporary parting from his family.

> A lure there is for us,
> In far horizons, dreamed-of, misty lands
> A voice that calls us.[25]

'Love, death and separation may seem to us the mere commonplaces of existence until they touch us personally, and at that moment the individual becomes the protagonist of humanity', he wrote in maturity.[26] In 1898 he was as yet too young to understand those commonplaces. Yet only ten years later he would write in *The Vigil of Brunhild*:

> But all these fleeting voices of our life,
> The loves and sensual desires of earth,
> Our joy in childhood, are but memories
> Of innocence in sheltered Paradise. [p. 34]

5

Abroad

AFTER SIX WEEKS at sea, the ocean barrier having been crossed, the great goal was achieved. The palaces, the churches, the monuments of the imperial city spoke to an eager provincial of the grandeur of the past; the shops, the cafes, the crowds, the concert halls and theatres of an exciting present. The middle-aged scholar, with his colonial pupil in tow, began to look up old friends. Literary London had regained its calm after the Wildean catastrophe. A city of so many writers, so many journals, so many circles and publishers could cover a gap quickly. The decadents had died or dispersed. Wilde was in exile in France; *The Yellow Book*, that journal so notorious in reputation, so comparatively mild in content—except for Aubrey Beardsley's drawings—had closed in 1897 and Beardsley died in March 1898, aged twenty-five. Arthur Galton's particular group of friends and mentors was gone. John Addington Symonds had died in 1893, Pater in 1894, Lionel Johnson, almost a recluse, appeared to be drinking himself to death, and Herbert Horne was now living in Florence, making a reputation as an expert on Italian art.

But Arthur Symons, that symbolist poet so much disliked by Galton, had survived and was still active, W. B. Yeats, Thomas Hardy and A. E. Housman had published new volumes of verse; and the great novelists, James, Conrad, Hardy and Kipling, were at work, undisturbed by any passing scandals. The new novelists like Wells and Bennett were making a mark, and George Bernard Shaw was replacing the disgraced Oscar as the leading dramatist. But Galton's narrow entrée into literary circles had become, after his years of exile, narrower, although the *Hobby Horse* group held firm in Fitzroy Street and some of his Oxford acquaintances were establishing literary reputations.

A former protégé of his Oxford days, twenty-nine-year-old poet and scholar, Laurence Binyon, had won a post at the British Museum and was prepared to help and encourage other writers. Another Oxford contact, Max Beerbohm, had made a name already and had taken over from George

Bernard Shaw as theatre critic on the *Saturday Review* that year. The 'incomparable Max', witty contributor to *The Yellow Book*, the *enfant terrible* who had complained in 1895 that he felt outmoded at the age of twenty-three as he belonged to the the Beardsley period, had worshipped the wit and style of Wilde.The scandal had shaken him badly, for behind the mask of the flippant dandy lay a core of cool, guarded commonsense, and a strong dislike of excess and vulgarity. His parody of Wildean wickedness, *The Happy Hypocrite* (1897), showed where he stood, for he inverted the Dorian Gray story so that his wicked Lord George Hell, putting on a mask of goodness, finally becomes a good and happy man.

Such a declared preference as this for innocence and gentleness over luridness and decadence, combined with his light-hearted wit, made him a fit, as well as a dazzlingly smart, companion for a naïve young colonial. Manning recalled attending the first night of Shaw's play, *You Never Can Tell*, in 1899 with Beerbohm and two other urbane and guarded dandies, thirty-one-year-old George Street, who had satirized the hangers-on of the aesthetes in his novel, *The Autobiography of a Boy*, and ironic A. B. Walkley, the drama critic of *The Times*. It was part of the dream of every young man from the provinces; and during the interval the three men discussed how it might be possible, with a series of articles, to bring Shaw even more to public notice. Manning, looking back, saw his sixteen-year-old self as having been at the birth of a vogue, the cult of Shavianism.[1] The elusive Max, however, 'both shy and egotistic'[2] remained largely a literary acquaintance for a number of years. Galtonian solemnity did not accord with his very determined lightheartedness, and there were many young poets like Manning, all too anxious to befriend him.

With literary circles interlocking and overlapping, one acquaintance led to another. In July, Galton (and possibly Fred) accompanied his old friend Horne, visiting from Italy, to Friday's Hill, Haslemere, Surrey, a centre of young writers, artists and musicians and the home of the non-conforming Pearsall Smith family.[3] The parents had been evangelist preachers in America, then had lost their faith. The son, Logan, a friend of Beerbohm, Galton and Johnson at Oxford, was a writer, an exquisite and a scholar, who, in later life, made no secret of his homosexuality. One daughter, Alys, had married Bertrand Russell in 1894 against the wishes of his parents; and the other, Mary Costelloe, had left her husband in 1891 to live with Bernard Berenson. Galton picked up his acquaintanceship with Berenson again and in 1899 Fred saw Berenson in Florence.[4] These were exciting years for a provincial adolescent, meeting unusual people of varied talents.

In general, however, these tangential contacts did not lead to closer relationships. Galton's severity, not to say priggishness, set him apart from the wits and dandies, and from the connoisseurs. Now quite middle aged, he had lost five years in the colony; any small reputation he had made in *Hobby Horse* circles was outdated. Old friends were dead or had taken other paths. Lionel Johnson, in particular, had become more and more eccentric and withdrawn from life. Expelled from Fitzroy Street because of his drunkenness (he was said to drink two pints of whisky a day), he now lived in solitude, in an alcoholic haze, seeing nobody but a few fellow Catholics. He remained, however, a devoted artist. Brooding over the past, burning with Irish nationalism and praying for the conversion of his old non-Catholic friends, this intense melancholic had nothing in common now with the friend of his youth, the ever brisk and determined Galton.

Johnson evinced, all the same, a modicum of interest in the new disciple, writing to Fred during a period the boy spent at Calverton rectory, Buckinghamshire, with the Reverend G. E. Willes.[5] But Manning did not appear to take to this weird friend of his tutor for in 1920 he wrote a blistering review of Johnson's *Some Winchester Letters*, in which he accused the poet of an 'intellectual dishonesty which characterised Lionel Johnson through life, and acted as a solvent for all moral obligations that might seem irksome or tedious to him'.[6] It sounds rather like the loud, moralistic voice of Galton speaking. Yet, whatever the dissensions between this Johnson and his old friend, he mustered enough respect from the past to bequeath Galton his papers. (Galton at one stage thought of writing a memoir from them, and Manning in later life did some work on them.) For 'the wonderful child' died prematurely, in 1902, aged thirty-four, after a fall from a bar stool in one of his favourite pubs. The fall was brought on, it would appear, by a cerebral haemorrhage, not drunkenness.

To be on the fringes of such circles, to have the interest of Beerbohm and Binyon and Johnson, was exhilarating to a would-be young poet; but to these men of some distinction Fred must have appeared just one of many such aspirants; a shy colonial lad, of no specially grand status, saddled with a dogmatic, boring guardian. The first genuine friend Frederic Manning made in England was not one of Galton's old university associates, but a beautiful and kindly young woman in her early thirties, a cousin of Johnson, and through that connection, a friend of Arthur Galton. Her name was Olivia Shakespear, née Tucker.

This dark-haired beauty, of a Greek regularity of features and an exquisite taste in dress, was married to a wealthy solicitor fifteen years her senior, Henry Hope Shakespear, and was the mother of a small daughter, Dorothy, born 14 September 1886. Olivia, cultured and literary, was known as the author of several romantic novels, and was one of the few women present at the dinner given in 1894 to launch *The Yellow Book*. At another literary dinner in 1895, Lionel Johnson introduced his lovely cousin to the handsome young Irish poet, W. B. Yeats. Yeats's sister, Lily, noted in her diary for August–September that year that 'Willy's latest admiration was the very pretty, young and nice Mrs Shakespear'.[7] Olivia soon became Yeats's mistress, meeting him discreetly, at first in Arthur Symons's flat near the Temple, then at an apartment in Woburn Buildings. She was, for a time, estranged from her husband and there was talk of the lovers running away together. Olivia, however, was no Bohemian. She lacked the passionate temperament to lose the world for love; and there were her child, her husband, her pleasant home, her standing in society to balance against what might have been, on both sides, a passing infatuation. When the affair ended, after a year or so, she remained a life-long friend of Yeats, becoming a kind of step-aunt to her former lover when he married Georgie Hyde-Lees, the step-daughter of Olivia's brother. Beautiful Olivia was the 'lovely face' of Yeats's poem 'Memory', and appeared in his memoirs as Diana Vernon. When she died he wrote that she had been the centre of his London life for more than forty years.[8]

As Galton had been in Sydney when Olivia was involved with Yeats he may not have known of the affair; it is unlikely that he would have retailed such gossip to his charge in any case. But kindly, beautiful Olivia, with or without a romantic past, was a woman to charm a gentle boy. At her pleasant home at 12 Brunswick Gardens, Kensington, she began to foster a genteel little salon, encouraging young writers and poets. Fred was soon a frequent visitor, and Olivia became to this lonely boy 'a beloved aunt', a substitute for his own dear mother, and a life-long friend. And as little Dorothy grew, she too became a friend of importance to him.

Meanwhile Manning's father substitute, after renewing various acquaintanceships and having failed to win a place in the literary world, was contemplating another twist in his career. Late in 1898 Arthur Galton, presumably with his protégé, returned to his family home in quiet Worcestershire to prepare for his reception back into the Church of England. During this time of reorganization he corresponded with his distant cousin, J. H. Shorthouse, author of a one-time bestseller on the evil of Jesuit intrigue, *John Inglesant*, a bitter enemy of the Papacy and a doughty champion of Anglicanism. Galton could give vent to him on his religious prejudices, as well as sharing his interest in Piranesi etchings and the church plate of Humbleton Church.[9] It was a final discarding of the unpleasant colonial years, a return to the culture of Englishness and Anglicanism.

On 19 December 1898 Arthur Galton was received back into the church of his birth. And on the basis of his Roman ordination he was admitted to the Anglican ministry. With some panache, he returned in 1899 to Windemere, where he had formerly been a Catholic priest. This time he went only as Anglican curate to the small parish of St Martin's, to a house called Cleabarrow. It seems likely that the sixteen-year-old apprentice spent some time with him there, for Fred was still too young and his health too poor to fend for himself and Galton remained *in loco parentis*. Such arrangements were not unusual in Victorian England. Philosopher Goldsworthy Lowes Dickinson remembered meeting a whole string of American youths in pupilage to the local scholarly vicar, during his childhood in the 1860s, though that gentleman was married. Manning's whereabouts in these early years in England are not well documented. Australian literary historian Percival Serle says he was at school there for six months.[10] He seems to have moved around a little for he also spent some time in London.

Artist William Rothenstein was approached at his studio in the first year of the new century by a nervous youth who asked to be drawn.

> Frederic Manning was his name; he admired the poets and and writers I knew, Max (Beerbohm) especially, and since I had drawn so many poets he sought me out. He was an attractive youth, a little precious and frail, looking wise for his years. I found him to be very intelligent; He came almost daily, then he disappeared. Manning had no money it transpired. He believed his father would pay for the drawing I did of him and for other extravagances; not so his father. And now he was afraid lest I might take proceedings against him. I reassured him, his father would pay some day; if not, what matter.[11]

Manning later described this drawing as a full-length portrait of a slender youth of somewhat prepossessing appearance dressed in the prevailing fashion of the year, 1900.[12] The extravagances referred to may have ranged from betting to book-collecting, both hobbies of the mature Manning, who loved horses and fine books.

Good-natured Rothenstein had a certain affection for Australia. A precociously early achiever, as a seventeen-year-old art student in Paris he had shared a studio with Phil May, former *Bulletin* cartoonist, had held his first exhibition in conjunction with Charles Conder, a member of the Heidelberg School, and he had been drawn by Australian portraitist, John Longstaff. But in 1900, at the peak of his profession, a member of the New English Art Club, he was a little too busy and important to spend much time on a unknown colonial youth. Manning's pride was hurt by the artist's apparent indifference and he nursed a grievance for many years, referring to kindly Will as 'my ancient enemy, Rothenstein'. The breach was mended during the war and Manning, looking back from 1915, saw the boy he had been as 'a young extremist . . . foolish and spoilt'.[13] With his vanity fed by the patronage of a man who had been the friend of Arnold and Pater, his desire for a literary career funded by an indulgent father, his acceptance at such an early age as a companion by successful sophisticates like Beerbohm and Berenson, it is small wonder if he felt the world was waiting for what he had to offer. The future, it seemed, glowed with his promise but Rothenstein had ignored it.

Not everyone he met had the painter's kindness or the elegant charm of Beerbohm. As late as November 1908 he still felt such distaste for a writer he met, it seems, soon after his arrival in London, that he stormed about this man with almost hysterical rage in a letter to a friend. Usually so balanced and slightly reserved in his correspondence, this letter indicates an angry distaste, though the fact that he was exhausted when he wrote it may explain some of the heat. The man involved was Arthur Machen, author of some popular horror stories, the best known being *The Great God Pan*, published in 1894. Machen, a translator of pornography, an acquaintance of Wilde, was attracted by the dregs of the decadence, and by the murky sensationalism and demonology of the satanist and black magician, Aleister Crowley. Manning's aversion was probably partly personal, partly intellectual. He included in his diatribe those two close friends of Wilde: Robert Ross, who claimed to have been, at sixteen, the first seducer of Wilde, and Lord Alfred Douglas. 'That holy trinity are a loathsome set,' Manning wrote,

canaille écrivante, the worst type of decadent, parasites infesting a pretty rotten body of one who was not great; except perhaps as an actor . . . Wilde's life after all was only a vulgar melodrama, and his literature, except in one or two places, is quite superficial and imitative . . . I do not mind passion, quite naked animal passion, but I detest prurience; and that vile Machen, converted from the diabolism of Huysmans to Roman Catholicism (Real Presence and 'culte de la viérge') is only a little more blasphemous and repulsive than he was twelve years ago. What vermin cover this earth, as thick as the lice in the rags of a Neapolitan beggar.[14]

His anger may have contained some literary jealousy on behalf of his mentor, for around the time the letter was written, Douglas became editor of the *Academy* magazine and Machen, a Roman Catholic, became contributor on religious matters, enough to send Galton into a frenzy. But the fastidious boy in the 1890s was deeply shocked, it is clear, by the decadents and by Machen's mixture of cosy black magic and rather pornographic voluptuousness. The severe intellectualism encouraged by Arthur Galton would have scorned Machen's brand of sticky, supernatural sentimentality, well illustrated later by that writer's story of the Great War, 'The Bowmen', in which St George and his ghostly bowmen come to the aid of some British Tommies in the trenches and are greeted with this bit of realistic dialogue: 'Ha! Messire; ha sweet Saint, grant us good deliverance. St George for Merry England!' Religious and patriotic bathos as a solution to the anguish of the soldier would have no appeal for the author of *Her Privates We*. Vance Palmer also reacted against Machen's 'complacent pride at having created'[15] the 'Angel of Mons' legend, another piece of sacrilegious balderdash, appealing more to the credulous civilian than to the soldier in the field.

Manning's disgust with Machen and the decadents fitted the rigorous standards set for him by his tutor. Galton was very fond of Pater's epigram: 'The way to perfection is through a series of disgusts'.[16] Severity and sobriety in scholarship, verging on pedantry, were his watchwords. In quiet Windermere the new curate could avoid the frivolity of the Café Royal literary set and settle down to what he enjoyed doing most, teaching and preaching from pulpit and page. In 1899 he published *The Message and Position of the Church of England*. Rome was his target, and Englishness his armour. The enmity between Rome and England, for him, was not merely religious; it was 'racial'. 'It is caused by a deep repugnance of nature which cannot be got over', he wrote in 1900 when he launched another missile in his campaign: *Rome and Romanizing: some experiences and a warning.* He followed this in 1901 with *The Protestantism of the Reformed and Catholic Church in England*, and a lecture, 'The Catholicity of the Reformed Church of England'. He was obsessed with the topic, and his view of the religion in which his pupil had been raised was so emotional that it would not have been possible to be under this autocratic influence without taking up some of these anti-Catholic attitudes.

Manning came to disdain, for many years, the church of his childhood and even the people of his ancestry, under the Anglicizing influence, both national and religious, of his teacher. Galton accused the Sydney Catholic diocese of Tammany Hall methods and his pupil wrote: 'An Irishman suffers from a natural disinclination to tell the truth, but an Irish ecclesiastic finds it physically impossible to utter anything but a lie: at least that is my experience of them (the diocese of Sydney being governed entirely by the Irish and Home Rule being taught as a dogma second only to Infallibility.)'.[17]

Under Galton's rule, however, no Index or censorship barred the student's path. Narrow in doctrine and in personal sympathies, the area of his scholarship was reasonably wide. He was as devoted to the modern French writers of the day, especially Anatole France, as to Biblical criticism. But the zealotry he brought to religion was only one aspect of his fiery, domineering nature. He was also arrogant in personal style. As Richard Aldington said: '[Manning's] association with Galton was not altogether an unmixed blessing. Galton was certainly a scholar and disciple of Matthew Arnold, and, so far as I know his writings, seemed even more priggish than that celebrated Oxford prig'.[18] Yet he obviously possessed some magnetism for his pupil. Despite being authoritarian and irascible, he commanded the younger man's affection and allegiance.

Manning in later life became obsessed with writing an historical romance which began as the story of the adventures of a boy and an abbé who come to the court of Rome in the seventeenth century. In the course of rewriting, the boy became a young woman, Madame Sainte Claire, but the parallel between Galton and himself and the original pair is obvious. Although the manuscript was never published, and most of it is lost, the energy and time that Manning put into the book show how much the subject meant to him. The pair had formed a strong bond in these early years which could survive separation and withstand parental disapproval.

Sir William Manning, as the Rothenstein incident indicated, was growing impatient with his long-absent son and his dilettante life style; and he may well have been shocked by Galton's becoming an Anglican priest. It was time for Fred to return home, to think again about his future, to settle down. And Galton was making changes in his own life. In 1901 he moved from the quiet of the curacy to the post of domestic chaplain to the Bishop of Ripon. It was a step forward for a pamphleteering cleric, determined to push his message, to be at elbow of a bishop, in touch with what was happening in the episcopal level of the church; and W. Boyd Carpenter, the bishop, author of *Popular History of the Church of England* shared some of Galton's crusading spirit. Galton took up residence in the Bishop's Palace of the small Yorkshire town; but the palace was no place for an acolyte. Meanwhile Sir William, Lady Manning and one of their daughters had visited England and collected Fred. The family arrived back in Sydney on the *Himalaya* in September 1900[19] in time to join in the preparations for the celebrations to be held in January 1901 to mark the federation of the six colonies into the Commonwealth of Australia.

Was it possible that a new age was dawning, a new utopia arising in the southern seas? Not, it would seem, for a young aesthete. While Fred praised Ibsen in the *Daily Telegraph* (3 November 1900), *Hedda Gabler* played at Her Majesty's for only two nights, to audiences of women in the main. But even an eighteen-year-old cosmopolitan might be touched by euphoria amid the decorations, the illuminations, the processions, the fireworks and the rhetoric of Federation. When the nationalistic fervour died down, Fred Manning could consider his future and reconsider his native land.

6

Exodus

IT ALL LOOKED much the same. The harbour and beaches were as beautiful as ever, the days as sun filled. Norman Lindsay, who moved north from Melbourne in 1901 to join the *Bulletin*, thought that Sydney was then at its best, a city that would never be seen on earth again. He was enchanted by the colour of this South Seas port with sailors from all the world milling round Circular Quay, and the masts of sailing ships reaching skywards. With its sunshine and its waters it was a city of pleasure-lovers, from the factory hands of Waterloo to the elegant gentlemen of Woollahra. While the would-be socialites, whom D. H. Souter drew with so much wit and style, flirted at balls and gossiped in restaurants, the masses crowded the beaches, the races, the pubs and the vaudeville; and the young and daring of all classes threw themselves into the new and exciting craze of surfing from the golden beaches.

Bernhard Wise analysed his fellow citizens of this first decade after the Federation. He saw the Sydneysider as 'the easy-going sun loving philosopher who does his work without fuss or show and tries to get the most from life';[1] and he contrasted all the carefree indulgence of Sydney with the gloom of the Sabbath in Melbourne. He rejoiced in the sight of the harbour, white with sails on a Sunday, with smoke rising from campfires in the many coves. At the same time he admitted that his home town retained some sadly provincial aspects such as the absence of capsicums and aubergines from the dull cuisine, and the preference for beer and tea over coffee and the local wine.

The malaise was not simply a matter of menus. The delight in the physical, in sport and the outdoors, combined somewhat oddly with much primness on sexual matters, and a great deal of narrow-mindedness in intellectual. Novelist Louis Stone, himself English-born, observed the Sydney middle classes during this decade and the simplicity of their life style, where a Plain and Fancy Dress Ball (dry, of course) at the Oddfellows

Hall in Queen Street, Woollahra, was a highlight.² Their sexual puritanism and suburban respectability contrasted with the less inhibited, cruder, working-class mores of his novel, *Jonah*.

English visitors continued to be shocked by this callow and self-satisfied society. Valerie Desmond's sharp, amusing attack on the Australian way of life did not appear until 1911 but her criticisms are the timeless ones of the English visitor: the weird accent, 'causing actual pain on a first hearing'; the uncouth vowels of all classes; the 'public be dammed' bad manners; the parvenu yet snobbish society, with its worship of money; the lazy civil servants, the illiterate politicians, loafing drunkards and the lack of culture. 'There are many coming Australians', she observed acidly, 'but none of them ever seem to do any arriving'.³ Visitors did not have a monopoly in criticism. One local writer summing up her city said: 'Sydney is a little, quiet, ignorant, provincial town'.⁴

Frederic Manning, after more than two years abroad, must have been struck by the jingoistic insularity. In early 1902, with Federation a fact, the High Court near establishment and the vote about to be won by women, public emotion and attention were split evenly between the Boer War and the coming cricket series against England. The deeds of Australian troopers on the veld were matched by the gallantry of Victor Trumper at the crease. The South African war was only another kind of heroic game if one viewed it from a distance, and any protest against it was letting down the side. When George Arnold Wood, Professor of History at the University of Sydney, opposed the war he was attacked by his colleagues, as well as by the citizenry; and while the *Bulletin* lent him some support, its pacifist moralizing was tainted by the blatant nastiness of its anti-Semitism, for it blamed the financiers of 'Jewhannesburg' for the war. The intelligent discussion of opposing viewpoints which could take place in England had little room in this emotional, intolerant town.

Whatever his viewpoint on the war Manning should have agreed with 'The Bookfellow' in the *Bulletin* (15 February 1902): 'The truth is that Australia, in point of intelligence, is still little more than a large parish. Parochial is written large over every discussion of public opinion'. The writer went on to compare the treatment of dissenting opinion holders in Australia with the situation in England where even 'Jingo' newspapers would not dream of questioning the right of utterance. 'So great a country is Australia, so small a parish.' For a young man to whom the mind was paramount, his native land might look a stony desert, very lacking in cultural nourishment.

But there was, initially, the pleasure of a fond reunion with his family. The Mannings were living in some style, as usual, having taken up residence in another fine Verge-designed mansion, Tusculum, at 83 Macleay Street, Potts Point.⁵ Sir William, still fascinated by politics, stood for the Senate in 1901 and the City Council in 1902, both attempts being unsuccessful. He continued to hope for a place in Federal Parliament and had trimmed his past pro-Britishism to a more nationalist shape. There was, he said, 'an insidious attempt being made to dominate the Australian states, not this time from Downing Street but from Lombard Street'.[6] Since he was addressing a St Patrick's Day banquet, presided over by Cardinal Moran, he may have been suiting his sentiments to his audience. Still a leading citizen, he was prominent on public occasions such as the functions held for the Japanese naval squadron visiting that year. It may have been in these years in Sydney that Fred, taking an interest in the Pacific, made the visit to Tahiti that he mentioned later to Ezra Pound.

Sir William's older children were establishing themselves. Harry, a fine debater, who had won blues for cricket and rowing at the University of Sydney, was called to the Sydney Bar in July 1902, and would make a distinguished legal and political career. William and Jack would be lawyers in the family firm, while Charlie, still at Grammar in 1902, would go on the land in Queensland. Only Frederic, among the boys, with his strong intellectual interests and literary bent, found his country frustrating, although his sisters Edith and Dot also asserted their independence by choosing to live abroad for many years. Sydney, brash, smug and small, lacked the range of journals, opinions and people necessary for the kind of intellectual and literary life Fred had enjoyed in England. A. G. Stephens struggled, almost single handedly, on his Red Page in the *Bulletin*, to cover the best in European as well as in Australian writing, mixing news, reviews, political, social and literary comment, plus an occasional poem, into a stimulating brew. But while Stephens was encouraging local writers on one page, Louise Mack, an Australian resident in London, was undermining them on another. 'If ever an Australian artist-singer, writer, painter, returns to Australia it is because he has failed', she pontificated, 'because he could not live over here. Nothing but failure drives them home' (19 July 1902). It was a statement to irk any recent home-comer who had literary ambitions, including Frederic Manning; and it must have twisted the knife in the back of unhappy Henry Lawson, just returned from the London venture which ended in personal tragedy. But it was only the insensitive reiteration of a prevalent view. Even nationalistic Katharine Susannah Prichard felt it was necessary for a young writer to go to England because it was there that reputations were made.[7]

With the loss of the validity of the bush myth for Australian writers soon after the turn of the century, to which Chris Wallace-Crabbe[8] and other critics have pointed, 'overseas' became the fashionable goal, even for patriots like Vance Palmer and Nettie Higgins. There they could learn and test themselves, before returning to help build an Australian literature. Disillusion also fuelled the flight abroad. As more of the disenchanted moved from the sunlit plains to the city in the wake of drought and depression, as the bush legend lost its life, a chapter in Australian literature closed. With the publication of two masterpieces in the genre, Henry Lawson's *Joe Wilson and His Mates* in 1901, and Joseph Furphy's *Such is*

Life in 1903, there seemed little more to say on what had been the main stimulus to Australian writing.

Aiding the collapse of the myth was the exposure of what bush life meant to women. Barbara Baynton and Miles Franklin, both bush-reared, had suffered in their girlhood from the brutalities of this harsh, narrow and essentially male-based society. Baynton's *Bush Studies*, published in book form in 1902, dealt with the primitive nature of male–female relationships among the most squalid of the bush peasantry. Franklin's *My Brilliant Career*, published in 1901, while lighter in tone, emphasized the unhappiness of a bright, ambitious girl trapped in the mindless drudgery of a poverty-stricken dairy farm. Both women escaped overseas, Baynton to London by 1904 and Franklin to Chicago in 1906.

Well before her departure, Baynton outlined in some biting lines what she was leaving:

> A wind-blown, shimmering, awful waste
> Fringed by a broken edge of green and grey—
> A ghastly field for devilish winds at play
> A pitiful tale of desperate men that faced
> The ghostly hell, of hard-won pathways traced
> In dull white bones, of a race whose long decay
> Gives warning to the pallid crowd today
> To seek a land by greener beauty graced.[9]

Disenchanted Baynton ended her plaint with a line to enrage the starry-eyed nationalists celebrating Federation by describing their land as: 'Mother of slaves who dare not speak their thoughts'.

The pride and hope expressed at the declaration of nationhood on 26 January 1901 could not prevent the exodus of talent in the decade before the Great War. There had always been comings and goings between the colony and the mother country; now the pace quickened. The many artists overseas in this period, either permanently or for a number of years included Tom Roberts, Arthur Streeton, E. Phillips Fox, George Lambert, Max Meldrum, Rupert Bunny, Septimus Power, John Russell, Blamire Young, John Longstaff, Will Dyson, Ruby Lind, Margaret Preston (then Rose Macpherson), Penleigh Boyd and Stella Bowen. Among writers living abroad, permanently or on long visits, were Henry Handel Richardson, Rosa Praed, Louise Mack, Katharine Susannah Prichard, Vance Palmer, Nettie Higgins (Palmer), Dorothea Mackellar, Louis Becke, Randolph Bedford, Frank Fox, John H. Abbott, Arthur Adams, William Baylebridge, C. W. Bean, Miles Franklin and Barbara Baynton. Many, when they went, intended to return. Many did return. Some, like Richardson, were determined expatriates.

A few strong-minded individualists, having sampled life overseas, settled for their homeland; such were Henry Lawson, Norman Lindsay, and Christopher Brennan, who wrote:

> Surely I do not foolishly desire to go
> hither and thither upon the earth and grow weary
> with seeing many lands and peoples and the sea.[10]

That was a bleak, experienced view. To most young artists travel was an exciting prospect, an escape from homeland dullness. T. S. Eliot, in the *Egoist* of March 1918, described his pre-war native land as a large, flat country that nobody wanted to visit. How much more fitting a summing up of Australia than of the United States, to those who longed for intellectual and artistic stimulation. Painter Stella Bowen saw her native Adelaide as: 'a queer little backwater of intellectual timidity, a kind of hangover of Victorian provincialism'.[11] Martin Boyd, who acknowledged Melbourne's 'culture', still longed for unseen Europe,[12] and Louise Mack, author of a popular novel for juveniles, *Teens*, described what drove her abroad in 1901, in spite of her local success:

> Every afternoon, away in far Australia, there comes over us all a half-past-two-in-the-afternoon feeling, an intolerable ennui, a sense of emptiness and discontent . . . It is our remoteness that pains us, a sudden sense of our great distance from the full intellectual life of the old world, from music and art . . . go back to Australia and the whole world vanishes like a dream.[13]

The world had vanished in such a way for Fred Manning. To regain it he must return to Europe. That fear of being buried alive in the provinces which seized Henry Handel Richardson's young musician, *Maurice Guest*, who came, after all, from a provincial town in England, not from the edge of the world, would stiffen the resolve of the gentlest young artist. The exciting years abroad had alienated Manning from his family a little, as well as from his country. His interests were very different, as were his friendships, and his allegiance to the faith of his parents had been undermined badly by the influence and arguments of Galton. To a young man who had known Beerbohm and Berenson, who had brushed shoulders with the friends of Oscar Wilde and the poets of the 1890s, Sydney was a literary village offering little future to his talents. He had published nothing since his review of Ibsen, though he continued to write.

For Frederic Manning, now an adult of twenty-one, Europe offered freedom from family pressures, a literary milieu and the additional happiness of being reunited with his intellectual alter ego, Arthur Galton. Sydney had not forgotten 'our Arthur'. The *Bulletin* noted in March 1902 that this militant champion of Anglicanism was now private chaplain to the Bishop of Ripon, and, in February 1903, that he was writing a memoir of that 'true poet', Lionel Johnson. And Galton had kept the editor of the *Sydney Morning Herald* informed, privately, of his current views on Romanism.[14] Whether Sir William and Lady Manning understood the strength of Fred's attachment to his old tutor or not, it was clear that this unusual son would not settle into a business career in Sydney, that he was determined to be a writer, and that the best place to practise that profession was England. He had finished a

Sir William Patrick Manning, Frederic Manning's father, managed 'an adroit balancing act between his simple Irish ancestry and his membership of the Anglo-Saxon establishment'.

Lady Manning in the 1890s, Frederic Manning dedicated Scenes and Portraits *to 'matri carissimae'.*

Manning's home in the 1890s, Elizabeth Bay House today; he later wrote that he 'always felt the character of a house'.

The 'earnest, austere . . . ambitious Arthur Galton' during his time in Australia

book which he hoped Heinemann would publish. This must have heartened busy and ambitious Sir William. Fred might well make good, with a small allowance from his father to tide him over until he was established. They would miss him but their money made it possible for them to holiday in Europe regularly. Ties would not be broken completely.

Arthur Galton also was changing his way of life again. Duties at the palace did not leave much time for his own writing. He had published *Our Attitude towards English Roman Catholics and the Papal Court* (1902) in his time there. He was also Jowett Lecturer at Oxford in 1903. But a quiet country living would give him more time for his special interests of modernist theology and Biblical criticism. There may well have been some personal problems too. After his disastrous time with Sir Robert Duff at Government House, it is surprising that Galton should have taken on another post involving a close, day-to-day, almost master-servant relationship. His choleric temperament was not fitted to being a subordinate. And the bishop had strong opinions too. He was, later, President of the National Council on Public Morals, and President of the National Council of Psychic Research. It is unlikely that the popular spiritualism of the day held any appeal for an austere intellectual like Galton. Worse, Bishop Carpenter was of a trusting, peace-seeking temperament, seeing even the Kaiser as a lover of peace who desired to promote the welfare of humanity, while Galton had become almost pathologically anti-German after visiting France in the wake of the Franco–Prussian war.

Whatever the reason for his going, Galton left the palace to take on the role of country vicar and the move provided the opportunity for a reunion with Fred. On 24 October 1903, Frederic Manning set out again for Europe, telling the *Bulletin* that he intended to spend some time in Italy.[15] His final destination, however, was the remote village of Edenham, deep in the Lincolnshire countryside, where he would be reunited with Mr Galton. For the older man it was a chance to create a writer, a protégé, who would be his justification and compensation. Under his care and guidance Fred would be reborn as a English scholar and aesthete, his hampering colonial birth forgotten. But although he might direct Manning's thought on religion, politics and literature, might polish up his dress and speech and manners to an almost English gloss, he could not wipe out the past.

As he matured, Frederic Manning showed far more understanding of the mystery of personality and the unvanquishable strength of early impressions than his cerebral and rigid mentor. Frederic Manning could not become a truly English Englishman. As he wrote:

All that we have seen, all that we have touched, the experience of our senses, the illusions of the brain, the desires of our heart, our ancestors, our companions, our country and our occupations, all move and work mysteriously in our being . . . Beneath what you seem to be lies what you think you are, and beneath that again, lies what you are indeed.[16]

But by the end of 1903 both Manning and Galton, united by personal affection, shared a common, somewhat simplistic, purpose. With study, diligence, practice, guidance, the brilliant youth would become the great English writer Galton had hoped once to be. It was only a matter of will and time, and the future would reward their dedication.

7

Edenham

AGAINST THE background of the quiet, flat, green, Lincolnshire countryside, Frederic Manning began his new life. The city-bred youth might now enjoy the pleasures of rural living in England, from the slow pace of village life with its gossipy, human interest and simple diversions to the beauty of the well-differentiated seasons, so striking to an Australian. He loved the northern winter especially 'from the last flame of autumn to the first reticent delicacy of spring'.[1] In summer he enjoyed, at times, hay-making with the farm labourers; in spring, long walks down leafy lanes. It was a society where eveything had its place in a traditional pattern, in contrast to the fluidity of the emergent bourgeoisie of his colonial childhood.

Except for a battered petrol pump, Edenham today must look very much as it did in Manning's years there: a few stone cottages, a small inn, the tall, grey church set in its little churchyard, where great trees shelter the tombstones. A few sheep graze in the fields beside the road, some cattle stand statue still. Even on a morning in early summer wisps of mist curl round the edges of the barns and farmhouses in the distance. There is a touch of clamminess in the fenland air. Not, one might think, the best climate for an asthmatic.

Cheek-by-jowl with the church stood the red, ivy-hung vicarage, Manning's new home. From the windows he might have studied St Michael's, so large and impressive a building for such a hamlet, with room for a congregation of four hundred, and in itself a lesson in English ecclesiastical history, containing vestiges of an Anglo-Saxon church, and a twelfth-century font, a thirteenth-century nave, a fourteenth-century porch and a high tower raised in the fifteenth and sixteenth centuries. Under its tall roof eight wooden angels gazed down at the tombs and memorials of the great lords and ladies of the district of former eras. Here was a sense of the past to impress and tantalize an almost traditionless colonial. Seeking some link with this past, Manning came to take pride in the fact that, only

55

a few kilometres away, in the little market town of Bourne, in the once-great abbey there, another Mannyng, a monk named Robert, had been the first to write in English as we know it. He wrote, this monk said, 'in simple speech for love of simple men'. Manning Road, in Bourne, commemorates him.

In Bourne were the shops, the market, the railway station and a large inn, the Burghley Arms, where William Cecil, first Baron Burghley and chief adviser to Queen Elizabeth I, had been born. Another local boast was that Charles Kingsley had written his story of a favourite son of Lincolnshire, the outlaw Hereward the Wake, in the vicarage at Edenham. Galton took special pleasure in this, surely, for Kingsley was famous as being as stout an anti-papist as could be found. It was to Bourne that young Fred went by carrier's cart to make small purchases, to have his hair cut, to meet the occasional visitor or to take the train for the two-hour trip to London. His affection for the place is shown by his choice of its name as that of the hero of his novel.

What was the life style of the pair in their new home? The stipend for the living was very modest in comparison with the income of other gentlemen, even of non-landholders in the professions: only £200 a year, with the reasonably commodious vicarage.[2] But in a time when a farm-worker with a wife and children to support was very lucky if he earned one pound a week, Galton could contrive to live in the fashion of a modest gentleman. In 1901 only 400 000 people declared their income at more than £400 a year, and £200 has been calculated as at about the least on which middle-class gentility could be maintained.[3] Galton, however, no doubt also enjoyed some small private income, as Manning did. And living was cheaper in the country. Dress, for instance, was simpler. They could avoid much of the extravagance of Edwardian upper-class codes which dictated special out-fits for every occasion and a change of attire at least three times a day. They could evade, too, the round of dinners, balls and teas of the city, the kind of life which Galton had found so tedious at Government House. Theatres, restaurants, concerts and entertaining would not be the drain they would be in city life. Servants, too, were cheaper in the country. For only a few shillings a week each, villagers coming in as daily helps would see to coal fires, laundry, cleaning, gardening. The pair would have enough for a civilized establishment, with a housekeeper to ensure that they could concentrate on their intellectual and artistic tasks in the privacy of their respective studies. Given Galton's high-handed manner, there were some-times problems with the servants but, in general, their way of life in these early years appears to have been comfortable, even privileged, despite a certain tumble-down quality about the vicarage and the chill of the fenlands.

The new vicar, although he had no curate (which at least ensured privacy), had sufficient leisure to follow his own interests. There were, nominally, five hundred souls to minister to in the parish but, except for the children in choir and Sunday School, most of these would not have been regular churchgoers, if they fitted the pattern of the times. The poverty of rural labourers, to whom every halfpenny counted, meant that many avoided church services, involving collection boxes and distinctions of dress. The clergyman would officiate, of course, at the ceremonies connected with birth, confirmation, marriage and death, and he was expected to visit the sick and dying of his congregation, in the squalid cottages of farm labourers, as well as in the properous farm houses and the manor. Being Galton he would preach a thundering sermon on Sunday, to a fair-sized congregation.

For while the lower classes were turning away from the churches, the upper classes in the country were still punctilious about religious observances. It was, after all, something to do; and the mistress of the great house of the district, as well as attending with some of her guests, would see to it that the Edwardian train of black-clad maids wended its way to church on Sunday too. In these services, class barriers were strong. The lord and lady of the manor went up to Communion first, followed by the doctor and the farmers, then the tradesmen, such as the blacksmith and the wheelwright, then, finally, the servants and farm labourers. What did Catholic-born, colonial-raised young Fred, used to Australian egalitarianism, think of it all? In general he seems to have accepted Arthur Galton's high Tory views at this stage.

Galton appears to have enjoyed his role as country vicar in these first years. The great family of the Edenham district and the patrons of his living were the recently created Earls of Ancaster. Galton, with his public school and Oxbridge education, his family coat of arms, his connections, however slight, with the Duke of Fife and the Duff family, was accepted by the Ancasters as a gentleman. Vicars, in general, held a higher standing with the aristocracy than other professionals. They were deemed worthy of being invited to dinner. Lawyers and doctors were asked only to luncheon. Galton not only dined at the Ancaster seat, Grimsthorpe Castle, one of the finest houses in Lincolnshire, a huge mansion set in a great park; he also joined at least one of the typical Edwardian shooting parties there, when four hundred brace of pheasants and partidges were slaughtered. On that occasion he made a strong impression on another guest, the American Ambassador. (Fred, no sportsman, was left at home.)

As for the vicar's pupil, his arrival must have been a matter of intense interest in a community where the tiniest incident was the subject of gossip. How the villagers and even the Ancasters must have wondered, at first, at the delicate lad, from far away Australia. Still, colonials from wealthy families, like their American counterparts, were inscrutable, unclassifiable mysteries with ways of their own. And the English, especially the upper classes, accepted eccentrics and unusual life styles with more equanimity than middle-class Australians. Freedom of thought and action, for people with means, was a mark of Edwardian society. Ex-clergyman Edward Carpenter, campaigner for more enlightened sexual attitudes and author of

Homogenic Love (1894), which dealt with 'the intermediate sex', shared his country cottage in Derbyshire with working-class George Merrill for thirty years without awkwardness. And in this case there seemed little cause for gossip. Bachelor scholar-clergymen were well-accepted members of English society; and young Fred Manning, the vicar's pupil—a gentleman it appeared, his father being a knight of means and some kind of colonial official—was accepted as part of the vicarage household and of the village.

There was even the occasional invitation to dinner at Grimsthorpe Castle for Fred. His first visit there must have been memorable, with the uniformed footmen, the great rooms, the protocol, the general magnificence of such establishments. As an incipient aesthete, he was delighted, surely, by the north front, built by Sir John Vanbrugh, by the huge hall with a double staircase at each end and by the great picture galleries, with their canvases by Lawrence, Reynolds and Van Dyck. The Countess of Ancaster, grandmother of a young boy, must have shown this shy young newcomer a special kindness and he established a friendly relationship with her, presenting her with a copy of his first book in November 1908 and dedicating his collection of verse, *Eidola*, to her in 1917. The diversions at the castle were infrequent, however. Like other such families, the Ancasters would have spent the season in London and some time abroad in winter. Neither, judging from Manning's extant letters, did Galton go in for the picnics, dinners and teas, usually a feature of country vicarage life. Reading, thinking, writing, talking together were their scholarly pleasures, while Galton's tendency to gout meant, for him at least, a temperate life style.

The great virtue of country life, for them, was its quietness, its freedom from the noise and stress and distractions of the city. And, for Galton, certainly, there was enough to do to escape boredom. As well as his parish duties to attend to, he had the instruction of his pupil, his own writing, including the weekly sermon and an occasional letter to *The Times*. He travelled a little, visiting Fox How in the Lakes district every year to see Miss Arnold, his idol's youngest sister. Fred did not accompany him there, but the pair visited Galton's old Worcestershire haunts during the Edenham years, for Lady Sandys of Humbleton Manor, Droitwich, told Jonathan Marwil that she remembered meeting Fred in pre-war days. Galton also enjoyed trips, alone, to Oxford, to hear a lecture, or, on one occasion, to give one, standing in for his cousin, Francis Galton. He stayed there with his old friend, Charles Shadwell, the Provost of Oriel, a close disciple of Pater. He visited London too, at times, for a Turkish bath and a night at his club, the Athenaeum. When Galton was absent young Fred acted as host to the visiting clergyman who carried out Galton's duties. The colonial lad was beginning to take on the persona of the Edwardian English country gentleman, happy in the peace of his book-lined study, working toward the future he and his tutor had planned.

Outside this quiet retreat, Edward VII and his train of pleasure lovers were pursuing their frivolous pastimes, shaking off the heaviness of late Victorianism, obliterating the image of the old Queen, with her worthy dullness. By 1904, however, signs of more fundamental changes were becoming clearer to the sharp-eyed. Mrs Emmeline Pankhurst and her militant daughter, Christabel, were organizing the latent power of women in the Women's Social and Political Union; the Russo–Japanese War drew attention to the rising power of that surprising and unknown element, the East. In January 1905 the Bloody Sunday uprising of the workers of St Petersburg gave an early warning to the tsar of what might lie in the future, while the first Moroccan crisis in March that year made plain the increasing tension between France and the Kaiser, heading a prosperous, demanding Germany. To meet the threat of the dangerously powerful new German Navy, Admiral Jackie Fisher, the new broom, was making sweeping changes, ruthlessly reorganizing the Royal Navy, bent on introducing a great modern weapon of war, the mighty dreadnought battleships, so speedy and so heavily armed.

Society in general was being shaken up as new ideas in science and morals appeared. Bertrand Russell's *The Principles of Mathematics* and George Moore's handbook to a new morality, *Principia Ethica*, were published in 1903; Albert Einstein stated his first theory of relativity in 1905. Industry grew and the cities swelled, as agriculture and traditional country life declined. Mass papers, mass transport, mass housing, mass entertainment, mass communications and mass household gadgets began to feed the needs of mass populations. All the aspects of modernity which so concerned E. M. Forster in his novel, *Howard's End* (1910), were starting to manifest themselves. An old society was dying, a new world emerging.

In secluded Edenham, however, the tide of life still flowed slowly and peacefully, much as it had done in the Victorian age; broken only, for Fred and Galton (apart from small problems with the servants), by long, quiet holidays with Galton's friend Llewellyn Hacon, another former associate of Wilde, and his wife Ryllis (Amaryllis Bradshaw, a former artist's model), who lived at Dornoch, Scotland, and by much shorter visits to London. Such pleasures took their proper place after work had been completed. As Galton wrote: 'The novice who would command the secrets of the Art must submit himself to a long apprenticeship and to the most rigorous training'.[4] The occasional visitor was welcome, as bringing some variety, provided he were of the proper scholarly temperament. Such a one was Albert Houtin, a French intellectual and dissident priest, who had much in common with Galton. He came to stay when Fred was twenty-two.

Houtin, in his past, had studied theology with the French Benedictines, had visited the Anglican community at Cowley and had developed a passion for the works of Newman. His views, however, had clashed with those of his church superiors, and he left his diocese in 1901. But religion, theology and biblical criticism remained his field of study. He was deeply impressed with the vast philosophic and historical learning of this young sage of Edenham, and he wrote of him: 'Perhaps another Walter Pater, and even more if he wants to work',[5] taking a rather pedantic view of literary inspiration and achievement. Middle-aged, obsessed with theological debates, possessed of little creative flair, his sympathies lay with the older partner in the relationship. The teacher would be little known, he thought, but the pupil would be his fruit. When one studied the genius of Manning, one would find Galton. Such reflections reveal some of the hopes Galton entertained at this time for his disciple and must have discussed with Houtin. The Frenchman also became an adviser to the brilliant youth. He and Fred exchanged letters until Houtin's death, and his help, in particular, with the Renan chapter in Manning's *Scenes and Portraits* was acknowledged by the author in the Preface. Some fifteen years older than Fred, fussy and pedantic, Houtin was a friend of the mind to the young man, another mentor, not a soul-mate, though the pair grew closer over the years.

He was well aware, however, of the force of Galton's determination and his whole-heartedness. 'He has given him [Manning] everything',[6] he wrote, implying that the clergyman had sacrificed his own career for the good of his disciple. This may well contain an echo of complaints by Galton, stemming from his imperious vanity. Galton, it might be more truly said, had failed in his own ambitions and was determined that Fred, his creation, should succeed. Houtin says no word about the sacrifices made by Fred, of youth, of freedom, of individuality. Imprisoned in a middle-aged world, cut off from the daily company of his peers in age, separated from his family, far from his country, his life was confined to the bounds of Art set by one dogmatic individual. In youth, however, all was still promise, and the sacrifice must have seemed worth while. In addition, to bring something of the brightness of young spirits into his life he had the friendship of beautiful, carefree Dorothy Shakespear, who, in 1905, was nineteen.

Dorothy's mother was a writer and her father an amateur painter, so Dorothy had been brought up to enjoy intellectual and artistic interests. As well as being widely read, she sketched and painted. She had also spent a year in Geneva, perfecting her French in the traditions of the English upper middle class. Cut off from her youthful, light-hearted company, except for the short visits to London often in the care of watch-dog Galton, Fred reached out to this charming girl in whimsical, summery letters, treating of village gossip, domestic trifles, his moods, his literary plans and the antics of his only youthful companion, his kitten, Kim. He signed himself, 'Always yours, Fred'. Like most young men of literary aspirations he thought of himself as a poet and in July 1905, after a visit to the Shakespears which seems to have gone awry because of problems associated with his bad health, he sent flowers and berries to Olivia as a peace offering, while to Dorothy he sent some verses, 'Dawn Music':

Dawn and the dawning of song
Leaping with Joy into light:
Flinging their notes to prolong
Echoes of stars, that the night
Wore in her dusk-coloured hair,
Larks with their souls winged to flight
Shout in the virginal air.

Leaping with Joy into light
Golden, that gleams over gray
Song that is swifter than flight
Up to the heaven of day
Rises in ecstasy, rent,
Breaks into musical spray
With the last rapture content
Song and the dawning of day.[7]

The verses were musical and well-crafted enough but not something to overwhelm Dorothy with poetic vitality. Just as Fred, physically, gave an impression of frailty and lack of vigour, his poetry, too, looked anaemic. The journey back from London by train, only a matter of a couple of hours, had taxed him badly in this case; and such difficult health, combined with his narrow existence, led to a chafing of spirits at times, as he admitted to Dorothy in a letter: 'When I am bored with other people I run away; at present the difficulty is that I am bored with myself, and it is impossible to run away from the fellow, who is quite impedible and bores me to death'.[8] Then he attempted to turn his mood, joking and punning, mainly about his 'perfectly charming' cat, his main source of entertainment and companionship. No wonder he could be found at times, as the years progressed, at the village inn.

In another letter he wrote: 'Oh! such a tragedy has happened! Cats were created by the devil, they are possessed by the devil, whose name is Legion; they have no morals, no manners, no respect for the property of others or the inspirations of the Muse ... Let them be anathema, maranatha'. He went on to detail the cat's misdoings, which had resulted in various magazines and manuscripts having to be burnt, including his book of Valiance, containing nearly three hundred aphorisms. And he concluded: 'But pity me that the B. of V. should have such an unhappy end. Eheu! O Absalom, my son! my son!'[9] His bright spirits might be dulled by loneliness and unending study but they were not extinguished. However, for a girl eager for life and romance, aphorisms must have seemed a rather unexciting form of literature. A few such aphorisms survive in a notebook in his papers in the Mitchell Library, titled 'Virtú'.

Galton was busy with his writing also. *The Appeal of the Church of England* appeared in 1905, and *Church and State in France* (which was republished in 1972) in 1907. The two led a disciplined, hard-working life; but the fixed opinions, the dislike of novelty and the overbearing manner of his

tutor kept Manning a prisoner of the past, so that the verses he was
writing at this time, such as 'Ad Cynaram', which he sent to Dorothy in
December 1905, lay in the shadow of the dead 1890s, as did his first published poems, 'Bal Masque' in *Outlook* (9 May 1906) and the Boston
Living Age (1 September), and 'The Secret' in the same journals (16 June
and 20 October). These were in the style perhaps favoured by Galton, with
his fond memories of the young Lionel Johnson. But Fred Manning lacked
his predecessor's poetic gifts, the lyrical intensity, the classicism. They
reflected, however, something of the personality of the poet. Dorothy
Shakespear, decades later, told Professor L. T. Hergenhan that she found
Fred Manning a nervous, entertaining character, seeming to belong to the
1890s rather than to the twentieth century.[10] In his fragile, artificial verses
he was not in tune even with the Edwardian mood, for the popular
Edwardian poets like Henry Newbolt, John Masefield and William Watson
were writing hearty, middlebrow ballads about patriotism and the sea.

A youth spent in an isolated little village, under the domination of a
middle-aged man of strong will and firm views, meant, inevitably, that the
younger, weaker partner, lacking any experience of the world, took on
some of the colour of the older man, at least in opinions. Galton, that proud
Englishman, no doubt emphasized heavily and continually the glories of
English history, literature and religion. Yet he was also an ardent
Francophile, devoted especially to modern French writing; and Manning
became one too. He was an expert on the relations between Church and
State in France; Manning supported his views in a letter to *The Times* (19
January 1907). Galton despised everything German; Manning followed
suit. Galton, forgetting his *Hobby Horse* days when, under Johnson's influence, he had espoused briefly the Celtic Twilight movement, took a
strongly conservative stand on Irish Home Rule. His pupil, regardless of
his ancestry, did the same. Galton had written on St Francis of Assisi in the
Hobby Horse, had produced a book on Thomas Cromwell and admired the
French historian and philosopher, Ernest Renan. All these influences
appeared in Manning later. On most intellectual and social matters the two
were in agreement; in character they were very different, Galton so domineering and aggressive, Fred so nervous and amiable; Galton, at this time,
so sure of his Anglicanism and his Englishness, Fred, the uncertain, doubting expatriate; Galton so vain and confident, Fred so modest and diffident.

Dependent Fred, seeking support and affection, clung to his gentler
friendships with Olivia and Dorothy Shakespear. Both women were literary
confidantes, reading his unpublished work, offering advice and criticism.
He told his friend James Fairfax that Olivia compared some short stories he
showed her in 1905 (possibly part of *Scenes and Portraits*) to the writing
of the French novelist, Pierre Louÿs, friend of André Gide and Oscar Wilde.
She thought Manning used the English language as a means of writing in
French.[11] She may have meant that he wrote with French clarity, irony and
precison, or that his writing had an affinity with Louÿs's musical, delicate

prose. Manning, however, had none of Louÿs's concern with sensuality and sexuality. Dorothy gave her views in 1905 on a story he called 'The Scarlet Masque', and in December 1907 he told her of some ideas he had for a set of stories (his *Scenes and Portraits*), and outlined the underlying religious thought: 'It seems to me that true Christianity is not a dead body of dogma but an order of progress and free enquiry, continually developing beyond the limits of all creeds'.[12]

Both Dorothy and Olivia Shakespear were immensely important to Fred Manning in these early years. (Indeed the family believed that he stayed abroad because of Olivia.) They offered friendship to a lonely youth, separated from family and in some kind of thrall to a dogmatic, bullying older man. Galton, too, was devoted to both women in his own way. And through the Shakespears and Olivia's salon, Manning made other friends, in particular one who was, according to Olivia, 'the most fascinating woman she had ever met'.[13] As Olivia had mixed in London literary circles for a number of years, her judgement is a tribute to the personality of Eva Fowler, who, as the years passed, was to become almost as important as Galton to Manning among his friends in England. Unfortunately she is a sketchy figure. None of their letters appear to have survived. Did Manning destroy them, in his passion for secrecy? Yet she meant so much to him that, years later, he was buried only a few feet from her grave. Whatever the impediments to their relationship in life, he joined her in death, in a gesture that was touchingly sentimental, given his lifetime reserve.

Californian-born Eva, the eldest daughter of a Prussian-born naturalized American, Paul Neumann, at one time Attorney-General in Hawaii, was brought up in those then distant and exotic islands. She married in 1890 a wealthy Welsh engineer, Alfred (Taffy) Fowler, who manufactured steam ploughs, and had settled with him in London. As a breezy middle-class American, married to a *nouveau riche* manufacturer, she was unlikely to find an easy entrée into snobbish Edwardian society. But Edwardian women, in general, were discovering an independence in politics and the arts, and Eva was not one, it seems, to be satisified with playing fashionable auction bridge or doing good works. Instead, like Olivia, she cultivated artistic and intellectual interests, building up a small salon at her London house at 124 Knightsbridge, London, and becoming the confidante and patron of young talent. Affectionate and generous, she also invited her protégés on literary and artistic holidays to her country cottage, Daisy Meadow, near Brasted, Kent. And she was sufficiently rich and impressive to be sketched later by John Singer Sargent. (This charcoal drawing of Mrs Fowler was exhibited at the Royal Academy in 1926.)

She met Frederic Manning in mid-1908, when Manning could lay claim to being a published poet. There were certain aspects of their lives to make a bond. Both were expatriates who had left a distant provincial homeland to seek a place in the metropolis; both were therefore outside the mainstream of English life. Like Manning, Eva was a searching, doubting Catholic, keenly interested in biblical criticism, she said, although her dabbling in the spiritualism popular at the time would not have been in tune with Manning's sceptical nature. Under the influence of W. B. Yeats she even lent her cottage in Kent to experiments in spiritualism featuring the well-known medium, Elizabeth Radcliffe.

When she and Manning met she was in her middle thirties, he in his early twenties. It was not a conventional romantic attachment. He called her, as he did Olivia, 'beloved aunt'. Yet it was a deep and lasting affection. For her part, handsome, childless Eva must have felt a real tenderness towards this witty, charming young man of the nervous manner and delicate health, for she was kind to him; 'a person it is sometimes difficult to be kind to',[14] he judged, regretting his bursts of fretfulness and petulance. She even helped in the typing of his manuscripts. He was still, in some ways, a lost child missing his mother, as the number of mother-centred poems show. Galton could not be be described as kind and young Fred needed a gentleness which his mentor might have derided as sentimental. What, one wonders, did caustic Galton make of this poem?

> Sweet white mother of rose-white dreams
> Through my windows the song of birds pours in
> And the sunlight on to my table streams.
>
> As a clear globe prisons the golden light,
> So I prison the dreams you shed on me,
> Sweet white mother of dreams rose-white.
>
> In a crystal globe I prison all things:
> Sound is frozen to silence there;
> Cover me over with wide white wings,
> Prison my life in thy crystal sphere,
> As a clear globe prisons the golden light,
> Sweet white mother of dreams rose-white.[15]

When in London, Fred often stayed with the Fowlers, and through Eva he met her younger sisters, Anita Focke, Ynez Stackable and Lillie Bird, to whom he dedicated poems. Lillie, in her early twenties and married to an Englishman, lacked, for Manning, the sympathetic nature of her eldest sister. He wished her 'a little gentler, a little wiser'.[16] There was obviously less tension in the company of older women who were prepared to mother him a little. He became friendly with another rich American hostess, Mrs W. N. Macmillan of Berkeley Square, and dedicated a poem to her. And he sometimes spent a night, when in London, with Lady Russell, the elderly widow of his father's old employer, Sir Peter Nicol Russell. Other women with whom he was in friendly contact in the pre-war years included Dora Curtis, an illustrator of children's books, Mrs Charles Fairfax, a former resident of Sydney, and Lady Dunsany, wife of the Irish writer, Edward Dunsany. From 1906 his elder sister, Edith, an independent individualist, lived mostly in England, and his friendship with Ryllis Hacon lasted for many years, long past her husband's death. He was also acquainted with Rachel Annand Taylor, a Scottish poet and aesthete, with May Sinclair, the feminist and novelist, and was a friend of the novelist Una Taylor, daughter of the Victorian man-of-letters, Sir Henry Taylor.

Manning clearly enjoyed the company of women and depended somewhat on their interest and support. He discussed his work with Olivia, Dorothy and Eva. He saw them whenever he was in London. He stayed with them, lunched and dined with them, and holidayed at Daisy Meadow. Yet he kept even Eva Fowler at a distance despite his warm regard for her, and his family in Sydney knew nothing of her. Some years later, Eva gave Dorothy 'quite a serious warning, (oh! so subtly)' against 'the artistic temperament' in men, causing the girl to speculate whether the older woman had suffered severely from it herself.[17] Had Eva hoped for something in her relationship with Fred which did not eventuate? When, some years later, Dorothy finally decided to marry penniless young poet Ezra Pound, some in the Shakespear circle were concerned. But Eva declared that she might have done it herself. In Manning's papers in the Mitchell Library there is the outline of a curious play about an older spinster's love for a young man who is in love with a young girl, which concludes with the quotation: 'Crabbed age and youth cannot live together'. The theme may have been prompted by his relationships with Eva and Dorothy, though fussy Galton appears the more likely inspiration. Were Manning and Eva held back from a conventional affair by their difficulties and delicacies? Eva, like Olivia, was bourgeois rather than bohemian. She might not be able to aspire to the social heights of Lady St Helier's salon in Portland Place but there seemed nothing in her group of the touch of raffishness which marked some literary sets, such as that of Ford Madox Ford's lover, Violet Hunt. On the other hand she was not narrow minded. She was open to new movements and, like Olivia, was quick to welcome Ezra Pound to London.

And, for his part, Manning, while needing the security of her kindness, possessed a deep reserve, a secretiveness, and preferred to guard against too much closeness. When he dedicated a series of poems to Eva under the title 'Les Heures Isolées', in his *Poems* (1910), he prefaced it with a quotation from the French symbolist, Henri de Régnier—a delicate versifier on melancholy themes—asserting the pleasures of loneliness, to the effect that, in explaining himself a man diminishes himself. Each must keep his own secret, and the beautiful life consists in hours spent alone. Years later, in a letter to T. E. Lawrence, he used the phrase again: 'On se doit son propre secret'. And the last words of *Her Privates We* are: 'They sat there silent; each man keeping his own secret'. The sense of a unique, hidden self, to be protected even from those who loved him, and whom he loved, was fundamental. The relationship between Eva Fowler and Frederic Manning, while enduring and strong, was complex.

Sheer physical weakness may have been the basis of his guardedness. He depended for survival on a quiet life. When he visited London he found the noise and stress unendurable, and maintained that he would never go there, except that his friends were there and he had to see his friends. It may be that he felt he had to protect himself from draining emotional relationships; Galton's hot temper was exhausting enough. Manning, with his dangerous asthma, was perhaps a special case; but Ronald Pearsall has contrasted the energy of Edwardian women, the feminists in particular, with the apathy of the men of that period.[18] Olivia and Eva were not strictly feminists. But their energy and strength may have been rather overwhelming, a little too much for Manning. He may have resented the will and power of Edwardian women, although, at the same time, he was fascinated by strong women like Brunhild and Cleopatra, who: 'though completely evil in the ordinary sense . . . redeem themselves and win our sympathy by a moment of heroic fortitude, or of supreme and consuming anguish'.[19] Where more ordinary women were concerned he was more critical: 'Women must always be stimulating some man's ambition', thinks his hero Bourne, in the interlude with a French girl. As a very young man Manning himself had found Ibsen's heroines too managing. 'Woman will have her finger in a man's destiny. Is there trouble? "*Cherchez la femme*".'[20]

Slightly built, dandyish in dress, mannered in style, fastidious and reticent in personality, the Fred Manning of these pre-war years liked to treat women with a touch of chivalrous ceremony. Eva, so dear to him, was always Mrs Fowler in his letters. His Edwardian verses have something of the character of a mask, a stylized defence against strong emotions and a too turbulent life. The delicate, melancholy love poems he was writing seem to reflect an image of Martin Green's typical Pierrot figure, 'pale, woebegone, listless', delicate in sensibilites and in health, sighing over his wistful verses:

> Love is but a wind that blows
> Over waves, or fields of corn,
> Floating petals, falling snows,
> The swift passing of the dawn.
>
> These are all Love's signs, perchance,
> Floating, fragile, drifting things!
> Dead leaves are we in the dance,
> Moved by his unresting wings.
>
> Love is light within thine eyes,
> Dearest! Love is all thy tears.
> Let us for this hour be wise:
> What have we to hope from years?[21]

It was one of a series dedicated to E. F.

But in his chosen life of monk-like seclusion in the vicarage he not only wrote such verses. He studied, he wrote prose pieces, he thought about theology and philosophy, he conversed with Galton on these matters, and wrote to Houtin. He shared the simple daily contacts of village life. The visits to London kept him in touch with friends and provided a stimulus. He wrote to Laurence Binyon at the British Museum, was acquainted with Selwyn Image and Lord Dunsany, had Beerbohm's address at 48 Upper Berkeley Street.[22] He kept his ties with his family in Australia. It was, however, largely a world of words on paper, with only one real companion, a rather elderly one for someone in his early twenties. Other young men of his age were revelling in talk, company, love, sport, parties, entertainments, friendships: all the delights of youth discovering itself. It may have been the tedium of his sequestered life which led to his habit of chain-smoking, to his problems with alcohol and his pleasure in gambling. Richard Aldington was harsh in post-war years about Manning's drinking[23] and Manning's alter-ego, Bourne, is a prodigious drinker, able to hold his liquor to the extent that he can drink sergeant-majors under the table. He longs 'to go on a big drunk somewhere, and break this bloody monotony'. Bourne, however, knows wines, and is discriminating about them. He also has no objections to a bet (a flutter on the game of 'crown and anchor'), like Manning, who even wrote in later life of the marriage of two friends as appealing to his 'gambling instinct'.[24] He found relaxation in studying form guides and placing modest wagers. But both Bourne and Manning combined their gambling streak with a love and knowledge of horses and horsemanship; witness Manning's war poem 'Transport' in *Eidola*. And even when a child in poor health, Manning rode well.

Whatever its small pleasures, Frederic Manning, in his middle twenties, was living a very quiet and restricted life. It was a happy chance that from around 1907 he was able to take pleasure in a friendship with a young man near his own age, a handsome, happy-natured Oxford undergraduate, who shared Manning's interest in languages, literature, poetry and ideas. This young man was, moreover, a fellow countryman. His name was James Griffyth Fairfax, and he was to become a true friend and deeply important to Frederic Manning in the pre-war years, a balance to the austerity and solemnity of Galton.

8

Best Friends

JIM OR JIMMIE, as Manning called him, was born in Sydney in 1886 and was, therefore, four years the younger. His father, Charles, the eldest son of Sir James Fairfax of the great Sydney newspaper company, left the *Sydney Morning Herald* to settle permanently in England in 1904. Jim after a period at Winchester (a bow to the shade of poor Lionel Johnson?) went on to Oxford, to Galton's old haunt, New College. The correspondence with Manning began in his undergraduate years. As leading families in a small city, the Fairfaxes and the Mannings, although belonging to very different traditions, attended the same public functions and were, at the least, aware of each other. Possibly the two young men had known each other in their home town. They could share memories of their homeland as well as a passion for poetry, and a united stand against overwhelming Englishness.

In his first years abroad Manning, who had come to maturity in the fervour of nationhood, still thought of himself as very much an Australian. Criticism by Englishman Herbert A. Strong—a former classics professor in Melbourne—of the White Australia policy in the political and literary journal, the *Outlook* (8 April 1905), evoked a protest from the expatriate at Strong's 'maladroitness and apparent animus'.[1] Manning took the view that Australia must increase its population by every possible method, but preferably by birth rather than by alien immigration. If today his stand seems prejudiced at that time it was shared by most Australians, by socialists as much as conservatives. The great historian of Australians at war, C. E. W. Bean, a 'small l' liberal, defended the White Australia policy in the *Spectator* (13 July 1907), and the Sydney magazine *Lone Hand* featured a series of articles by progressive playwright, Louis Esson on the 'asiatic menace' in 1908; notions of anti-Semitism and xenophobia were fostered by the socialist, republican, egalitarian *Bulletin*. It was the unhappy insularity of the times.

Manning was also concerned that his country should be self-reliant in defence. If Britain withdrew her naval support then 'We Australians should be compelled to form a small navy for ourselves'. He was probably the colonial Ezra Pound met at a tea-party in London before the Great War who pointed out that one cruiser could interrupt all the Indian trade. He was quite proud of the military training scheme of his homeland where almost every schoolboy learned to use a rifle, and he predicted that 'a volunteer army of Australians would be far more efficient in the field than a volunteer army of Englishmen whose Liberal demagogues have so far prevented even an elementary instruction in military art'. Although a conservative in disposition he defended the Australian Labor Party against the charge of larrikinism, levelled by the English, and he thought *The Times* misrepresented Australian matters.[2]

He could discuss such matters with Jim and reminisce with him, if in sentimental mood, about their childhood. But Jim was more in the image of what the English expected the son of wealthy and important colonials to be. He was handsome, robust, solidly built, with the smooth look of a bourgeois romantic hero in his well-cut tweeds and bowtie. Like that other model colonial, Bernie Wise, he could claim an English public school and university, could in time seem very English. Frail, shy, scholarly Manning was harder to place as an Anglo-Australian colonial abroad. Yet kindly, somewhat Establishment Jim was dedicated to poetry and literature with almost as much ardour as his delicate friend, and could boast of a letter of introduction to George Bernard Shaw from Henry Champion, the English editor of the Australian journal, *Booklover.*

To the exile in Edenham the friendship was tremendously important. Jim was 'animae dimidium meae' to him (half of my soul); when they had passed two years of their comradeship Manning wrote: 'I'm not a gregarious animal . . . There are only yourself and a few others who are real to me'. There were longed-for visits to Edenham and discussions of their work. 'When you come here we shall lie under the mulberry tree smoking cigarettes with just that abandonment to the moment, "yielding to one brief, sweet luxuriance".'[3] There were meetings in London, where Jim's mother, Florence Fairfax, lived and brief summer holidays with Eva Fowler's artistic set in Kent. His relationship with Jim was the closest Fred came, in his isolation, to the typical undergraduate friendship, with its mixture of affection and intellectual stimulation. Cut off by his asthma and by Galton's sway, he could have no share in the kind of life depicted by E. M. Forster in his novel of the Cambridge of the period, *The Longest Journey* (1907). He could only read about the *badinage*, the discussions, the luncheon and tea parties, the hours on the river, the walking and reading tours, the company of a group of young and lively minds: all the pleasures that Jim and other young people of similar interests, abilities and backgrounds enjoyed.

From a distance he observed wistfully the high spirits and freedom of

Fairfax's rowdy Oxford set: 'Your Bacchanalia is a subject of envy to me. Was there no Proctor, another Pentheus to intrude upon these orgiastic rites?'; and on another occasion he mocked at himself for being elderly and professorial in his advice and style. It came, he said, from having lived always with people much older.[4] The deprivation he felt at the lack of a youthful, undergraduate life may have led to a touch of envy at the lot of those more fortunate. He showed an ambivalent attitude in later years to Oxford, loving its beauty but fearing the influence of some of its dons; classicist and fellow expatriate, Gilbert Murray, in particular. He disliked also the plummy Oxford accent. His own voice probably retained traces of the almost ineradicable mark of his birthplace, which could be an emotional trigger abroad. Anglo-Australian expatriate Martin Boyd was roused to fury by the English scorn for the Australian accent. But happy with Jim, compatriot and fellow poet, Manning could share at least some of the joys of youth. Fairfax, who could enjoy all the diversions of the university to the full, with his looks, his health, his money, must have found Fred, somewhat older than his undergraduate associates, a charming and interesting companion, to make the journey to Edenham fairly frequently. Jim seemed, too, to have the good will of of Arthur Galton, who visited the undergraduate on his trips to Oxford and took an interest in his poetry. Fairfax was, after all, at the clergyman's old college, which made a bond, and he probably took an interest in Australians who had fled that shore. The friendship with Fairfax, some youthful company, would keep his pupil happier than a complete isolation.

Manning's health was certainly poor, but given the fact of his later army service, his incarceration seems unnecessary. London, with its crowds and noise and pace, was beyond him but could he not have lived a quiet, studious life among his peers at Oxford or Cambridge? To isolate him, to deprive this highly intelligent young man of a broader experience, of a range of friendships, a testing of his abilities, indicates a narrow possessiveness, a selfishness, on Galton's part, as well as a great vanity.

He certainly domineered over and dictated to his acolyte. In June 1907, when Manning was almost twenty-five, he expressed to Fairfax his disappointment that he would not be able to be present at Jim's twenty-first birthday party on 15 July, 'so great a festival'. The reason was that he was behind in his work and Galton was consequently in a bad mood. Fred's family had been visiting, and he had suffered a bad asthma attack, but such excuses were not acceptable to the taskmaster. The work must be done. Young Fairfax had published already a first book of verse, *The Gates of Sleep and Other Poems* (1906). Manning was falling behind. Galton's tyranny may well have provoked Manning's asthma. On this special occasion however, all ended happily. In late June, Manning felt he might be able to get a day in town, if Galton recovered from his irritation over the poems not being ready for the publisher. By 12 July he had sent the poems off, and was free to join the celebration.[5] Galton's passion for his protégé's

success, backed by his formidable temper and possibly a streak of possess-
ive jealousy, induced in the gentle, frail, younger man a certain subservi-
ence. Richard Aldington, a friend of later years, thought that as a writer
Manning always needed direction or else his indolence, partly a product of
his physique, would take charge. In living with Galton there was also the
question of keeping the peace. Yet Manning, in his letters, never let slip a
word of crticism of his mentor. Nor did he speak of him as a friend, as
Arthur. It was almost always Mr Galton, sometimes A. G.

At last Arthur Galton, at the end of 1907, had some result from his
tutelage: Manning's first book, a long narrative poem, *The Vigil of
Brunhild*, appeared in December that year. For a young man to whom a
trip to London was an ordeal, the subject was an odd choice. Brunhild was
the warrior queen of Austrasia, who waged war on her brother-in-law,
Chilperic, and his second wife, Fredegonde, seeking vengeance for her
sister's murder. She took her step-nephew Merow, or Merovee, as her lover,
was imprisoned finally by her rebellious nobles and dragged to death by
wild horses in 613 A.D. at the age of eighty. But Manning was fascinated
by her and would hear no word against her, he told Jim in early June. He
admired the old Queen for her courage, her will, and her struggle to create
some order after the collapse of the Roman Empire. The themes of passion,
murder and battle suggest that for all his quiet exterior the young poet was
drawn by the flamboyance, danger, violence and adventure of the heroic
life, by all he had no part in, by, as he wrote in the poem:

> . . . A life of war and love;
> Passions that shake the soul; bright, ruddy flames
> Devouring speedily this fretful flesh:
> A life of clamour, shouting, dust and heat . . .

The mild reception of this first work must have been an anti-climax for
Arthur Galton. The *Times Literary Supplement* (23 January 1908),
reviewed it briefly, along with seven other volumes by names unknown
today, saying it lacked grandeur and passion, though it was clearly the
work of one with a sensitive ear and fine taste. In most reviews Tennyson
was seen as an influence. This irritated Manning, for he was glad that poet
was not mentioned in a review by Fairfax which he sent his father. He
cared, it was clear, about his father's opinions on his work.

It was more than a year before the most generous appreciation of the
work appeared in the *Book News Monthly* (April 1909), when another
young poet praised the old Saxon vigour and medieval glamour of such
lines as:

> But in this little moment which is mine
> While all my foes are sleeping, drunkenly,
> Amid the dying lights, the broken meats,
> Which the dogs tear upon the rush strewn floor
> While even the moonlight sleeps upon the hills,

> I build again, out of my memories,
> The storm and splendour of my troubled life.

The reviewer, Ezra Pound, was enchanted by medievalism, and had recently met, and liked, Frederic Manning.

Sales were sluggish and struck some rather special obstacles in Sydney, where his eldest sister organized a public reading and sale at the Women's Club, which was misinterpreted. 'Poor Brunhild', the author wrote to Houtin, 'An ecclesiastic of the diocese of Sydney has been spreading a stupid story to the effect that the book was put upon the Index, and that my father ashamed of his heretical son, bought up all the copies in Sydney'.[6]

He had been working hard on his second book for some time and was drained of energy. Never physically at ease, his constant pain under pressure of work led to bouts of peevishness and despondency of which he felt ashamed. There were other spells of good health when he felt robust and cheerful as in the spring of 1908, when despite his physical frailty he got up at dawn to walk four miles, and then walked another three after a day's work. Asthma, insomnia, neuralgia, a poor digestion and a bad back meant that he was more often than not physically miserable. With Jim he could be really happy, could forget his pain, and he so enjoyed their holiday together at Daisy Meadow in July that he had no wish to go alone the following year when Jim could not come. A devotee of Swinburne, Fairfax wrote a derivative ode to celebrate his friend's twenty-sixth birthday in July 1908.

> Come, all ye Muses over the foaming ways,
> To Albion's blanched coast.
> There dwelleth he, who all his rose-white days
> Falleth in prayer and praise,
> The minister of your eternal host.[7]

At this stage in their relationship Manning took a generous view of his friend's talents. 'Swinburne is dead, and you are the heir of all his music. But we look for something from you which he lacked', he wrote in April 1909, with all the enthusiastic sincerity of the young, determined that their generation will set the world alight and outstrip their older friends. Jim might have missed winning the Newdigate prize for poetry that year, but was it worth the having? As Manning wrote to Jim (9 May 1908), 'a kind of paralysing academic formalism seems the chief quality of all who win it'.

How earnest and high-minded, how determinedly literary and intellectual they were, talking of their work and their ambitions, of metre and cadence, of Ariadne and Stheneboea, of Judith and Circe, as they sprawled on the grass under the mulberry tree, while Galton, who liked to be there when Jim visited, pondered, in his study, on the threat of Rome.

Country life stood still in Edenham; the scene before them was familiarly idyllic, even to city-reared colonials:

The full ewes call to the lambs;
Lowing, the cattle come
To drink at the reed-fringed pool,
Bending, they drink, and lift
Dripping muzzles, to gaze
With patient, satisified eyes
Over the plenteous earth.
While slowly out of the fens,
And heavy plough-lands the mist
Rises to greet thee, and spires
Of thin blue smoke, that ascend
Trembling into the calm
Windless air, and float
From the habitations of man.[8]

The rich green calm of the Lincolnshire fields, so very different from the heat and harshness of the countryside of their native land, was no mere pretty picture for serious-minded Fred. For this grandson of a farmer, it evoked an aspect of the eternal, the yoke of the seasons, the peasant cycle of birth, work, death:

. . . And his children forget,
Even they, too, that he was.
They turn to their toil, and eat,
Sleep, drink, as of old he did.[9]

In this quiet, secluded life in Edenham, except for the rare dinner at the castle, there was nothing for Fred of the frivolous world of the Edwardian legend: the house parties with their servants, dressing up, love affairs; the shooting parties in Scotland and Norfolk; the dinners, the balls, the strict manners and loose morals. It was a world far removed, too, from the booming middle-class suburbs happy in their sports clubs, gramophone dances, musical comedies, ping-pong tournaments, and household gadgets like the vacuum cleaner. It had little awareness of the slums and sweated labour of the industrial cities, of the drunkenness, the gambling, the food 'on tick', the desperation and growing resentment as the rich grew richer and the poor poorer. The most vigorous Edwardian novelists, Arnold Bennett, H. G. Wells, John Galsworthy, even G. K. Chesterton, were responding to the movement in society, writing of socialism, Fabianism, provincial life, free love, feminism, matters of class and money; and left-wing ideas were being circulated especially by the radical magazine *New Age* first published by A. R. Orage in 1907.

The young recluse of Edenham, cut off from such change, seemed afloat in time; and in space as well, as the years weakened the bonds with his homeland. He evinced none of that nostalgia for the land of his birth which led some compatriots to congregate together in a an Anglo-Australian club dubbed Dingo Dell by Barbara Baynton;[10] to cooee to each other across the street; or to sniff crushed eucalypt leaves in the manner of a homesick

Louise Mack heroine. Even Henry Handel Richardson, so settled in expatriate life, could be swept back into the past by a scent: 'To this day I have
only to catch a whiff of mimosa in a dingy London street, and I am once
again a small girl, sitting on a fallen tree under the bluest of skies, with all
around me these golden, almost stupefyingly-sweet masses of blossom'.[11]
Martin Boyd, so very Anglo-Australian, so long an expatriate, took delight
in recalling his childhood home: 'I think I was happiest at Yarra Glen than
I have been at any other time in my life . . . I remember it as a place of perpetual sunlight—sunlight on the distant hills, sunlight filtering through
the vines and nectarine trees that enclosed the verandah, and through the
wattle branches on the riverbank'.[12] If Manning were ever overtaken by
such rushes of memory he kept them to himself, apart from some reticent
references to the irrecoverable past. Reflective and wistful, sighing to the
moon over his derivative verses (a mixture of Rossetti, Swinburne and
Dowson as Julian Symons put it),[13] shut off from his past and from the
vital, elemental present, he must have seemed destined to live out his days
as a sad tailender to the poets of the 1890s. This impression ignored the
fact that behind the slight verses there was a strong mind and a sympathetic sensibility, which combined to make him seem much older than his
years, and a strength of will and capacity for endurance.

When a friend of Eva Fowler's died in 1908, he grieved for her loss, for
her sake, since she had been so kind to him, experiencing, as he looked at
the fact of death 'a sense of intimate communion and sympathy with our
fellows, when we reflect that we are all liable, sooner or later, to suffer the
same loss, to come to the same mystery . . . It is the one thing that draws
us all together, and shows us how necessary we are to each other'.[14] When
Eva's much-loved youngest sister, Lillie Bird, died suddenly in Mexico, a
year later, aged twenty-four, Manning, three years older, commented: 'she
was such a child and did not understand that life is a weary business'. Well
aware of 'the limits which life imposes'[15] he had formulated a creed of
acceptance and love.

> What I do know about life and death is simply that we must trust something,
> whether in ourselves or beyond ourselves I do not know—which seems to tell us
> that we are all one, that in spite of all revolt on our parts, we do what we were
> sent here to do, and that we are not wasted. I have no kind of creed beyond that.
> Our lives seem to blend and mix into others', nothing seems to be lost but
> merely to flow through all things, to escape from our sight for a little while, but
> never to be very far away from us, in a thousand unsuspected thoughts and
> actions we suddenly become conscious of the dead, perhaps more intensely con-
> scious of them than we ever were while they lived. To trust both life and death,
> that is our only way. I believe that it is really the Christian way: it softens us and
> makes us sympathise with and love each other.[16]

This was the manner of his thinking in his early years with Arthur
Galton. He reflected on suffering and death, on the existence of God, on the

role of religion in history; and he talked his ideas over with the older man. The result of his preoccupations, and of his background reading of the Greek philosophers, in particular, as well as of Martial, Pliny the Younger, St Paul, Machiavelli and Ernest Renan among many others, was his second book *Scenes and Portraits*, a little collection of short stories. He was so exhausted in the last stages of his writing that in October 1908 he felt like lying down on one of the tombstones outside the dining room window. The book, the essence of his unusual being, was immensely important to him. 'I shall be quite heart broken if it is not a success,' he told Jim in November 1908. He was encouraged, however, by the high praise for it by Henry Newbolt, poet, lawyer, patriot and man-of-letters, who had read *Brunhild* for the publisher, John Murray, and recommended it. A member of the leading literary circles, Newbolt had been shown the new manuscript by Laurence Binyon and again acted as Murray's reader. Manning hastened to send a copy of Newbolt's letter to Eva, and hoped 'to appease his father' with it. He lunched with this important new friend at the Savile Club in early December.[17]

It was an odd and idiosyncratic work. While the other Edwardian writers were concentrating on the scene before them, the movements in a changing society, this naïve young man presumed to tackle eternal questions in a series of philosophic dialogues, flimsily disguised as stories. But except for his friendships with Dorothy and Jim was serious, isolated, over-protected Frederic Manning ever really young? Prematurely aged by the lack of youthful company and by the stress of his illness, he found his freedom for development largely in the area of ideas. The views he had reached on life and death in this early work remained his views, and underlie the novel of his maturity. The friendship with Jim brightened his lonely life and lightened his spirits at times, but did not influence his serious work. Yet the friendship was enormously important to him, keeping him from despondency, giving him a youthful ally against the over-bearing ways of his older friend. He could gossip to him light-heartedly in letters, or confide his depressed moods, with an expectation of understanding and sympathy. Without the friendship of Jim, idyllic Edenham may well have seemed just a beautiful prison, instead of furnishing that security of 'home' which he needed. Sending New Year greetings to Houtin in 1908 he wished him 'the best gifts of the best Gods, who are little and familiar Gods, living "chez nous", and full of kindliness for mortals'. His way of life, despite its narrow ambit, seemed to content him still.

9

Scenes and Portraits

MANNING HAD read widely when preparing his second book. It owed something to Pater's reflective, historical fantasies, *Imaginary Portraits*, with their emphasis on death and suffering; something to Walter Savage Landor's *Imaginary Conversations*, his dialogues between the great dead; much to advice from Galton and Houtin; and most to his own interpretation of the Greek philosophers, particularly Socrates, as well as to other writers ranging from Lucretius, Martial, Pliny the Younger and St Paul to Machiavelli, Anatole France and Ernest Renan. Beerbohm caricatured Manning as 'A Ventriloquist', using his puppets to express his own views; one of the most used words in the reviews was original. In its seriousness the work may well have seemed to Arthur Galton the realization of the ideal John Addington Symonds had set him: 'could you not produce in concert with your friends a book which should arrest attention by its worth and weight'.[1]

The basic formula of the book was to 'envisage from slightly different standpoints the same, or cognate ideas'.[2] Manning was looking at the idea of religion at different stages in world history. Pater's *Marius the Epicurean*, set in the breakdown of the Roman Empire and highlighting the confrontation between the old religions and Christianity, had used such a theme. Manning expanded the idea, placing each of his stories at a crucial stage in the development of religious thought. He drew the clear-cut conclusion that there were only two basic religious attitudes, the faith of the simple believers, 'the humble folk', and the scepticism of the tolerant doubter. He saw religion as an attempt to understand death and suffering. 'Death is the great fact of life' for, with even the greatest, 'Time is his master, and he cannot find a remedy against death'. (p. 8) But does God exist? And if He exists does He care?

In the first story, 'The King of Uruk', an account of Adam and Eve set in 4000 B.C., Bagoas, a Sumerian priest and adviser to the great king of ancient Iraq, Merodach, meets naked, innocent Adam in an outpost of the

Empire, the Garden of Eden. Adam believes that God exists and that man is good; world-weary Bagoas is a pessimistic agnostic who sees man's life as 'a little heap of withered leaves suddenly caught up in a windy dance; a little flame flickering ere it goes out into darkness'. The King covets Adam's garden and it is Bagoas, not the serpent, who tempts Eve before she and Adam flee before the forces of the King. Yet Bagoas forecasts that Adam, the believer, will be one day father of a race that will revolutionize the world. The might of Merodach will be swallowed up in sand but the legend of Adam will live for ever. The originality of the subject and the exotic grace of the style won this story most acclaim from critics. E. M. Forster called it, more than twenty years later, 'perhaps the most exquisite of short stories of our century'[3] and termed Manning 'a master of irony'.

With each change of period, Manning changed his style to suit. The setting of 'At the House of Euripides' is in Athens, in the fifth century B.C., where a confrontation is looming between the state and Socratic thought. Here Manning attempts a skit on a Platonic dialogue. Socrates and Protagoras discuss the notion of divinity. 'If mankind with its blind follies makes me doubt the existence of a God', says Euripides, 'its miseries make me believe in one'. Protagoras is more cynical: 'if there be a god, he is careless of the fate of man'. It is a dangerous discussion, for one of the company threatens to report it as part of the irreverent sophistry he thinks is destroying Athens. Protagoras is concerned about the reaction which is developing, yet maintains that 'Socrates, of course, will survive it'.

The subject of 'The Friend of Paul', which was dedicated to Eva Fowler, is the rise of Christianity. Here Manning writes more freely, in a warmer, more personal style, creating the character of Serenus, a provincial Roman who lives a pleasant life on his beautiful estates in Spain in the first century A.D. Serenus is an Epicurean, glad of the small pleasures of life, seeing nothing beyond death. He believes that the gods take no interest in human anguish, although he condemns the Stoics for their lack of love and pity, their apathy about human misery.

The Roman Empire is cracking. Some new spirit is in the air. 'The gods are dead', says one of his soldier companions. 'They are not dead', answers Serenus gently; 'but they have changed their names'.

For Serenus is aware of Christianity. In Corinth, the city of pleasure, nine years before, he had met Paul, the apostle of the new religion. Although drawn to the doctrine of peace and love and the notion of eternal life, Serenus, even when beset by great personal tragedy, cannot believe . . . 'faith, belief is not an act of volition'. For him life is 'a little pleasure, and then darkness and silence'. But the force of Christianity, with its doctrine of hope for the lowliest, cannot be withstood. After telling of his encounter with the magnetic preacher, Serenus walks towards his house and 'looking through the low branches, he thought he discovered in the uncertain light, the figure and features of Paul, surrounded by the slaves of the household'.

The time of the next story 'The Jesters of the Lord' is the early thirteenth century. The new spirit, the sweetness and simplicity of St Francis of Assisi, 'God's fool', battles the entrenched power of the Catholic Church. Pope Innocent is concerned that the ingenuousness of St Francis and his followers may threaten the stability and authority of the church: 'how often have the most beautiful ideals led men into abominable heresies and destroyed the peace of the church', says the scourge of the Albigensians. St Francis, however, wins the qualified support of the Pope, who is also a lover of frugality. A cynical cardinal smiles at the comedy played by these rival idealists, his ironic attitude being 'the tribute which small imaginations pay to the great'. In contrast, the protagonists of 'At San Casciano' are total cynics. Thomas Cromwell, born 1485, executed 1540, an adviser to young King Henry VIII of England, visits Niccolo Machiavelli, who is living in retirement after losing power. He finds the exiled Florentine polishing up a little treatise or manual for princes. They discuss the approaching confrontation between the great states and the church. Machiavelli is clear-sighted about the outcome: 'those who fight in the cause of liberty are fighting for their own establishment in power and, being established, they seek to protect themselves, and fortify their position as the central authority'. Cromwell, pragmatic, full of ambition, suggests cautiously that the minister, to protect himself, may have to become greater than his master, the king. 'Machiavelli shifted a little in his chair, and the darkness hid an ironic smile.'

The last dialogue in the 1909 edition takes place between the spirits of Ernest Renan, French historian and philosopher, and Pope Leo XIII in 'The Paradise of the Disillusioned'. It centres around the great religious debates of the nineteenth century, the doubts raised by scientific discoveries, and the doctrine of the Infallibility of the Pope. The two earthly opponents meet in the afterlife and exchange aphorisms and paradoxes.

'Ah, M. Renan', says Leo, 'why are you here? You were always a believer at heart; one might say almost a scholastic. You invented a system of doubt, as others might a system of faith; even your doubts were affirmations'.

And the historian replies: 'Doubts must be systematic, but there is no need for system in religion ... Science, in limiting the field of its researches, has increased the mystery which lies beyond. I became, as it were, the priest of an unknown God; and the first article of my creed was, that perhaps he did not exist at all'.

The ironical Pope is not to be outdone at this game. 'St Paul was a heretic. So was St Augustine. All the Fathers of the Church were heretics. So was St Francis. So were Lamennais, Lacordaire and Newman.'[4] It is more an exchange of intellectual wise-cracks than a story. Manning's witty, cynical pair ramble through the topics of socialism, the faith of the peasantry, the French Revolution, eugenics, democracy and the state of the Catholic Church. And both are amused to hear finally that ironic Leo has been succeeded by a severe moralist, basically a simple parish priest, Pius X. Yet sceptical Renan can be passionate about the French Revolution, the great tragedy that produced a terrible grandeur. Manning, in his Preface, paid tribute to the double-minded quality he saw in great men: the doubters who could appreciate the force of the mystic and the religious impulses in life; the men of reason who understood the power of the emotional and the irrational.

Scenes and Portraits has been seen by Professor Richard Cody as anticipating, in all but neurosis, the historical intelligence of T. S. Eliot's *The Waste Land*.[5] Its tension between doubt and belief, its awareness of human suffering, its wit and irony and lack of illusions form a link with the consciousness of the great modern classic but it has nothing of the innovative technique, the explosive, startling effects. Ironic, detached, pessimistic, doubting Manning wore the look of an old-fashioned aesthete, with his mannered style and smooth surface. Eliot found the book 'too literary and derivative',[6] and as Aldington put it 'the shade of Pater dims some of his best pages', although he praised 'The Paradise of the Disillusioned' as 'a most penetrating and prophetic study of modern thought . . . Beside that essay most political thought is incoherent and silly'.[7] But Manning's poetic prose can appear too ornate and dated for modern tastes:

> The days are blue and gold, blue and silver are the nights: and the birds are clamorous among the dripping boughs; why should we pause to think of fate? What does his wisdom profit him when in a little time he dies and is equal with us in the dust? The flowers bud, blossom, and seed, without thought for the departing year; the birds go delightfully upon the ways of the wind, though the arrows which shall bring them to earth are stored in the quiver. Shall we do otherwise? [p. 15]

For Manning, with his reflective vision and his little experience of life, it was impossible not to intellectualize. Consequently these stories are cerebral and static, lacking in life, weighed down with argument. 'The Friend of Paul', however, with its beautiful backgrounds in Spain and Corinth, its sketches of Serenus and of Paul, 'a thick-set, crook-backed man, ugly and mean', indicated that a novelist might break out of the philosopher in time. Manning, so intrigued by the double-natured, later diagnosed his own weakness: 'too much of a philosopher to be an artist, and too much of an artist to be a philosopher'.[8]

Frederic Manning was twenty-six when he finished *Scenes and Portraits*, and he had made his judgements on life; the attitudes which underlie the first book are to be found also in his war novel. In an era when the avant-garde views were socialist, Fabian, optimistic and utopian, he remained a doubter of both religion and heaven-on-earth faiths. As he has Machiavelli say: 'I marvel, always, Messer, that in spite of the overwhelming evidence of human depravity, men are to be found in every age who base their conceptions of the ideal state upon the hypothesis that mankind is naturally good'. Bagoas is similarly sceptical: 'Adam believes that all men are naturally good, and that it is society that makes them evil; he does not see that society cannot be different from what it is since it is a purely natural development'. Manning, for a young man, exhibits a deep pessimism. As Bagoas says: 'We are all idealists. All of us have excellent intentions but the world is so constituted that we can never carry them out'.

This stark view is softened in this early work, as in his war novel, by Manning's empathy with the inescapable sufferings of human beings. The feeling, as expressed by his Euripides, is not simply a Paterian anguish over the death of youth and beauty. It covers all. 'We would not, if we could, cut ourselves off from the dumb herd of humanity, with its obscure sufferings, its vague desires, its inarticulate and eternal pain.'

He looked wise beyond his years, Rothenstein said of him. Certainly sad beyond his years, carrying the burden passed on to him by Galton of the sense of tears in things, his mature pessimism marked him off from other young people; especially, if he had but known them, from the brilliant girls and promising young men who had begun meeting at 46 Gordon Square, Bloomsbury, in 1904. So witty, so free in language, so emancipated in attitude to sexual matters, so confidently rationalist, so modern, they briskly repudiated any notion of original sin, of the imperfectibility of humanity, which weighed on Manning. As John Maynard Keynes wrote of his pre-war group: 'We were not aware that civilisation was a thin and precarious crust erected by the personality and will of a few, and only maintained by rules and conventions skilfully put across and guilefully preserved . . . we completely misunderstood human nature, including own own'.[9] So it appeared to Keynes after the catastrophe of 1914. However, everything seemed possible in the progressive, modern pre-war world emerging towards the end of the first decade of the twentieth century, a world of cars, motor buses, underground railways, moving pictures, vacuum cleaners, neon lights and submarines. Even the aeroplane and the wireless were realities; what other wonders lay in the future, as the world continued to improve?

Manning's individual angst might be attributed, at least partly, to his constricted circumstances, to his loneliness, to his poor health and fatigue. His spirits were up and down with the state of his body. Early in January 1909, after an illness, he was somewhat depressed, writing to Fairfax that tragic things were more permanent than joy. Yet by early February, he was much more cheerful. He had pulled himself together, and hoped to keep an equilibrium of mind in future. The change in attitude, the declaration for optimism, coincided with his making a new friend, an energetic young American poet—Ezra Pound. Jim remained close to him, and their friendship lasted beyond the war, but where the old friend was solid, respectable, trustworthy, the new friend was exciting, unpredictable, explosive. Manning, the old-fashioned exquisite, had encountered the young American who would become the personification of emergent modernism. What, for his part, would dynamic, ambitious Ezra Pound make of the delicacy, the fine sensibility, the *passé* aestheticism of this last exquisite?

10

The Last Exquisite

THE WORD so often used about Manning by his closer friends was exquisite: 'exquisite and pathetic',[1] 'an exquisite and an exquisite writer',[2] and 'an exquisite scholar' of 'exquisite taste'.[3] His early reputation for delicacy as a writer rested largely on *Scenes and Portraits*, with its highly polished, delicately wrought surface, its fragile sensibilities and its thoughtful argument.

A number of the sheerly descriptive passages are so finely drawn that they resemble some highly enamelled, brightly coloured little paintings, as in the description of Serenus's estate in Spain, where Manning's concentration on colour is marked.

Passing out of the library through the atrium the friends crossed the small courtyard enclosed on three sides, and turning sharp to the left began to climb the slope which sheltered the house. The walk was shaded by a thick hedge of ilex, and there were tall, slim cypresses at irregular intervals. Leaving the path, they crossed a plot of grass, starry with little flowers, and, passing through a thicket of myrtles, came presently to a semicircular stone seat shaded by beeches which stood, eastward, a little way behind it. Falling water tinkled like little silver bells somewhere close to them; and the leaves made a pleasant whispering noise. Lysis covered the seats with rugs, and left them. The seat faced westward, overlooking the olive-yards which the winds flushed to silver; and the friends had a magnificent view of the Atlantic. In the declining light the distant promontories, blue and lemon, seemed to jut out into a bath of liquid colours, as if suspended in the vague; and the horizon was indeterminate. A fleet of fishing-boats, some miles from the shore, seemed like small brown moths with motionless wings that had settled upon a flat screen of transparent blue gauze, and about them the light gleamed and flickered upon innumerable little dancing waves. It was all blue and green, but so pale and silent as to seem a mirage.[4]

The scene is supposedly European, but did some diffuse memory of his native city and its headlands, its 'red-tiled' roofs and its 'green lizards' emerge from childhood in his description of Serenus's estate? And the view over the Atlantic from Serenus's house might hold aspects for him of the ocean of his boyhood, the Pacific: 'From the windows in the upper storey Serenus could see this wide expanse of waters, never completely the same, but always restless and troubled, with caprice in sunlight, or anger in storms'.

In contrast the exotic, dreamlike landscape of 'The King of Uruk', coloured like some Persian miniature, is wholly of the imagination, the Valley of Eden.

> I had strayed into a pleasant valley, where the Euphrates flows between level meadows of wild wheat, enclosed like an amphitheatre by well-wooded hills, which had already taken on the tawny and golden tints of autumn.
>
> On the lower slopes grew mulberries and oranges; above them, threaded with opulent colouring, plane-trees and sycamores, yellowing oaks, and the beautiful level boughs of dusky cedars ... The sunlit fields of ripe wheat swayed in the wind like an undulating sea; the river gleamed as silver, and many coloured lilies grew beside the brimming water, filling the air with a delicate perfume ... It seemed a place sacred from the profaning feet of man. At the same time, I had a curious sense of being watched; and presently a young man rose out of the wild wheat before me, and stood watching me with an expression of curiosity qualified with distrust ... 'It was Adam', said Merodach. [pp. 16-17]

The world of nature, however beautiful and however glowingly described, however loved, is for Manning only the backdrop for humanity and for its fundamental problems.

The delicacy of his descriptive writing is more than matched by the nuances of sensibility in his dealings with the pain of human life; he contrasts continually the beauty of nature, of the life-giving earth, with the misery of man, the plaything of mysterious forces. His sympathies, as in *Her Privates We*, are bound up with ordinary people: 'the doings of men seem to be more the result of the conditions of life than of their own wickedness', says Euripides.

> If men err it is through ignorance; but they suffer quite independently of their deserts ... Man struggles all his his life with the fluctuations and vicissitudes of fortune; his pleasures are but phantoms and visions which elude his grasp; the one certainty before him is death: an unknown terror ... The best happiness we can find in life is resignation, a folding of the hands, a withdrawal into the interior peace of our own minds, the serene heights which the Muses inhabit. Those who have gained that sanctuary have at least the happiness which comes from a knowledge of the limitations of life; they have learned to desire little, to delight in natural and simple things, the bright air, the coolness of forests, wind rippling the waves of corn and setting the poplar leaves a-tremble; but, alas! behind even this serenity of mind is the shadow of human suffering. So few are the wise, and so many the miserable. [pp. 65-6]

Manning's hypersensitivity to the pain of others prevents his adoption of the more rugged solution of the Stoic school of philosophers. '[Stoicism] is

at once raw, crude and narrow; [says Serenus] it coarsens our natural appe-
tites instead of refining them. For Stoicism the human emotions, love and
pity, are but weaknesses which it denies and attempts to stifle. It is very far
from the secret of human sympathy'. For Manning, this sympathy is all
important, especially in relation to the simplest people, the peasants following their traditional life, as his ancestors had done in Ireland. These are
the innocents of the world, God's fools, like St Francis and the early
Christians. He sympathizes, however, with the suffering of all people, as
in this instance where wealthy Serenus has lost to sudden death his wife
and child:

> In my weakness and grief my hands went forth and groped in the darkness
> seeking the hands of those who had also suffered, seeking for the little familiar,
> commonplace things, that twine themselves round our being and are the main-
> stays of life . . . Philosophy, religion, discipline, every vain convention which we
> imagine may buttress our will in moments of great spiritual weakness, fell away
> from me like garments, and the only thing remaining was a sense of human
> sympathy, a craving for human consolation. [pp. 123-4]

This understanding of suffering in a young man who had suffered, it
would seem on the surface, no great blows of fate, except poor health, is an
indication of the exquisite sensibility remarked upon by his friends. The
other side to this tenderness of feeling was a certain toughness and
subtlety of mind. In all the stories, and especially in 'At San Casciano',
Manning shows an ironical scepticism about the never-ending struggle for
power, for control, whether by King, Church or State; he has no faith in
'new orders'. Speaking of the conflict between the Senate and the people of
Rome, Machiavelli, the arch cynic, says:

> Marius having been made the champion of liberty is followed by Sulla the
> master of reaction; the fight is is long, bitter, and when, finally, the people tri-
> umph, they find themselves under the absolute rule of one man. Now this
> results from the fact that men worship the name of freedom, rather than the
> thing itself . . . having been raised up by the popular voice, they are stronger
> than the power they have supplanted; thus it happens that people warring
> against their government in the cause of liberty do but increase the power which
> they aimed to destroy. [p. 217]

And of the struggle between Church and State Manning has the Florentine
statesman say:

> The liberty of the State will be achieved, at least in a great measure; but the
> State being stronger will be more absolute, more tyrannous. The solvent of the
> new learning, as you call it, will be smiled upon by kings, so long as it doth help
> them to rid themselves of the Pope; but it will be repressed the moment that it
> shows any desire to alter or limit the power of the states. [p. 218]

His thought is deeply conservative, no doubt influenced by Galton, but his nature is extremely sensitive, even passionate at times, as when his political conservatism is modified by the burst of idealism about the French Revolution, which Renan expresses in 'The Paradise of the Disillusioned'.

> There is the chief glory of the human race [says Renan]. They will sacrifice themselves for an impossible ideal. None of us can contemplate that great tragedy of the French Revolution without feeling cleansed by it. The enthusiasm of the people has a kind of terrible grandeur. In such moments of divine delirium all men assume heroic proportions. We may pity it for its fanaticism; we may pity it for being so easily duped; but it is impossible to deny its magnificent devotion to an ideal . . . Men seemed for a moment to become the incarnations of ideas. Oh, on both sides. [pp. 244-5]

The passage was written some years before the enthusiasm of the people, on both sides, for the terrible grandeur of the Great War with its heroic devotion to ideals, as well as its monstrous suffering and loss. It taps a hidden depth of emotion in Manning which was such that, despite his deeply ironic nature, he responded to what appeared the idealism of the cause when war came.

His highly developed consciousness, of himself and of others, and his careful artistry with words earned the Manning of this period the description of 'exquisite'. But there are other styles of the exquisite. What would young Fred, with his delicate sympathies have made of that other young contemporary who might lay claim to the title 'the last exquisite', Ronald Firbank? Firbank, like Manning, came of a recently enriched family; but there was much more money, and it went a generation further back. Like Manning, he was a sickly child, cosseted by his mother, and spent only a term or two at school at Uppingham. Spoiled and richly indulged, Europe became both his study and his playground as a boy. In 1906, when Manning was working hard in the monastic quiet of Edenham vicarage, Ronald Firbank found his perfect setting at Cambridge. Here he could express his bizarre tastes and attitudes to the full. If Manning represented the last breath of the aestheticism of high seriousness in the tradition of Pater, Newman and Arnold, Firbank, at this stage, could be called the last gasp of the decadence represented by Wilde.

His Cambridge rooms, stuffed with flowers, candles, *objets d'art*, red silk curtains and cushions, bric-à-brac and incense, were the obverse of the tumbledown austerity of Edenham. He, too, was a Catholic of sorts, having been converted in 1907, but his many fervid enthusiasms: J. K. Huysmans, evil, the stage, drugs, fortune-tellers, homosexuality, drink, studied artificiality, were hardly those of a simple son of the church. A dandy and a snob, a narcissist about his personal appearance, with stained finger nails and powdered face, he presented what Edmund Wilson called a nostalgic caricature of the aesthetes of the Beardesley–Wilde period. But there was more to Firbank than his eccentricities and his startling manifold poses. He,

*Olivia Shakespear in 1897;
Manning called the woman loved
by W. B. Yeats 'My beloved aunt'.*

*Dorothy Shakespear at the time of
her engagement to Ezra Pound in
1914; 'The lovers regarded "poor
Fred" with a mixture of respect,
affection and amusement'.*

*Grimsthorpe Castle, the Ancasters' residence near Edenham; Manning
dedicated* Eidola *to the grandmotherly Countess of Ancaster.*

Frederic Manning in 1909 at the time of his first success

like Manning, was a dedicated artist, taking the decadence to a final high note in his work as well as in his life. Where the essence of Frederic Manning was moral seriousness, Firbank's was the avoidance of solemnity. His writing, as opposed to Manning's, was original, innovative in its use of inconsequential dialogue, in its oblique narration and its play with the absurd. Exotic, brittle, witty, his influence extended even into the future, into the cynical 1920s where he seemed at home with the Sitwells and Evelyn Waugh. Although E. M. Forster termed him an interesting example of literary conservatism and saw him as fundamentally unserious, Edmund Wilson saw anguish behind the laughter.[5] The interest lies in the contrast Firbank presents to Manning: in his determined avoidance in his novels—from his *Vainglory* in 1915 to his works of the 1920s, *The Flower Beneath the Foot* and *Prancing Nigger* (the British title is *Sorrow in Sunlight*)—of the kind of thoughtful seriousness about life and suffering which was absolutely essential to Manning. To Firbank that was boring, perhaps pretentious. He feared feeling, as much as vulgarity and the mob, in life and in art. He was so odd that, as Siegfried Sassoon said, it was impossible to have an ordinary conversation with him.[6] Shy, nervous, giggling, lonely, ill, he spent his time in travel and the London cafés, the Café Royal, the Tour Eiffel and at the theatres. Unfit for service, he passed the war years in Oxford, ignoring the war, and died in Rome in 1926. It is not a question of setting these two artists against one another. Each expressed his own vision, devoted his talents and life to his art. Both were determined aesthetes, if in total contradistinction. The interest, for those who care for Manning, lies in that contrast. The two, with certain similarities of background, had taken such different paths in the field of aesthetics. Extraordinary in every way, Ronald Firbank, with his odd imagination, his determined weirdness, his absurdities, might be best described as 'the last fantastic', whereas Manning with his guarded nature, his control, his subtlety and scholarship, his double sensibility, his old-fashioned aura, was, in essence, 'the last exquisite'.

His subtle mind was drawn to balance and order. In his Preface to the 1909 edition of *Scenes and Portraits* (omitted from the 1930 edition) Manning laid stress on his theory of the double nature of the world's greatest men and on the double-sidedness of beliefs.

> Take for example, the curious paradox of Epicureanism, which counsels a temperate pleasure, and yet condemns the whole of life as being merely the pursuit of an unattainable desire; reconciling us to life by the prospect of death, and to death by showing us the vain efforts and innumerable vexations of life.

Bonamy Dobrée, in a review of the second edition of the book, termed Manning a Catholic Epicurean, 'a happy sceptic'[7] so calling attention to Manning's own brand of double-sidedness, his delight in beauty and the pleasures of life, on the one hand; his concern with the moral problems and sufferings of human existence on the other. As well as these two aspects of the exquisite, there was also a third Manning, who perhaps became more obvious in maturity: the ironic observer, the realist, also with a word in the Preface: 'I am perfectly willing to take a thing for what it is and not to grumble at it for not being other than it is'. But the irony of the young Manning is witty rather than grim; he is not quite a Christian, but he is not a cynic himself. In the Preface his particular heroes are the balanced doubters, Renan and Euripides:

> Unbound by any system, moving easily in all, they sought by the free exercise of reason and a profound irony to cleanse their ages of much perilous stuff; and though Renan was not a Christian in the common sense of the word and though Euripides turned away from the gods of his own day, yet each tried to save out of the ruins of their faiths the subtile [*sic*] and elusive spirit which had informed them; that divine light and inspiration which is continually expressing itself in new figures and cannot be imprisoned in any vessel of human fashioning. *Anima naturaliter Christiana* we can say of each.

Scenes and Portraits is the work of a young man of intelligence and sensitivity, well aware of the sorrows of the world, though not yet oppressed by his own; and it is the work of a young aesthete, delighting in the beauty of language and nature. It is markedly different to most of the poems he was writing around the same time, with their vague personal melancholy, their themes of loss and diffuse yearnings, their thinness, their total lack of irony. Galton preferred Manning's poems to his prose.[8] Perhaps he meant the more vigorous verse of *Brunhild* or possibly he hoped to keep his pupil as a substitute Johnson, a lyricist in the style of the 1890s, and could see that Manning was developing more individuality in his prose. His pupil's style, when it was ornate and mannered, ran counter to Galton's view that English prose should be plain and pungent. Yet Manning's poetic talents were possibly better suited to descriptive verse, somewhat akin to the prose poems of *Scenes and Portraits*, than to lyrics. A poem, representing Manning in this mode as the pure, verging on sensuous, aesthete, is the unusual (for him) 'Still Life':

> Pale globes of fragrant ripeness, amber grapes
> And purple, on a silver dish; a glass
> Of wine, in which light glows, and fires to pass
> Staining the damask, and in dance escapes;
> Two Venice goblets wrought in graceful shapes,
> A bowl of velvet pansies, wherein mass
> Blues, mauves, and purples; plumes of meadow-grass;
> And one ripe pomegranate, that splits and gapes,
> Protruding ruby seeds: a feast for eyes
> Better than all those topaz, beryl fruits
> Aladdin saw and coveted: these call,
> To minds contented and in leisure wise,
> Visions of blossoming boughs, and mossy roots,
> And peaches ripening on a sunny wall.

It was this poem, static as a painting itself, which Richard Aldington chose to include in his *Religion of Beauty*, a selection from the aesthetes. Here Manning is seen almost wholly as the painter with words, using the deliberate literary artistry, so much part of *Scenes and Portraits*, which has won him the description, 'exquisite'. The aestheticism of words is only one side of him, however. Style was the surface for his preoccupations. The decorative facade needed also his delicacy of sensibility, subtlety of mind and gentleness of spirit in order to earn from his admirers that distinctive, if limiting, epithet.

Now this ironic, conservative young aesthete, apparently set in his ways at the age of twenty-six, who tended to value only the achievements of the past, and to be sceptical of the possibilities of the future, was about to fall into an unusual friendship with that scourge of the very Victorian high-mindedness and 1890s fastidiousness which had formed him as an artist, that literary revolutionary, Ezra Pound.

11

Ezra Pound

Twenty-three-year-old Ezra Pound, looking the paradigm of the young poet in velveteen suit and open-neck shirt, pale of face, reddish of hair, swept into Edwardian London in the autumn of 1908, with only three pounds in his pocket, and knowing no one. Starting from meetings with Laurence Binyon and Selwyn Image at Elkin Mathews's bookshop, within six months he knew all the major literary figures, from Ford Madox Ford to W. B. Yeats, from historical novelist Maurice Hewlett to symbolist poet Arthur Symons, from feminist writer May Sinclair to philosopher and poet T. E. Hulme. Rushing at life with American energy and eagerness, determined from the age of fifteen to be a poet, he was, as Richard Aldington says: 'a small but persistent volcano in the dim levels of pre-war London literary society'.[1]

Passionate about the literature of Europe, spurning the introversion and world-wearinesss of the 1890s poets and the dullness of Victorianism, he soon reinforced his flamboyant appearance with a reputation for brash outspokenness. So unmistakeably alien among the Oxford-Cambridge littérateurs and the inturned Little Englanders, his fresh breeziness was to stir up languid Edwardians like Fred Manning. While Fred had struggled with each day, Ezra had raced through his short life with gusto. Being born in a frontier town in Idaho (on 30 October 1885), may have set the note, though he grew up in the east, in Pennsylvania. He made two trips to Europe as a boy, in 1898 and 1902, studied at the University of Pennsylvania and at Hamilton College, Clinton, New York, met a fellow student-poet William Carlos Williams, fell in love with, and, in 1905, became engaged to, Hilda Doolittle, the future Imagist poet, H.D., spent some time in Spain in 1906, was sacked from his post as instructor at Wabash College, Indiana, for sheltering a homeless girl in his room in 1907 and travelled to Venice in 1908, where he published his first volume of verse, *A Lume Spento*, at his own expense. Then he set out to conquer London. This energy, ambition and dedication to the hard, penurious existence of the artist made Fred's Edenham life look pampered, prissy and empty of event.

Generous natured in his search for talent, still under the influence of Rossetti and Browning himself, Pound praised Jim Fairfax to William Carlos Williams in May 1909, as one of those of 'the second rank' doing 'damned good work'.[2] In January 1909 Pound, Fairfax and Manning met at Eva Fowler's salon and became good friends, though the American was to change his mind about the worth of the kind of poetry the two Australians were writing then. 'In 1908 London was full of "gargoyles", that is, with high reputations, most of whose work has since gone into the discard', he wrote later.[3] But in those pre-war years, for Americans, as for British colonials, London was the real centre of the cultural world: 'the U.S. was then a colony of London as far as culture was concerned. London was the capital of the U.S. as far as art and letters and thought were concerned'.[4] In 1909 Pound was happy to meet these two scholarly colonials, cultural exiles like himself. He also met Olivia Shakespear, whom he judged undoubtedly the most charming woman in London.[5]

Soon after the first meeting, both he and Fred Manning were asked to tea at the Shakespears. It was a significant occasion. Dorothy, swept away by the romantic ideal of the reckless Bohemian poet, was enchanted by his looks and his genius, and fell headlong in love with the dynamic American. Her mother, too, was much charmed; both women enrolled at a course Pound gave later in the year at the London Polytechnic on Dante and the troubadours, and they took their new favourite to meet W. B. Yeats at Woburn Buildings. In April, Pound's *Personae* was published, making a definite impression. He seemed bound for success in this citadel of culture.

But Manning by April was recovering from another bout of depression following Lillie Bird's death and more bad health, regretting 'letting this stupid body of mine and all its clumsy apparatus get in the way of my own and other people's enjoyment of life'[6] and reaffirming his devotion to Jim. Yet the free-wheeling, unquenchable American attracted him, and Manning's dry wit pleased Pound.

They were an unlikely pair of friends: Pound so vital, Manning almost an invalid, Pound all drive and fiery enthusiasm, Manning all diffidence and irony, Pound so quarrelsome and excitable, Manning so quiet and calmly conservative. But both were devoted to their art and recognized this in each other. Both were in flight from a native Philistia, both were absorbed in the classics and European literature, and both were provincial strangers in an imperial capital, which was markedly supercilious about 'colonials'. Vance Palmer noted, a few years later, an acute hostility in English circles to new countries, for instance, G. K. Chesterton, the apostle of 'Merry England', made no secret of his dislike of Australian and American writers.[7] Just not being English was an intangible bond between Pound and Manning, for neither could share authentically in that romantic passion for the English landscape, inbred in the emerging Georgian poets and visible even in the urbane E. M. Forster, who said of his favourite county in *The Longest Journey*: 'The fibres of England unite in Wiltshire, and did we condescend to worship her, here we should expect our national shrine'. Looking back angrily from 1938 to his twelve years in 'Gomorrah on Thames', Pound said he 'never found an Englishman who knew anything, save those who had come from the edges of Empire'.[8] It was something of a belated tribute to Manning. These two expatriates, spurning the parochial, and the middlebrow—exemplified to Pound by the poet Lascelles Abercrombie, and to Manning by the man-of-letters Edmund Gosse, whom he called 'the incarnation of fatuous mediocrity'[9]—turned to the broader prospect of European culture.

Both young men were well read in French literature. Pound admired to excess the contemporary poet and aesthete, Remy de Gourmont; possibly he saw scholarly Manning as a kind of English equivalent. Pound passed on his enthusiasm for the medieval Provençal troubadours to his new friend and Manning sent a copy of Pound's poem 'A Quinzaine for this Yule' to his recently acquired mentor, Henry Newbolt, hoping he would like it as much as he did himself.[10] Newbolt approved. Closer to home, Galton was not likely to have been an admirer of the cocky, raw American. Even Manning was troubled by his new friend's irregular cadences and innovatory approach. 'What a damnable thing is this craving for originality', he complained to Fairfax, 'which . . . makes Pound write as if no one had written before him. I like Pound very much, but he will certainly be dammed'.[11] While the astonishing Ezra was certainly intriguing, Jim was a far more stable friend.

May 1909 saw the publication and critical success of *Scenes and Portraits*. The book was widely and favourably reviewed, in *The Times* (27 May); in the *Observer* (30 May); and in the *Manchester Guardian* (2 June), which remarked on the book's French lucidity and originality. And *Mercure de France* (16 July), in a brief note, drew some comparisons with the idol of the French aesthetes—and Pound—Remy de Gourmont. Manning expressed his pleasure with the reception to Newbolt.[12] His father and brother Charlie, who were visiting so that farmer Charlie could examine sheep, bulls, crops and agricultural machinery, could join in the rejoicing at this pleasant success, but Fred regretted that the dearest mother, 'matri carissimae', to whom the book was dedicated, could not be with him.[13]

The odd little volume had a small vogue among some well-known writers. Max Beerbohm told Will Rothenstein that he knew of no better stories in English.[14] Years later Pound claimed he could still quote the opening paragraph from 'The King of Uruk' from memory;[15] and T. E. Lawrence avowed he read the entire book over and over, particularly the Preface.[16] It did not appeal to all tastes. The *Athenaeum* reviewer (9 October) said it lacked the wit of Wilde and the malice of Anatole France, and was wearied by 'the monotone of agnosticism'. The *Bookman* (4 August), impressed as it was by the beauty, wisdom and originality of the book, was more impressed, perhaps, by the courage of this young writer, for it thought it perilous to put words into the mouth of Socrates: 'Those who do not care for Socrates will not care overmuch for your performance, those who care for Socrates will have a thousand arrows waiting for you'. It ran with its review the portrait of a most serious young man, with huge dark eyes and a strong nose, which seemed to capture a certain underlying sadness in Manning.

For Arthur Galton the most joy in the reviews must have sprung from the *Edinburgh Review* (October 1909), for it said: 'Since Mr Arnold there has been no such ironist in this country as the author of *Scenes and Portraits*'. Here was, at last, his reward: to have his pupil compared with his great idol. 'Irony is not an English quality', the reviewer continued, 'and Mr Manning's is distinctly not an English book. It is Latin in its intelligence, in its disregard for consequences, in its presentation of the pure idea. If Lucian, Landor, Renan and Anatole France could have collaborated the result would be some such as this'. In its style, its ideas, its influences the work may have been Latin; but irony was also an Australian quality in that era—as Joseph Furphy made plain in *Such is Life*.

With such great names invoked, it seemed the opening phase in a notable literary career for a young man of twenty-six. He had already begun work on a new project, 'a kind of "roman comique" about ecclesiastics in the 17th century'[17] and in July his poem 'Noon' appeared in the *Atlantic Monthly*. When Fairfax took his first-class degree in Literature in June Manning's congratulations were a trifle perfunctory; perhaps a little envy lingered about Oxford, perhaps he was too taken up with his own small triumph, excited about the future and his new friend. Fairfax sailed home on a visit in the autumn and in October Manning invited Pound to spend a few days at Edenham, to discuss with the two Latinists there Pound's proposed book of criticism, *The Spirit of Romance*, which contained a section on the Latin poets of the Renaissance. Pound spent an enjoyable week at the vicarage in November. If the American's verve and irreverence disturbed Manning, they must have infuriated Galton. These two great egotists shared a liking for forceful prose and a hatred of rhetoric but the dogmatic clergyman and the iconoclastic poet were bound to strike sparks off each other. Hating novelty, Galton disliked Pound. And while Pound admired Galton's prose and his scholarship, he became contemptuous of him as an atheist masquerading as a clergyman.[18] It must have been a difficult week for quiet Fred, eased by his ironic amusement at the pair. Pound's outrageousness was entertaining. 'He is not as other men', Fred wrote drily to Olivia in November. 'He has seen the Beatific Vision. Which is an extenuating circumstance.'[19]

The phrase lodged in Pound's memory to emerge years later in a letter to Wyndham Lewis, written when he was confined in St Elizabeth's Hospital, Washington. 'Yu allus were a lousy correspondent but as Fred Manning once remarked, there are or perhaps in the singular, is what the hell was it "extenuating circumstance".' On another occasion he passed on an amusing squib Manning had written:

> How much mist c[ou]ld
> A mystic stick
> If a mystic c[ou]ld
> Stick mist.[20]

He enjoyed Fred's wit and liked his parodies in particular, being delighted by Manning's mocking of his 'Ballad of the Goodly Fere' in 'The Ballad of the Goodly Hair'.

As for Manning, he must have developed from an early age in his years with Galton his defences against bad temper and explosiveness. Tolerant and peace-loving, Manning, while often irritated by Ezra, could forgive usually his friend's idiosyncrasies. As he wrote about his heroine in the romance he was working on: '[Madame de Sainte Claire] had never learned in fact that the perfect charity and tolerance in friendship are very largely based upon our recognition of the comic element in each other. She did not understand the humour that is half a caress'.[21] Caught between these two egotists, each determined to have his own way, he might smile at the comedy most of the time.

And Pound was generous and helpful. Impressed by *Scenes and Portraits*, he sent a poem by Manning to the *English Review*, edited by Ford Madox Ford, saying it was quite beautiful and urging its publication. The poem, originally entitled 'Kore', appeared as 'Persephone' in the December 1909 issue.

The classic figure of Kore, Persephone or Proserpine, the maiden daughter of Demeter, seized from a flowery field by Hades and taken to rule in the underworld as his queen for the period of the winter months of each year, has a long history in English literature, appearing in Chaucer, Shakespeare and Milton. The appeal of the myth to Manning was so great that he thought 'the most beautiful and moving lines Milton ever wrote were: 'Proserpine gathering flowers,/Herself a fairer flower'.[22] The legend was popular among the nineteenth-century aesthetes. Ruskin made use of it and Pater gave two lectures on 'The Myth of Demeter and Persephone' in November 1875. Swinburne, in 'The Garden of Proserpine', portrayed the maiden as symbolizing the death that waits for all humanity and John Addington Symonds wrote of 'Sombre Persephone, Dread goddess with the sanguine pomegranite'.[23]

This myth, blending love, separation and death, with the themes of the lost child, the mourning, searching mother, the exile, the double personality, reached to Manning's core. The poem, despite its Pre-Raphaelite style, has a sombre strength, compared to his other verses of these years, grounded in its symbolism of 'the yearly slain', the never-ending roll-call of the dead.

Only I saw the shadow on her brows,
Only I knew her for the yearly slain,
And wept; and weep until she come again.

It remained Manning's favourite pre-war poem.[24] And that Pound found it
so appealing is evidence that the future modernist was, at this stage, still
under the influence of Dante Gabriel Rossetti, that he had not yet thrown
off the romantic influence of the troubadours. The theorist of modernism,
of austerity and precision, was as yet largely an Edwardian. He not only
praised Manning's poem but he also responded to it, with a more forceful,
more complex exercise in the same genre in the *English Review* (January
1910): 'A Canzon, The Yearly Slain', dedicated to both Dorothy and Olivia
Shakespear. He included 'Kore' in his own *Provença* that year[25] and he was
to use Persephone in his own work as a symbol of radiant youth before its
death.

In Manning's life, 1909 was a significant year. His book was a critical
success, he was preparing a volume of poems, working on his historical
novel and, at the end of the year, in tribute to his new-found literary standing, began a period as leading reviewer for the *Spectator*, the most widely
read of the political and literary weeklies. Another promising young writer,
Lytton Strachey, had left the magazine that year because he found the
chore of reviewing 'pretty sickening' and that it kept him from real writing.
This was to be Manning's view in time but, initially, to be Manning 'of the
Spectator' was a small triumph. Galton, who was an old friend of the
editor St Loe Strachey (a nephew of John Addington Symonds and a cousin
of Lytton), was also turning out articles for the magazine.

The new post was some compensation to Fred for the disappointment he
suffered when the type of *Scenes and Portraits* was distributed, though a
second edition was later set up.[26] The first edition had sold out but a series
of philosophical dialogues in the thin guise of stories was not best-selling
material, even in bookish Edwardian days. He published two more poems
on classical themes in the *English Review* (May 1910), 'Hera Parthenia'
and 'To Artemis the Destroyer', and another, 'Hecate' in the *Spectator* (12
March). All were in his artificial, studied mode. 'Mine eyes have seen the
veiled bride of the night' was his salutation to the moon. His *Poems*, which
appeared in 1910, dedicated 'to Lle and Ryllis, with my love' met a formally polite response. The *Spectator* praised them for their very conven-
tionality, for their freedom from 'the captious revolt which disfigures much
modern poetry'. The *Times Literary Supplement* (23 June 1910) found
some positive virtues, calling the verses 'much alive and not imitative at
all', the work of a mind with 'the experiencing gift', and finished: 'it is the
effect given by the whole volume of constant pressure from within of a
highly responsive imagination, rather than any single poem, which seems
to us the significant feature of Mr Manning's work'. Walter de la Mare,
however, regretted the lack of the wit and irony of *Scenes and Portraits*.[27]
The verses were mostly bitter-sweet reflections on love, solitude, the past,

memory and death, well-crafted and musical if flimsy: 'the spirit of spring and passion throbs behind the delicate words' said the *Spectator*. 'Helgi of Lithend' and 'Theseus and Hippolyta', both in the more robust, narrative manner of *Brunhild*, found less favour. Manning's persona was still akin to the wan Pierrot, gentle and touching, as in 'To a Bush-Baby,' which calls to mind his favourite saint, St Francis of Assisi.

> Little hands that cling to me,
> Helpless as mine own, and weak,
> What in this world's mystery
> Do we seek?

Manning regretted that his parody 'Death of a Mad Pound' did not appear in the collection. It would have been quite out of place, but it might have pleased Pound as a change of pace. Manning had heard reports of the American's unfavourable reactions to his poems and was hurt. Granted these reports were accurate, isolated Manning was too thin-skinned, perhaps, for the give-and-take of the outside world. Mercurial Pound, who according to Aldington, quarrelled with everybody, was given to rash remarks and vehement see-sawing opinions. Manning attacked back, writing to Fairfax:

> Poor devil, I am sorry for him, and I do like some of his work, but the conceit is beyond endurance . . . He is welcome to say what he likes of me and my work: that simply does not interest me. His mixture of cock-sureness and stupidity over others does irritate me. And all the while the poor devil looks like a mixture of Alfred Jingle and St Francis of Assisi: or Mr Mantolini returned from his colonial farm![28]

It was as well for the friendship between Fred and Ezra that Pound visited the United States that summer of 1910. Manning was glad to see him go, owning that there was a nice side to him and he did not want to quarrel over nothing, making light of whatever had upset him. The summer was a happy one for him, as, still glowing from his small success, he once more holidayed at Daisy Meadow with Jim. And he made another new friend, the critic and biographer, Percy Lubbock, a typical scholarly English man-of-letters, product of Eton and King's College, Cambridge; very much of a change from wild Ezra. Then Manning spent a gentlemanly time at Oxford, staying with the elderly Provost of Oriel, Charles Shadwell, a dignified old scholar, friend and devoted disciple of Pater, and his even more old-worldly brother, Lionel, enjoying their eighteenth-century courtesy. In October he was Binyon's guest at Netherhampton. To a modern eye it looks a leisurely, peaceful life, if narrow in range. But Manning, hoping to publish his romance by June the next year, was working hard. In a friendly letter to Pound he wrote on 30 August 1910 that his reviewing and his work on the romance left him with a hatred of pen and ink.

On Christmas Day, Frederic Manning left for Paris to meet his youngest sister, Trix, who was visiting Europe for the forthcoming Coronation celebrations of George V. He planned to look up Houtin who had been so helpful to him in his chapter on Renan; and he looked forward to being shown Paris by him. They arranged to lunch together but the Frenchman did not appear, and Manning was upset. Such mishaps may have stemmed from a nervous awkwardness and his inexperience with people, which Pound had noticed, for he had told Dorothy that Frederic Manning had no sense of relations with people, no idea of whom to talk to about what.[29] Reserved Fred was loved within his own circles for his charm and talent but venturing into the wider world was more difficult and could, indeed, be agonizing to one lacking in experience and in social self-confidence. In this case Manning may simply have made some mistake in the arrangements. The Houtin incident in itself was a minor matter but it was an indication of what happened to Manning when he ventured too far into the world from the safe routines of Edenham. He lacked the physical strength and worldly assurance of Pound. From France he retreated back to the vicarage, to shoulder the burden of reviewing, necessary for financial reasons, since Galton's stipend was cut to a mere £50 by 1911.[30] The first Earl of Ancaster had died in 1910. Had the choleric clergyman fallen out with his son, the second Earl, had the atheism of which Pound accused Galton become alarmingly obvious, or were the Ancasters just economizing? In an enigmatic comment on the main relationship in his life, Fred wrote to Fairfax (4 November 1910): 'The cat is like me while Hans [the dog] takes after his own master'. Quiet, self-contained, keeping out of the way, Manning, whatever his troubles, could always find a refuge in working on his 'Golden Coach', an escape into an imaginary, romantic world, away from the dullness of the necessary and grinding chore of reviewing, and from the uncertain temper of his companion.

Virginia Woolf pin-pointed 1910 as the date of the arrival of the modern character. It was the year of Forster's *Howard's End*, mourning the death of the old English way of life as city and suburbia conquered. 'I love Shropshire, I hate London,' says the heroine Margaret Schlegel. It was the year of the post-Impressionist exhibition, when Londoners had their first view of Cezanne, Gaugin and Matisse, and marked the beginning of a cultural passage.

Pound, back in Europe in February 1911, was moving into new movements, new ideas, new friendships. He had met H.D. again in New York and she had followed him to Europe. There in 1912, the nineteen-year-old poet Richard Aldington fell in love with her and in the Vienna Cafe, handy to the British Museum, these three young poets, along with Thomas Sturge Moore and Wyndham Lewis discussed their new theories of Imagisme. Excess words were to stripped away, rhythm was to be free. The ideas had been put forward by T. E. Hulme around 1908; now they became a creed of the new movement, Vorticism, which also expressed its theories of energy and hard forms in painting. Pound, plunging into modernism, was leaving Manning behind in an Edwardian world unaffected by the new movements.

Manning still hoped to finish his novel by June 1911 and Olivia Shakespear praised what she saw of it, but this was not a productive year for him. Apart from his reviews he published only 'Danaë's Song' in *Forum* (February 1911), and 'Vision of Demeter' in the *English Review* (April 1911). Weakened by a bout of summer hay-fever, surrounded by books for reviewing because he 'could not afford to neglect them',[31] unable to complete the 'Golden Coach', his slight energies at a low point, he was no recruit for the iconoclasts. Not for him the London literary life, the lunches at the Eiffel Tower in Soho, the gatherings at Pound's rooms, the nights hosted by T. E. Hulme at 67 Frith Street, even the casual teas at the A.B.C. in Chancery Lane or some carousing at the Café Royal. One qualification for the literary life of those years was stamina, with the comings and goings, the meetings, the lectures, the web of personal encounters. Yet even in the midst of all his new excitements and new friendships Pound retained his affection for Fred Manning and a respect for his intelligence and his scholarship, if not for all of his poetry. Although the world was changing, the friendship continued to hold firm, perhaps to the surprise of both. It is a tribute to the quality of mind and the charm of personality of Fred Manning, that impatient, brash Ezra, meeting scores of people, involved in many enterprises, continued to admire his reclusive, scholarly friend for more than a decade.

12

Disappointments

Looking back from 1939, Ezra Pound saw 1911 as a turning point in his life. It was the year that Ford Madox Ford rolled on the floor over Pound's volume *Canzoni*, which showed the future modernist poet as still being in the grip of what Pound later called 'the arthritic milieu' of the respected critical circles—'Newbolt, the backwash of Lionel Johnson, Fred Manning, the Quarterlies and the rest of 'em.'[1] But this contempt for these writers was Pound's view in retrospect. Manning was still one of Pound's 'real early friends',[2] according to Aldington, and even as late as December 1911, Pound was praising Manning's poetry saying that Robert Bridges, Maurice Hewlett and Frederic Manning were in their different ways seriously concerned with overhauling the metre.[3] Nevertheless Ford's gleeful criticism of stilted Edwardianism accorded with the new directions in which Pound was moving by 1911.

Pound was spending more time with Ford, Wyndham Lewis and T. E. Hulme and was making such a name for himself that he was parodied in *Punch* in September. In November he began pouring out articles for A. R. Orage's radical journal, *New Age*. At the beginning of 1912 he met Aldington, then H.D. arrived in London. He was frantically busy, as the modernist began to emerge. And yet he still managed to find some time for his old-fashioned, scholarly friend. They corresponded during 1911 on the Italian medieval poet, Guido Cavalcanti, and considered co-operating on a translation of Dante, for which Manning suggested using as models the English verse of the fourteenth century: Piers Plowman, Chaucer and 'The Pearl'.[4] Manning's correspondence with Fairfax, who was preparing for the Bar, was dropping off. Now he clung to Pound in letters as he had to his earlier friend. From a poem of February 1911, 'Danäe's Song', with its sense of desolation and unhappiness, one might guess some personal hurt:

> Bitter thy fruit, O Love, thy crown is pain!
> Sweet were thy words to me, thy soft caresses.

Child of my heart, O gain beyond all gain.
Sleep, while I shelter thee with arms and tresses!
Sleep thou, my babe; and sleep, thou cruel sea;
And sleep, O grief, within the heart of me.

Some sourness seems to have invaded his previously sweet nature. His letters became a little sharper in tone. Although sister Trix and brother Harry were in England for the Coronation season, he took no joy in the celebrations, and was so oppressed by the fuss that he vowed it had made him a republican. He suggested that a wax doll be made to be taken out for occasional worship. 'Men will worship anything.'[5] In August he passed a 'damned dull' fortnight in London, met his 'ancient enemy, Rothenstein' (who had once been so kind to him) in company with Ryllis Hacon, and sent off 'a hostile and slightly contemptuous review' of R. L. Stevenson's letters, though, typically, he was reluctant to criticize harshly as he had a respect for human endeavour.[6] Given his dependence on the friendship of kind women like Eva Fowler and Olivia Shakespear, he displayed, in writing to his new adviser, Newbolt, an unexpectedly strong mysogynistic streak: 'a woman with the slightest trace of reason on her side will never admit to any on the other';[7] and he complained on 30 November to Newbolt, who seemed to bring out the worst in him, that he had had to feed so many old women at Mrs Fowler's musicale he did not have time to talk to Percy Lubbock. He had seemed irritable about the gift of a piece of wedding cake in a letter to Fairfax on 13 October: 'I was told to put it under my pillow and dream of my future wife, but I do not like nightmares, matrimonial or otherwise, and I'm not keen on matrimony. I hate bride cake'. As an attempt at his whimsical style, it fell flat.

Two things brightened his life: the Russian Ballet in *Carnaval* and *Scheherazade*: 'the most indecent as well as the most beautiful thing I have ever seen in my life',[8] and the relaxation he found in the friendship with Ezra. Jim, beside the 'small volcano', looked a little dull. The old friendship faded a little as Manning's admiration for Ezra grew. Where Manning was cool in his comments in late October 1911 about Fairfax's volume, *The Troubled Pool*, saying it was really charming in form and that the initial letters were jolly, he was very enthusiastic about his other friend in 'Some Contemporary Poets' in the *Cornish Illustrated Xmas Catalogue of Books* that year: 'Mr Ezra Pound's work is altogether extraordinary in its vigorous handling of human passion, its vivid dramatic qualities, its moments of exquisite tenderness coming sometimes among the stormier lights with wonderful effect'. The vigour and vitality of this poet held something of the same appeal that the passions of the Elizabethan dramatists had for him. Elemental Ezra may have been a factor in the warmth of Manning's review of *The Work of J. M. Synge* (1 April 1911), appealing to some primitive feelings which had been hidden under the mask of the aesthete.

He [Synge] saw . . . that to be a master of character a writer has to discover not the difference of one man from another, but the resemblance of one to all, and it is this elemental quality of his characters which gives to them an extended significance . . . they become for us types or personifications of man's eternal and unprofitable strife with fate. They are great because nothing stands between them and the direct shock of circumstance.

But where Pound was bounding forward, Mannning was falling behind, losing some of the small status he had won, beset by disappointment. The most bitter blow was the depressing mix-up over the Princess de Polignac Prize for 1910. Maurice Hewlett proposed *Scenes and Portraits* and it was chosen unanimously by the selection committee. Then Newbolt pointed out that the work was ineligible, having been published in 1909; the award was passed on to Walter de La Mare. Missing out on the one hundred pounds, which Manning needed, was bad enough. Much more upsetting was the loss of the critical recognition, the endorsement by the literary establishment. Then there was the matter of not being asked for a poem for the first *Georgian Poetry* anthology. He thought the editor, Edward Marsh, might have considered one or two of his poems.[9] He was badly mistaken. The hearty young Georgians, Rupert Brooke, Lascelles Abercrombie, Gordon Bottomley and others whom Marsh admired, were reacting against the Edwardian aestheticism that Manning represented. They were intent on being optimistic, realistic, and even a little brutal; on demolishing Edwardian langour and artificiality. Manning, in return, despised them except for Brooke. Pound, seen as new and vigorous, was asked for a poem; he refused. Manning was overlooked.

The small reputation he had made was already shrinking. The *Spectator* was seen as staid and puritanical; since reviewers had no by-line, St Loe Strachey being rigid about contributions being unsigned and using the royal 'we', Manning's name was little known. He was well aware of his lack of standing in the literary world. When Pound invited him to London to chair a meeting in March 1912 he replied: 'Would my name command any, even the smallest measure of respect'; he felt it needed someone who looked as if he knew everything. 'Newbolt would be a good man to get I should think. Imagine him, Sir Percival in trousers.' He had written a few formally polite letters to Newbolt after the fiasco of the prize but the tone of this sardonic vision of the martial poet as a knight of the round table indicates his disillusionment in this patron. 'Or perhaps Selwyn "the graven Image",' he continued.

With what respect do I always consider that placid and urbane countenance, that manner of perfect detachment, of Justice tempered by mercy. Here is the perfect symposiarch . . . a soul nourished not only upon the ambrosia and honey of the Muses, but upon the turtle and champagne of aldermanic banquets. I can imagine the neatness of his few remarks, the smile, the caressing voice, the well-chosen words.

The correspondence with Newbolt ended about this time; the old school tie patriot of 'Vitaï Lampada' and the ironic author of *Scenes and Portraits* really had little in common. And despite his protestations Manning was advertised as chairing Pound's lecture on Cavalcanti in March 1912.

The contact with exciting, lively Pound affected Manning strongly and he was grateful for the influence, writing in January 1912 that Pound had loosened something in him. Between priggish Galton and slightly pompous Jim, Manning was in need of some stimulus. Certainly the poem, 'The Mother', published in the *Spectator* (6 January 1912) shows him as emotionally freer, less guarded. He admitted a week later that he contrived to enjoy the radical *New Age* for which Pound wrote, finding its kind of socialism less objectionable than the futility and cant of liberalism. But, basically—'au fond tho', as he put it—he remained Galton's disciple. 'I'm a Tory and always shall be', he continued. Yet, he felt in March, as he indicated in another letter to Pound, that his articles on the Elizabethans and on Thomas Gray for the *Spectator* were an approach to Pound's theories, along different lines. However irritated he might be by Pound's egotism, however much they might argue, he responded to his vitality.

When in town in April he saw Eva Fowler and his South African friends, the Sargants. The Fowlers' nephew, Paul Hasson, whom he had known for several years, visited Edenham in May 1912. Manning liked young people. He was also on friendly terms with Eva's niece, her namesake, Eva Focke, and he later took a special interest in the Rothenstein children. In the eagerness and freshness of the young could be seen the brighter side of the Kore myth, the continual renewal of life.

The relationship between the four young friends, Fred, Ezra, Dorothy and Jim, was becoming more complicated. By 1911 the Shakespears were frowning on their daughter's obsession with the magnetic, but penniless, Ezra. It appears from Dorothy's little jokes that Fairfax, nicknamed by her 'Jim-Jam-jum-jam', was seen as a more acceptable suitor. But the girl thought that wealthy Jim should marry a title to give the £.s.d. (his money) *raison d'être*. Fred does not seem to have been considered as a possible husband, by either the parents or Dorothy. Her attitude towards 'poor Fred' was one of teasing affection. When that double-dyed Tory, Arthur Galton (labelled 'Mat-Mat' by Dorothy from his tendency to talk about his great hero, Matthew Arnold), decided, in June 1912, to live without servants to avoid being a tax gatherer for Lloyd George's National Insurance Bill, Dorothy, in a letter to Pound that month, pictured harassed Fred as an inadequate housemaid at Edenham.

She respected him, however, as an artist and admired his prose style. Writing to Ezra in December 1911, she hoped Pound would have a good influence on Fred's verse, and Fred a good influence on Pound's prose. Ezra himself even mentioned 'Our Frederic' in the same breath as Henry James and Anatole France.[10] Fairfax was much more of a target for jokes between the lovers, especially about his 'Shipwrecked Pool' as they termed his latest book. But they regarded 'poor Fred' with a mixture of respect, affection and amusement. It was probably left to the usually calm Manning to keep some sort of an uneasy peace between his friends, for Jim was touchy about his verses and perhaps saw Ezra as a rival for Dorothy, while Galton disliked Pound, and Ezra was continually and explosively quarrelling with absolutely everybody, even Fred. This was wearing on those of his friends who took his outbursts to heart, but as Dorothy said, Ezra scarcely noticed quarrels. Manning was both excited and exhausted by the relationship. Yet he hoped, as he indicated in a letter in March 1912, for a *modus vivendi* where they would be able to talk to one another for half an hour without their hackles rising. At times, however, his irritation took over from his admiration, and he turned again to Jim: 'As for poor Pound . . . well God must be delighted with his handiwork . . . for the pure comic give me the works of God. He means well, Pound does'.[11] All the same Manning could forgive many of his difficult friend's eccentricities for the sake of his generosity of spirit in those years, and the stimulus of his genius.

With articles on sixteen topics, 1912 was the peak year of Manning's *Spectator* reviewing. Money was short and he joked to Fairfax in late October about publishing the poems he had been working on, 'Ganhardine's Song' and 'The Shepherd's Carol of Bethlehem', under the title of 'Poems for an Overcoat'. (Both poems were reprinted in *Eidola*.) He found the reviewing heavy going, the only compensating factor being that he was allowed a free choice of books. As a disciple of the Greek critic, Longinus and his criticism of enthusiasm, Manning did not often review works he did not like and he was always reluctant to criticize harshly: 'I have a sort of respect for human endeavour, human vanity and human failures even, as being after all common to the whole of mankind', he wrote to Jim (11 November 1911). This did not stop him from attacking Lytton Strachey's *Landmarks in French Literature* which offended him by its dismissal of Montaigne, one of his special favourites.

He emphasized in his reviews the quality he admired, the dual nature of the artist, using Coleridge and Swift as particularly clear examples. The vital qualities were, for him, the personal emotion and the personal experience. Despite his mannered verses, in his lucid reviews he was for realism and emotion, against artificiality and rhetoric. He preferred the passion of J. M. Synge to what he termed the cerebrations of G. B. Shaw, the robustness of William Morris to the abstractions of Swinburne, the broadness and the tolerance of Hardy to what he saw as the superficiality and extravagance of Balzac. He approved both the elemental quality of the Elizabethans and the melancholy reticence of Thomas Gray. Unexpectedly George Sand won him with her enthusiasm: 'Her whole life was an *affaire de coeur*, but illusion succeeded to illusion and she was never disenchanted'.[12] His critical response was total and intuitive: 'In the greatest works of art the form, the style and the matter cannot be separated from each other; they cease to exist.'[13] For Manning a work of art was to be appreciated as a whole, not split into aspects. The whole was more than the sum of the parts.

There were several oddities among the works he chose to review, but none more so than *The Memoirs of the Countess Golovine*, the Russian countess who at twenty-six became the mentor of the teenage Grand Duchess, the future Empress Elizabeth. Was he striking some personal note, drawing some parallel with his own life, when he commented on the breaking of that friendship? 'It seems possible, too, that there was something in the nature of the friendship which rendered it exceptionally brittle: a passionate affection asks for so much that when it comes finally to the enigma which every person, in the ultimate resort, presents to it, it imagines that it has been betrayed.'[14]

Pressure of work, shortness of money, Manning's partiality for Pound, the abrasions of time, were putting strains, it would seem, on the friendship with Galton which had endured more than fifteen years. The older man had placed so much faith in his protégé, but the great success had not yet been achieved. Although Manning told Jim in a letter late in April 1912 that he longed to finish it, 'The Golden Coach' still loitered. Manning was scarcely known, while the young American iconoclast was becoming the talk of London. Galton was obviously not happy; passages from his sermons *A Thought for Each Day* (1911) show him in a ceaseless struggle with his own turbulent nature. Christianity, he says, does not promise that life shall be easy, that it shall be free from pain and care. It puts this life before us, on the contrary, as a discipline, as a bearing of the cross, as a journey along a steep and narrow way, as a time of warfare, of sobriety, of watching and self-denial—we must suffer a while. Pound, however difficult, was a life force, a beacon of light to a man not yet thirty, living in this gloomy atmosphere. And the clergyman's choler did not help. 'Good temper', Galton wrote, 'is one of the most important of the Christian virtues and one of the most difficult'. The hopes and happiness of the early Edenham years were shadowed by disillusion. 'Like all those who are engaged in a warfare, we must be continually on guard: ever sober, ever vigilant, always ready for a surprise.' The picture was not totally black, however. There were pleasures in life: visits to London, to the Stracheys at Guildford, a holiday at Daisy Meadow, and a happy little excursion for both Manning and Galton in July 1912 to Oxford, in the company of delightful Dorothy. She told Ezra in a letter that she found Fred most entertaining on that occasion.

Edenham for Fred was becoming less attractive. On his side, what was there to show for the fifteen years? Galton had instructed him, guided him, guarded him, but also had cut him off from other possibilities in life. The relationship dominated his life, for the book to which he was devoting his energies, 'The Golden Coach', seems to have had its beginnings in some fictional account of their association. Although the original protagonist, as the novel progressed, turned from a boy into a young woman, a curious scrap that remains from this lost work may give some clue to Manning's complicated feelings. His heroine was courted as a girl by an old man, Chapuys. When he dies an acquaintance urges her to marry again.

'Never', said Madame de Sainte-Claire with a shudder. 'Do not speak to me of it again . . . I shall be candid with you. M. Chapuys was always kind to me; he befriended me; I loved and respected him as though he were my father. It was not sufficient for him. I am sincerely grieved that he is dead. But, but it was an outrage.'[15]

Whatever the relationship between Fred and Mr Galton, it was extremely close. But devotion can wear thin. The emotional problems shown in Galton's sermons would be hard to live with as year succeeded year. The clegyman's agonizing seems genuine enough. It is unlikely that Frederic Manning would have spent all those years with a fake. It was a difficult period, though, with Galton questioning his faith in Christ as God, with both men disappointed in Fred's comparative literary failure, with the shadow of Lionel Johnson perhaps coming between them. Small wonder that Manning, in late November, looked forward with such zest to a week in London with Pound. 'It will be great fun.'

The dullness and the constraints of the Edenham life must have been accentuated by the flamboyant adventures of another friend of this period, whom Manning visited in August 1912 at his Somerset home, Pixton Park. Aubrey Herbert was a son of the Fourth Earl of Carnarvon and his Countess. Sir William Manning had managed this lady's Australian investments, which included whole streets of Sydney, and Herbert had visited Australia in 1908. As well as this connection, there was the bond of poetry, for Manning suggested to Harriet Monroe in a letter (9 October 1912) that she send a *Poetry* prospectus to Aubrey Herbert who possessed 'a simple but . . . true poetical gift'.

Herbert, a daring, sanguine adventurer, had travelled extensively in the dangerous Balkans and the Middle East, often accompanied by an undisciplined Albanian servant, learning the languages, confronting robbers, catching typhoid, enduring hardships, facing danger and charming all to such an extent that he was offered the throne of Albania. Back in England, he was elected Conservative Member of Parliament for Somerset in 1911. Yet this colourful aristocrat, Evelyn Waugh's future father-in-law and the model for 'Greenmantle' in John Buchan's novel of adventure and espionage, was almost blind. Surely Frederic Manning, in spite of his frailty and nervous temperament, could find a little more excitement in the world than the tensions in the vicarage in Edenham. Manning also believed about this time that his romance—'The Golden Coach'— might benefit from a visit to France.

On 14 October 1912 he wrote to his friend Albert Houtin asking for help in finding cheap, furnished rooms in Paris. He had made a decision to strike out for his own small adventure. He intended, he said, to stay in Paris 'a long time'.

13

Restless Days

W<small>HEN THE</small> *Titanic* sank on 14 April 1912, with the loss of 1600 lives, Frederic Manning reflected that he had come to consider bravery as a kind of saintliness. His shy and nervous temperament made the decision to settle in Paris for a time a minor act of courage on his part. It was also a small reflection of the growing mood of unrest in Europe, the desire for change, the longing to break up old patterns, to wreck the placidity of a boring existence. 'A long period of law and order, such as our generation had behind it, produces a real craving for the abnormal',[1] wrote young German ex-officer Ernst Jünger, looking back to before the war. In the United Kingdom, bitter strikes, militant feminism, the passions associated with Home Rule for Ireland and rebellious movements in the arts manifested a struggle to change what was seen as a complacent and dull society. The Georgian poets, in their initial phase, emphasized vitality, realism and toughness against the artificiality and aestheticism of the previous tradition.

The dandy writers, Saki and Max Beerbohm, intuited a mood of unease even in the youth of the upper classes, some vague rebellion against the status quo. Saki's 'untameable young lords' find they cannot settle into a dull world. Comus Bassington becomes the boy 'who throws away his life'.[2] In Beerbohm's *Zuleika Dobson* (1911) a generation of undergraduates follows its aristocratic leader into a mass suicide for an ideal: love of the divine Zuleika. 'It was ill to be down in that abominable sink of death. Abominable, yes, to them who discerned there death only; but sacramental and sweet enough to the men who were dying there for love.' Such young men were looking for something more, something out of the ordinary, even at the cost of life. In popular literature, Raffles, the gentleman cracksman, turns to crime largely for excitement.

The idea of violence as a good, as an explosion of life-giving energy, won followers in a mish-mash popularization of the ideas of Nietzsche, Shaw and Bergson. Karl Pearson's neo-Darwinism saw struggle, with accompanying violence as a natural force; George Sorel's *Reflections on Violence* provided an intellectual gloss to the use of force by trade unions. In Italy, Futurist Filippo Marinetti lauded violence in his 1909 manifesto and his lecture in London drew an audience which included Dorothy Shakespear. Among London's avant-garde, T. E. Hulme propounded that life is action. In a debasement of such ideas to the level of popular patriotism, Australian poet, William Baylebridge, then an expatriate, chided the Mother Country in the *Daily Mail* on Empire Day (24 May) 1909, for her lack of energy:

> England, thy loins have lost their fabled power
> Or wherefore ease in these too-pregnant times.
> A cancerous apathy o'er grows and devours
> Thy vital parts and through thy marrow climbs.

He, however, was an obsessed militarist and a believer in violence: 'Does not peace mean stagnation, which is death?'[3]

Manning was no such apostle of violence but he was a pessimist about the madness of human beings and he had been taught by Galton, who had observed the results of the Franco–Prussian War of 1870, to despise Germany. German industrial and military power were growing ominously; fear of the Kaiser and of invasion had taken hold of the popular imagination in England. Invasion novels were popular. General R. S. Baden-Powell had urged his Boy Scouts to 'Be Prepared'; and in Saki's bitter invasion novel, *When William Came* (1913), the Boy Scouts are seen as the hope of a defeated and occupied Britain.

The general atmosphere of anxiety was heightened by special tensions in the vicarage. Early in 1913 Arthur Galton was in a fury that the booksellers, Cornish Brothers, had cut a number of the essays he had written for their Christmas catalogue. As well as objecting to his remarks about Catholics, and the Quaker Cadbury family, they had found unpalatable his approval of epithets such as barbarians, uncivilized, envious, narrow, uncouth and tactless, when writing of the Germans. Vain and cranky, not to be crossed, sure of the rightness of his views, Galton reacted with almost paranoic rage. He was clearly a most unhappy man. He saw the ecclesiastical and political life as permeated by cant, and by 'sophistry, mental reservations and verbal jugglings'. For one who held a living as a clergyman he was sadly lacking in religious faith. He thought: 'There is not a religious system at present in the world in which any person can believe, without making reservations that are destructive to clear thinking and to clean language'.[4] His hope of earthly fame as the mentor of a brilliant writer was dimming. Manning was little known and seemed unable to complete his romance. When Galton published, in 1913, the essays Cornish Brothers had rejected, he dedicated them effusively, not to his close companion of many years, but to Dorothy Shakespear:

In memory of Dreaming Hours at Oxford,
With a hope of More Golden Realities in Rome.[5]

As for Manning, he ended nearly a decade of quiet country life late in 1912 with visions of violence and blood, expressed in a letter farewelling Fairfax, once more off to Sydney.

> By the time you think of returning Europe will be a red, wet mass of bloody slaughter . . . I have visions of myself trailing a puissant pike, in Pistol's phrase, spilling my blood, what little I've got, for my country and being compensated for it by, what would be the supreme satisfaction of my life: sticking a knife into the guts of a gor-bellied German until the fat closed around the haft, I really hate European democracy, and think, that, as it is impossible for us to teach the masses to despise and slaughter themselves, they should be incited to despise and slaughter each other. So you see I scent carnage from afar like an exultant vulture.[6]

There is something a little stagey about this blood-thirsty letter. The anger and bitterness seem real enough, the targets rather literary. Like the letter about Arthur Machen, this one has a touch of hysteria, as well as a heartlessness unusual in his correspondence. He had professed to Houtin on 31 December 1911 that he had never been so busy: with his romance, his reviewing, a quarrel in *The Times* (his letter of 21 December 1911 dealt with a review of J. W. Mackail's Lectures on Poetry) and a long poem in his head. But the realities of 1912 were that the novel did not progress, the envisaged poem was not written, and he was thirty in July. Pound was moving into new areas, Manning was stalled in his own career. Paris, by early 1913, represented an escape from his prison, an adventure of his own.

'I feel, Monsieur,' he wrote (in French) to Houtin,

> as if I were going into another world, or at least to China. All adventures, I believe, are more marvellous in thought than in reality, because nothing is impossible in thought. I feel like a little child, oh, what am I saying, like a doll in the hands of a little child, that terrible child Providence, who daily breaks her toys without any regret . . . Oh, well, monsieur, I ask your pardon in advance for a thousand pieces of childishness. At heart I know I will be very much at ease after six hours in Paris, but for some souls the unknown always has hidden perils.[7]

His feverish tone is an indication of how difficult he found what others took as pleasures.

He no doubt managed to hide such nervousness behind his languid, witty mask of Manning 'of the *Spectator*' at an evening at Eva's in early January 1913 where W. B. Yeats was also a guest, and at a farewell luncheon given by Dorothy on a few days before he set out. His South African friend, poet Edmund Sargant and his wife, Marie Don, were guests. So was Charles Whibley, the Tory scholar, critic, journalist and talker, who was a great favourite with Manning; one of the people, he said, whom he took to in five minutes. Whibley, who was to become an influential friend of T. S. Eliot, was a master of invective, and had won some notoriety with his scathing review in the *Scots Observer* in 1890 of Wilde's *The Picture of Dorian Gray*. A stout hater of puritanism, and of humbug, he quipped about the rejection by the *Spectator* of one of Manning's poems as 'improper', 'to the pure all things are impure'.[8] (For all his fastidiousness, Manning was not a prude.) Pound was not a guest that day and writing to him in late March about the occasion, Dorothy joked that she might go to Paris with Frederic Manning. It looked, at last, like some change of personality and a new phase in his life, a new beginning, free of the sway of Galton. He planned to arrive at the Hotel St James on 19 March, and he invited Houtin to dine with him that evening. But the Great Adventure turned into a complete disaster. The train was an hour late, the Customs a chaos. He was hours late reaching his hotel, and Houtin was not there. One week after his arrival in Paris Manning was preparing to leave his rooms at 69 Rue Raynouard (XVIème arrondissement) to return to Edenham, miserable with flu and failure. His dash for freedom and independence, for a new kind of life, had ended in collapse. His only Parisian contact, Houtin, was elderly and none too well himself. He had been unable to spend much time with this clinging Anglo-Saxon, whose French, while fitted for scholarship, was of little use in daily life. Manning, writing to the Frenchman (27 March 1913), felt guilty that Houtin had worn himself out in helping him in a search for lodgings in the chilly weather. It was a sad fact that living under the protection of Arthur Galton for so many years combined with his natural nervousness and weakness, had unfitted Manning for dealing with the strains of a foreign country.

Safely back in Edenham, after breaking his journey to stay with the Shakespears in London, he consoled himself with the thought that he had met many people and tasted several kinds of Parisian life. Although still very 'enrhumé' when writing to Houtin (14 April), he recollected some pleasanter aspects of his adventure, from the pretty women in their Paquin dresses at the Hotel Crillon to the artists and musicians of the Left Bank. But the pretty women were stupid and boring, and one editor's wife had insisted on playing the violincello after dinner. His only real regret was that he had not met Anatole France or Albert Loisy, an ex-priest and modernist Bible critic. He accepted that Houtin had done all he could. They had been unlucky. Nevertheless his bid to break the monotonous pattern of his life had ended in fiasco. Henceforth, he said, as far as travelling was concerned the best course of action was to stay at home, exploring new countries seated beside his fire. As for a little excitement, there were always the races, and he boasted to Pound in June 1913 that he had won on Louvois in the Two Thousand Guineas.

As a slight compensation for the Paris disaster he had three poems published in *Poetry* in April: 'The Faun's Call' (from a proposed longer poem, 'Demeter'), 'At Even' and 'Simaetha'. Harriet Monroe, the American editor of this Chicago-based magazine, had approached Pound for some of his work in 1912, and in September of that year Pound had become foreign editor. Manning was one of the poets whose work he recommended. He betrayed a growing anxiety about time by putting back his age two years in the biographical note he sent Monroe in mid-May 1913. That brought him below the barrier of thirty. Another poem, 'Passe-pied', published in the *Spectator* (26 April), showed him still caught in an artifical romantic web of language, with 'fairy hours that invite to the chace [*sic*]'. Yet Pound remained impressed, writing to Monroe: 'his name is respected', 'he is important aside from what he happens to contribute', he was a name worth having.[9] He also tried to promote the first chapters of the romance in the United States, and praised the parodies, 'The Ballad of the Goodly Hair' and 'Chocolate Creams who has forgotten them' to Monroe as things of lasting delight. But by July 1913, Pound was planning to send Manning's work, in future, to the *Smart Set*, advertised as the 'magazine of cleverness', designed for a sophisticated audience. Those clever men H. L. Mencken and George Jean Nathan were not yet the editors but they exerted considerable influence. Manning's old-fashioned aura was hardly smart set. Pound's well-meaning attempts on his friend's behalf had no result; his own life, however, continued to gather pace.

In June 1913 Pound became literary editor of the anti-Pankhurst feminist journal, the *New Freewoman*, edited nominally by Dora Marsden. Here he gained a platform for his ideas, especially for Imagism. Also in that year he met the twenty-one-year-old sculptor, outrageous, innovative Henri Gaudier-Brzeska. With Gaudier-Brzeska, Wyndham Lewis, sculptor Jacob Epstein, poets Richard Aldington and H.D., young writer Rebecca West and philosopher T. E. Hulme—the group described by Ford Madox Ford as 'the band of Les Jeunes'—Pound was 'planning to blow Parnassus to the moon',[10] with non-representational art, *vers libre* and disturbing ideas.

That year Frederic Manning published only five reviews in the *Spectator*. The small success of *Scenes and Portraits* was now some years in the past, his poems were dated; he was fading from the scene. Was Max Beerbohm thinking of his acquaintance, Fred Manning, when he wrote in 1914 the short story which immortalized in satire the type of the failed minor writer, 'Enoch Soames'? This dim poet is desperate for some acknowledgement and he sells his soul to the devil in return for an afternoon in the British Museum, in one hundred years time, when he may savour his posthumous fame. Alas, it is non-existent. 'A third-rait poet hoo beleevz imself a grate jeneus' is history's judgment, in Beerbohm's view.

Soames lives in the shadow of Pater and the poets of the 1890s (the story is set in the 1890s) and has many touches of Manning about him. He is a heavy smoker, with nicotine-stained fingers, he has a small private income, is in poor health, and on the edge of literary circles. He has written a book, *Negations*, which contains a dialogue between Pan and St Ursula. He is given to bouts of French phrases and his verse reads like a parody of

Manning, 'pale tunes irresolute and traces of old sounds'. Although he maintains that he cares not a sou for recognition, he is desperate to be drawn by Will Rothenstein. In fact Will has done a pastel of him at one time, but the painter finds it hard to remember this model. There was a similar situation in Rothenstein's relationship with Manning, for Manning wrote to Fairfax (2 September 1911) that he had met Rothenstein with Mrs Hacon, and recalled to him that they had met some years previously at an art exhibition, where the painter had failed to recognize his former model. 'His wife said precisely what you said at the time. "You would think he would recognize anyone whose portrait he had drawn," whereat I riposted: "No one has so far recognized the portrait".' Soames admires Milton's 'dark insight' as Manning did his 'angry shadow', and Beerbohm grants that he has a sort of music in his prose, acknowledging that Soames is an an artist, as far as he is anything, poor fellow. It is a sad and funny portrait, and may well have originated in Beerbohm's impish amusement at some aspects of 'poor Fred'. It leaves out, however, the intellect and the irony which were fundamental to Manning. Soames's driving passion is a mad and empty vanity, Manning's a dedication, however difficult and hopeless, to his art, to an unrealizable perfection. He was not, however, an exponent of art for art's sake. Instead he followed in the line of the exquiste but serious-minded aesthetes: Newman, Arnold, Pater, who used their art in trying to understand problems of life and thought.

To the literary world Manning might have seemed *passé*, but he did not lack persistence. He took up his task again, back in Edenham, haunted by his character of Madame Sainte Claire, a romantic vision of 'black velvet, old lace and bewitching eyes'.[11] For all its problems the relationship with Arthur Galton had its own happiness, a security, a sharing of ideas and interests, an affectionate understanding of this difficult man. In writing of Swift he could well have been thinking of his friend: 'his charm . . . his frank coarseness'; 'his misanthropy and odd streaks of idealism'; 'his cynicism, and his playful scoldings'.[12] Epicurean in outlook, Manning could savour the small pleasures of life: books, music, art, his writing, his friendships; he could accept his limitations, and endure his frustrations. His was a classic, not a romantic temperament—there were no permanent solutions—life was a mystery. As he had written some years before:

> We have all that sense of personal isolation, of our own impotence to withstand the blind forces which impel us toward certain actions, or the irresistable march of circumstance which thwarts our purpose, and we have all to steer our way among conflicting currents or dangerous shallows toward a future which we cannot discern, while at every tack we are hampered by our own disorderly appetites and desires, and are as often as not the victims of our virtues as of our vices.[13]

In the friendship of fifteen years, the well-loved village, the familiar countryside, he had a place. Turbulent Wyndham Lewis recalled the atmosphere of those pre-war days with his own mentor, Thomas Sturge Moore:

> How calm those days were before the epoch of wars and revolution, when you used to sit on one side of your work-table, and I on the other, and we would talk—with trees and creepers of the placid Hampstead domesticity beyond the windows and you used to grunt with a philosophical despondence I greatly enjoyed. It was the last days of the Victorian world of artificial peacefulness—of the RSPCA and London bobbies, of 'slumming' and Buzzard's cake.[14]

In Frederic Manning's life too, these were the last days of a sort of peace.

14

Another Friend

BECAUSE OF his particular circumstances and his tendency to take conservative positions, Frederic Manning had little to do personally with Pound's set of non-conformists. There was one exception, Richard Aldington. Dorothy Shakespear, mischievously wondering what they would make of one another, invited Aldington and his wife, Hilda Doolittle (the two had been married in October 1913) to tea to meet Manning in early January the following year. Aldington had recently been appointed assistant editor of the *Egoist*, formerly the *New Freewoman*, but now virtually the journal of the new Imagism, and Dorothy thought it an excellent idea that the three should meet, as she assured Olivia.

The picturesque Faun and his Hamadryad (so nicknamed by Olivia), both tall and handsome, emphasized by their build the slightness of 'poor Fred', just as their laconic Imagist poems threw into relief his outdatedness. Possibly H.D., an an uncompromising, unconventional American used to the outgoing personalities of Ezra and her husband, was the most perplexed of the three at this meeting with the nervous, dandyish Edwardian. Fred, friend of aeronautics pioneer Lawrence Hargrave, had been aeroplaning, according to a letter Dorothy wrote to Ezra (6–7 January 1914) and the excitement, she said, 'had stirred up his brain nicely'. Aldington, already an admirer of innovative, vigorous Pound, was won over to the discipleship of this very different writer, so cautious and conservative. The friendship, though never close, endured until well after the war.

It was an unexpected conquest of mind and personality, for the two had little in common at first sight. While Ezra and Fred were almost of an age and shared the experience of expatriatism, Richard Aldington, at twenty-one, was scarcely more than a boy, and came of a very English, middle-class, old Saxon family. He was born in July 1892, the son of a solicitor's clerk—a scholarly recluse—and a dominating mother whom he grew to hate so much that he refused later in life to attend her deathbed.[1] But, like

Fred, he had found his way to European culture, in particular to the love of French literature, through the interest and encouragement of an older man—in his case a scholarly dilettante of fifty, Dudley Gray. Rebelling against his mother's wish that he should enter a profession, he enrolled at University College, London, to study classics and literature. The other undergraduates were inclined to be Shavians and Fabians; Aldington, an enthusiast in nature and colourful in personality, found them somewhat philistine and dessicated, and became a leader of his own small group. Then, unable to complete his degree because of family circumstances, he took to the precarious life of writer and poet, and fell under the spell of Pound.

Boyish, frank, handsome with his rugged build and red beard, well set off by his customary velvet jacket and bow tie, passionate in his personal life and in his devotion to his art, full of zest for life, his style and character seemed at odds with Manning's deliberate guardedness and shyness. Yet he responded to the charm of the older man, 'an adorable fellow',[2] as he called him in 1917 after some years of acquaintance. He admired him as a writer of very beautiful prose, and was delighted, in particular, by 'The Friend of Paul'. Like Pound, Aldington was under the sway of the French aesthete, Remy de Gourmont, saying: 'he meant to us the type of the artist—the man who lived to create the work of art and to whom nothing else is of essential importance'.[3] Manning, so scholarly, so dedicated, so reclusive, seemed to him to be formed in much the same mould. The brash young Imagist poet, deeply involved in the new movement in poetry, was prepared to defend this new friend against the charge of being an outdated writer.

He put forward the view that Frederic Manning, Ford Madox Ford and Thomas Sturge Moore were the only three real critics of the day. He denied that Manning was merely a repetition of the 1890s: 'he has simply read the books of more languages and centuries, looked at more pictures, heard better music and thought more imaginatively than most of his contemporaries'.[4] He went on to emphasize his subject's disinterestedness and modesty. In his opinion, while Pater seemed always perfectly self-satisfied, Manning suffered from a perpetual sense of dissatisfaction, damned by the irony that was so fundamental to his thought—the irony that is 'the mark, the pleasure and the curse of distinguished minds'. And Aldington defended the prose style, saying that although it was sometimes too ornate and precious, it was never cheap. To be discussed so very enthusiastically and so discerningly by one of the leading new young writers was as much as Manning could hope for in those transitional times.

The support of Pound and Aldington buoyed up his sinking reputation, so that he was included in the guest list of poets invited to attend the Peacock Dinner (so called because of the menu) held in January 1914 in honour of Wilfred Scawen Blunt, the anti-colonial, pro-Home Rule for Ireland, poet and explorer. W. B. Yeats, the sponsor, and Ezra Pound, Richard Aldington, Thomas Sturge Moore, F. S. Flint and Victor Plarr all travelled down to Blunt's house, Newbuildings, Sussex, for the celebration. Pound read an address in verse, and the old poet was presented with a casket, engraved by Gaudier-Brzeska, containing a poem by each guest. Robert Bridges, the Poet Laureate, declined for political reasons, and John Masefield was unable to attend at the last minute. Manning also failed to arrive, though he had hoped to go.[5] Ill health was the usual reason for missing out on such festivities, but on this occasion the moral indignation of Arthur Galton at the idea of paying homage to a radical, womanizing, pro-Irish, anti-Britisher may have barred the path.

The invitation was a sign that the friendship of the American, the Australian and the young Englishman held firm despite the attendant quarrels and tensions largely due to Pound's explosive nature and his unawareness that he was upsetting people. They formed such a threesome that in March Manning proposed they should run their own magazine which would accept *vers libre* and Imagiste pieces, in opposition to the journal of the Georgian poets, *New Numbers*. He was trying to keep up with his modernist friends, admiring Jacob Epstein's sculptures at the Gimpel Gallery, attending recitals of Debussy by Pound's friend, the American pianist and composer, Walter Rummel. In early March he suggested the *Hellenist* as the name for the proposed magazine, but this surely carried too many Arnoldian resonances to suit the new mood, and Charles Whibley, whom he mentioned as a possible contributor, seemed too linked with the past. In any case Dorothy told Ezra that there were enough magazines already. Pound, however, was interested, suggesting to Dorothy in late March that such a review might balance Wyndham Lewis's provocative new project, *Blast*, a journal of Vorticism, which aimed at destroying old shibboleths and shaking up English complacency. Manning was prepared to accept the financial responsibility in a very modest way, and proposed only about eighty subscribers, with contributors also being guarantors. Nothing came of the plan. The would-be joint-editors, Pound and Manning, quarrelled, though Dorothy felt that Pound, as usual, was unaware that they had. Disagreements meant more to withdrawn Manning than to busy Pound.

Pound had many concerns that year, in particular the fact that the Shakespears, in February, finally gave their reluctant consent to an engagement. Pound's financial status had been the difficulty, for Olivia maintained that if Ezra only had £500 a year she would be delighted. Little appeared to have changed, except that the parents accepted that Dorothy was utterly set on the marriage. And Pound was making a name for himself, and held a job of sorts on the *Egoist*. Did Olivia succumb to the memory of her romance with Yeats? She had given up the greatest poet of the day. Dorothy's Ezra might prove even greater. While Eva Fowler was delighted with the news, according to Pound, some members of the Shakespear circle were less pleased. Previously latent feelings in relationships rose to the surface. Dorothy was concerned in early March that she had not heard from Fred since the announcement, and, what was worse,

Olivia had not heard from Galton. 'Do you think it's fury', she asked her fiancé, when writing to him. Then Dorothy received a letter from Fred which had been delayed in the post. On 6 March he had written:

My dear Dorothy,
I send you my blessing, and wish you and Ezra the best gifts of the best gods, who are those those of the hearth and the threshold. I quarrelled with him, a little while ago, but when I heard the news, I wrote to wish him luck, and in return he sent me a joyous epistle inviting me to attend you in saffron slippers, bearing torches and cantillate [chanting] . . . I should not have been astonished some years ago, if you had said you intended to marry Ezra, but I am rather surprised now. However I am less astonished than most people, and declare myself absolutely impenitent for having mocked in your presence his whiskers etc . . . Well, I have known you half my life, and have grown very fond of you, and I wish you the best happiness in the world . . .
Yours always,

Fred[6]

On 3 March he had written to Pound, congratulating him, despite 'the good deal of ill-feeling' he thought had developed between them of late. In writing to Fairfax, however, he felt free to express his doubts about the alliance. He was sorry for Dorothy, but not surprised, and thought Pound would prove an impossible husband. While he accepted that Pound was in love, he termed him 'practical'[7], in the sense, it would seem, of pragmatic. The news seems to have upset Jim more, although he congratulated Pound formally. He may have seen himself as a possible husband more acceptable to the Shakespears in style and circumstance. He appears to have been ruffled by her choice, for Dorothy told her fiancé, on 21 March, that she had had two priceless letters from Fairfax, which she would keep for him. Manning claimed, writing to Fairfax, that he was not horrified by the match, only a little amused. He admired the lovers for staking so much. Whether or not the matter touched him deeply, his stance towards his two friends was amused and gently affectionate.

'No reasonable person could look at the Apoxyomenos [the statue of a Greek athlete in the Vatican Museum] and then propose to marry Pound', he quipped to Jim, but he felt that Dorothy knew what she was doing and was content to be poor. Manning's apparent coolness in his acceptance of a *fait accompli* contrasted with Galton's livid reaction. The clergyman had known Dorothy from early childhood; she had teased and charmed him, won some tenderness from this curmudgeon. He and Pound, alike in their explosiveness, their dogmatic stands, were natural enemies, prophets of different causes. He called Dorothy's decision 'a monstrous piece of folly',[8] saying that 'Female human beings do anything that enters their stupid heads'.

Galton's passion ran counter to Manning's quiet acceptance. But Manning was not one to display his emotions. Was he crossed in love by Dorothy's choice? She was the only girl he was close to, a friend of many years, softly pretty, talented and with a buoyant spirit which could cheer even Galton. It is likely enough that Manning felt for her an unrequited tenderness akin to Bourne's attachment to the French peasant girl. That girl also was in love with the brusque masculinity of another man. Yet to Bourne the seemingly slight encounter was of tremendous importance. 'Bourne had a positive hatred of the excuse that "it does not matter" being given as the reason for any action: if something does not matter why do it? It matters enormously, but not necessarily to others, and the reasons why it matters to you are probably inexplicable to yourself'. (p. 120) At the very least Dorothy's decision underlined Manning's own loneliness: 'Well, I had better find a wife', he wrote in his letter to Jim. 'If Pound can manage it there should be hope for me.' One of his few extant aphorisms may reflect his mood then: 'Sex is everything . . . the sexless are the hopeless'.

The wedding took place on 20 April 1914, at St Mary Abbot, Kensington. Pound had resisted a church ceremony at first as he did not want an atheist like Galton to officiate, but a satisfactory clergyman must have been found. There were only six guests, mainly family. Manning was not present, having told Pound in a letter (11 March 1914) that he was doubtful whether he could get up to bear his hymenical torches. Probably Galton had vetoed Fred's attendance. The alliance of the beautiful, wellbred young lady and the brash Bohemian drew some quizzical comments. 'She is beautiful and well off and has the most charming manners', said the father of W. B. Yeats. 'As Willie remarks, when rich and fashionable people bring up a daughter to be intellectual, naturally she will turn away from the "curled darlings" of her own class and fall in love with intellect which is mostly to wed in poverty as well'.[9] Set beside the flamboyant American, unassuming Manning appeared even more frail and ineffective. In some ways he was a little like Dorothy herself. She also could be reserved and fastidious. Stella Bowen, a young Australian artist on the fringe of their circle, described her: 'Ezra's beautiful wife Dorothy . . . never attempted to keep up with her husband's exuberant pace and remained at home in somewhat lofty seclusion. It was a great compliment when she brought her cool detachment and charming presence to some of our studio dances'.[10] Yet Dorothy herself was a painter and designer of talent enough to have been accepted by these young artists quite apart from her relationship with Ezra.

The magnetism of Pound had worked on Manning as it had on Dorothy. Ezra was a perplexing, disturbing element in his life: 'hitherto I have felt an extraordinary restlessness, when he has been by me. I must sit on it', he confided to Jim in March. It was a time for retreat, now that he was losing his closeness with two of his few real friends as Dorothy and Ezra became a self-contained entity, the Pounds. The literary friendship continued, though it was more limited. Fred does not seem to have written again to Ezra until after the outbreak of war. As 1914 moved on Pound found more modern writers to excite him. In February 1914 he had begun serializing

James Joyce's *Portrait of the Artist as a Young Man* in the *Egoist*. In March the anthology, *Des Imagistes*, appeared, containing poems by (among others) H.D., Richard Aldington, Ford Madox Ford, William Carlos Williams, James Joyce, Amy Lowell and Pound. In June came the first issue of *Blast*, with contributions from Gaudier-Brzeska, Jacob Epstein, Pound and the editor, Wyndham Lewis. In July Pound warmly reviewed James Joyce's *Dubliners* in the *Egoist*, and in September he met T. S. Eliot. In October he was ablaze with excitement, having written to Harriet Monroe, on 30 September, of the best poem he had yet seen or had from an American: Eliot's 'The Love Song of J. Alfred Prufrock.' Meanwhile Manning, in his calm and lucid, if old-fashioned, manner reviewed books on William Blake (4 April), Cesare Borgia (25 April), Samuel Johnson (27 June), Edmund Spenser (16 May) and Francis Thompson (4 July). His dislike of self-pity, of hyper-emotionalism, roused in him a great distaste for Thompson's 'puling fear of death.' His image was of the balanced, thoughtful man-of-letters, rejecting rhetoric and sentimentality, excess and hysteria.

He was also rejecting modernism. While Pound and Eliot, both with their roots in the culture of Edwardian scholarship, were striving for new modes in their work and a new sensibility, Manning seemed to have no interest in the future, content to stay with the techniques of the past in his poetry. The most intriguing aspect of the bond between Pound and Manning was that it was not broken by all Pound's new interests. Manning obviously had his own charm. His quiet irony and his gentleness balanced Ezra's extravagant enthusiasms; his intelligence and his scholarship could match Pound's, his wit entertain him, his thought interest him. But though *Scenes and Portraits* had indicated a modern bent philosophically, he resisted innovations in form, and was little affected by most of the causes then arousing bitter debates. As far as the suffragette movement was concerned, he expressed the hope to Jim that the goddess would revenge herself for the attack on Velázquez's Rokeby Venus in the National Gallery in March 1914; snug in Edenham he avoided the worst affects of the great strikes by railway workers, dockers, sailors and miners; he took only a superficial interest in aspects of the new art, the new music, the new ballet. Ironical, detached, more absorbed in eternal questions than in the contemporary, he did not appear to be a man for strong public stands.

One public issue roused him, however, the most explosive of all: Ireland. His family heritage, his formal religion might have been expected to draw him to the side of Home Rule, but the influence of Galton, who supported Ulster against Dublin and who despised the Tammany Hall methods he had observed in Australia, won the day, allied with Manning's own assessment of the situation. On the Irish question he was an English Tory. In a letter to *The Times* (27 March 1914), he argued the case for the conservative British officers in Dublin who resigned rather than follow the orders of the British Government to move against the Ulster Volunteers. He took a high line against the politicians. 'Someone obviously should be punished. Either some officers should be dismissed, or some Ministers should be impeached. The fact remains that the action of these officers averted civil war.' As he saw it, that was an undoubted good.

His way of life in the first half of 1914 was much as it had been for years; he tinkered with his novel, he wrote five reviews for the *Spectator*, he saw his friends occasionally. The focus of his world remained, however, the man to whom, in a sense, he had dedicated his life. Richard Aldington, who had no love for Galton, later wrote of an anonymous pair who were surely Manning and Galton:

> Nothing is more unfortunate for a young and inexperienced author than a strong influence from older authors who have failed either as men or as artists. I have myself seen a writer of some promise ruined by an uncritical admiration and friendship for a disappointed senior who imbued the younger man with all his personal enmities, all his whims and fads, all his feelings of bitterness against the world. With the candor of youth the young writer accepted disappointed grumblings as sober facts and with the reckless generosity of youth, made this lost cause his own.[11]

At thirty-one Manning appeared set in his careful, narrow, valetudinarian, middle-aged ways: avoiding risks, accepting limitations, holding aloof from change. It was more than ten years since he had been home; his father, who had been proud, formerly, of his literary son, now disapproved of what he had done with his life. The rift must have caused Manning sorrow. Yet, in spite of all the problems, he had not lost his attachment to Galton, or his dedication to his art. It appeared in the first half of 1914 that his future would be an extension of his quiet past.

15

The Soldier

'THIS IS GOING to be the biggest thing in history. You Americans must stand by us', wrote Richard Aldington, three days after the declaration of war.[1] The future author of one of the most passionately anti-war novels, *Death of a Hero* was trying to join the Honourable Artillery, but this youthful and apparently robust volunteer was rejected on medical grounds. Other friends and acquaintances of Manning reacted with similar fervour, for most intellectuals and writers, on both sides, supported the war in its early stages.[2] There were exceptions. Max Beerbohm reflected on the sadness and absurdity of it all; and the tiny Bloomsbury group was astounded at being confronted with the fact that men were not rational, that other forces were involved in their actions.

Images of Housman's simple, golden lads, marching off to take the Queen's shilling, saving 'the sum of things for pay', and of Kipling's Irish rowdies defending a distant, exotic frontier had invested the life of the soldier with a hazy, romantic appeal. Avid for adventure, swept by love of country and by detestation of German militarism, the young men volunteered. 'To die will be an awfully big adventure', Peter Pan had told this generation as children. Somewhat older, more experienced men also came forward, seeing the war as a fundamental conflict of values. Satirist Saki, at the age of forty-three joined up as a ranker. Pound's friend, thirty-one-year-old radical conservative, T. E. Hulme, admired by Manning for his philosophic methods, was on his way to Flanders as a private by December. Hulme opposed romanticism about war, 'that is a stupidity we may leave to the Germans',[3] he wrote, but was convinced that a German victory would mean a military-based German domination of Europe and the end of European freedom. To him the question was as clear-cut as it was to the opponents of Nazism in World War II.

It was a view shared at that time by socialists, conservatives, trade unionists, feminists and many who would later be pacifists. Radical Will Dyson, working as a cartoonist for the *Daily Herald*, turned his anticapitalist figure, 'The Fat Man', into a gross and swinish Kaiser, threatening the world with terror and death, while German Culture knelt before Krupp, the arms king. The invasion of Belgium and the burning of Louvain aroused a horror akin to that felt by a later generation about Guernica. Australian Louise Mack, freelancing in Belgium for the *Daily Mail* was overcome by her on-the-spot experiences. 'Oh, Beethoven, Goethe, Heine. Not even out of respect for your undying genius can I hide the truth about Germans any longer. What I have seen I must believe.'[4] And back in Australia, *Bulletin* radicals became anti-German patriots, and republican bush balladists turned into sons of Empire. But, so far away, the Australian volunteers took on an air of light-hearted adventure. Sydney journalist turned Light Horseman, Oliver Hogue, for instance, enbraced his teenage sweetheart, Frances Anderson (later the great actress Dame Judith) and went off to war singing naïvely:

> Hurrah! Hurrah! We're off to Germany!
> Hurrah! Hurrah! The A.L.H. are we
> We're rounding up the bushmen from the Darling to the sea
> When we go marching through Germany.

Arthur Galton must have felt justified. His anti-German feelings were so rabid that in July St Loe Strachey had refused to publish a review in which the prophet of Edenham warned of 'the bestiality and treachery of the Prussian Government as I read them in history and remembered them in 1870'.[5] He had kindled a similar fiery contempt for German scholarship, philosophy and science in his pupil, so that the usually gentle Manning could call the enemy: 'lineal descendants of the Gadarene swine'.[6] Galton saw the war as 'a struggle of life or death for European liberty and civilization against a sinister and arrogant despotism which would inevitably destroy them both'.[7] Such passionate beliefs in the older man would have been hard to withstand and the general mood of the day backed them up. No doubt Galton, with his maxim 'oratory cannot save a state which has lost its military virtues',[8] urged his protégé on to military service.

Frederic Manning, however, seemed to be in the fight on his own account. At thirty-four, with a life-long medical history of poor health, he could well have stood back. His father was elderly and not in the best of health—Manning could have made a welcome return home and seen out the war in peaceful Australia. But now he was confronted with an opportunity for the elemental experience which fascinated him in literature, and which his life had lacked so far. Here he could escape the domination of his mentor, find some independence, test his courage, be truly himself. Possibly the exploits of his friend, Aubrey Herbert, encouraged him. Half-blind, knowing his eyesight would disqualify him from any formal enlistment, Herbert had managed to join up unofficially. He had donned the uniform of an officer in the Irish Guards, attached himself to a group of that regiment as it marched by, marched on to a troop train, then on to a boat, and into

France to the Battle of the Marne. Yet in the face of Galton's bombast, Manning maintained, privately, a certain ironic scepticism: 'Perhaps war and glory and liberty are stupidities', he wrote. Then the romantic, idealistic side of his nature asserted itself: 'but they are unavoidable stupidities, like love'.[9]

At first he hoped for a commission in the Flying Corps, an unrealizable ambition at his age, with his only qualification being that he had enjoyed flying. At this point there seems to have been no question of the ranks for this scholarly gentleman, despite the example of Hulme. The war was still a romance, though the death of Rupert Brooke from septicaemia on 23 April 1915 suddenly made real the tragedy of young deaths. Manning, who thought Brooke the best of the Georgians, was moved later to an epigram on this symbol of golden youth lost:

> Earth held thee not, whom now the gray seas hold
> By the blue Cyclades, and even the sea
> Palls but the mortal, for men's hearts enfold,
> Inviolate, the untamed youth of thee.[10]

He also grieved that month for his father, who died in Sydney on the twentieth, after what his son saw as a long and useful life with few disappointments or regrets. He may well have felt a sadness that he had been one of those disappointments. He did not foresee 'affluence' from his father's will, 'having been errant for so long',[11] though he expected some change in his financial situation. He was worried too, that month, that his sister Edith might be torpedoed on the way home; and for any Australian, even one who had been out of the country for more than a decade, the last days of April must have brought the emotions connected with the Anzac landing at Gallipoli, the pride and the sorrow. The tragedy may have given more strength to his own determination to enlist.

In May, while waiting for a hoped-for military billet, he repeatedly read Pound's *Cathay* which he loved, and joked to his friend that he had invented these purported renderings of Ernest Fenollosa's translations from the Chinese. Manning also told Pound that he was intent on getting a place in an Officer Training Corps (with the Inns of Court, Naval Brigade or Artists Rifles), seeing it as the quickest way to the trenches. The choice of regiments indicates that he was aiming high socially and had some interest in being with men who might have something in common with him: education, class, an interest in the arts. The war was still something of a fantasy. He could write to Pound (29 May) about 'slaying Germans to dung the earth of France', at the same time crying 'damn patriotism', and planning a journal with him—they hoped to take over the *Academy*— which would exclude unctuous Romans, Puritans and liberal Christians.

He published only one review in 1915, 'The Poet as Virtuoso'—on Swinburne—but pushed on with the 'Golden Coach', now about three-parts finished,[12] enjoying the greater freedom of handling imaginary characters. In June, Gaudier-Brzeska, who had joined the French Army, was killed, aged twenty-three. Pound, who had applauded the Battle of Ypres as 'the struggle for free life and free thought',[13] now became an embittered opponent of the war. Aldington (who would be called up in 1916) had also become sickened, comparing the crash of contemporary civilization to the overthrow of the Roman Empire in a letter to Harriet Monroe (7 June 1915). Manning remained firm, possibly influenced by Hulme, who argued his anti-pacifist position in the *New Age*, under the pseudonym 'North Staffs', from the cold misery of the trenches. After the war Manning wrote: 'I wish poor Hulme were alive to teach this idiotic age something of philosophy's methods . . .'[14] Hulme maintained that he opposed pacifism as a democrat, that, in his opinion, the dispute was between a grey and a very much blacker grey, and that liberty was an achievement. For him there were values above life itself. Like Hulme, Manning, at this time, seemed convinced that the war was being fought by the Allies against an aggressive militarism in the defence of civilization.

There still seemed no prospect of a commission for Manning. His slight physique, his lack of experience with men—even at school level—his nervous manner, his ill health, were hindrances to a position of command. And, despite Galton, he does not appear to have had the necessary connections. Martin Boyd, also a delicate aesthete, though younger and the product of an Australian private school, had no trouble gaining a commission among 'people of his own class' in the Inns of Court Regiment towards the end of 1915.

After a summer holiday at Daisy Meadow, Frederic Manning was accepted, finally, by the army, early in October 1915. His rank, though, was that of ordinary private in the King's Shropshire Regiment, 'the finest marching regiment in the British Army', he wrote proudly to Will Rothenstein (14 November), from his training camp at Pembroke Dock in Wales. (Manning, after their encounter late in 1911, had sent Rothenstein a copy of *Scenes and Portraits*. The painter, impressed by the spirit of this unlikely soldier, revived their old acquaintance by letter.)

Why should Manning choose this regiment rather than a local one? It would make a new start, of course, uncomplicated by any slight awkwardness that might be involved in serving beside the men who had cut his hair, or mended his shoes, or tended his garden in pre-war days. He would have complete anonymity. Some romantic literary sentiment about Housman's vision of the Shropshire Lad may also have influenced his choice. But the reality he encountered was a hard, noisy life full of dirt and discomfort. All his life he had enjoyed material ease and he had spent the last ten years, living with only one person, with the privacy of his own bedroom and study, in an atmosphere of country quiet. He had filled his leisurely days as he wished and had never worked with his hands. He had been spoiled a little by his women friends and had taken for granted a comfortable bed, hot water, clean clothes, good food and drink. He admitted in later years that he 'had a bad time in training and was not cheerful'.[15] As he wrote to Harriet Monroe in January 1916, soldiering left little time for the Muses.

Only a touch of this unhappiness appears in his letters to Rothenstein. Instead, he told Will in November 1915 that he could be happy in this life, which involved peeling potatoes, scrubbing floors, and becoming 'a beast of burden' on route marches where he carried sixty pounds weight for twelve or thirteen miles. He may not have enjoyed it, but he survived, showing an unexpected capacity for physical and mental endurance. And he came to love the men, although he was lonely in the crowded, noisy huts, where one was 'always lonely but never alone'. Sleeping on three planks and some straw, he could sit up with a cigarette after lights out, thinking his own thoughts, and experiencing a mysterious freedom. For the first time in his life he was his own man, unprotected. He showed no sign in his letters of the horror at the assault on an individual's dignity entailed in army life, as displayed by Somers in D. H. Lawrence's *Kangaroo*. He appeared to accept the practices and disciplines involved quietly. Perhaps, after living with Galton, he was armoured against sergeant-majors.

He told Rothenstein (26 December 1915), that he got on well with both NCOs and men, even after professing that he was a teetotaller for self-protection against the hard-drinking ways of army life: 'because I can go out with them and let them go as they please, without joining in their orgiastic rites, or seeming an outsider to them . . . These men are like children . . . "We be sinful men" they say and don't know how close that spirit is to the heart of religion'. He managed to be accepted by these hardy miners and farm labourers, among whom he was an alien in manner and background, for his style, his speech, his education, his interests must have made him an oddity, a mystery to his companions. Equable and quiet, he lacked the authority they expected of the best type of English gentleman, and the arrogance of the worst. But then he was a colonial; he was outside the system and his childhood in egalitarian Australia had preserved him from the deep-rooted attitudes of English class prejudice. As Leonard Mann has suggested, Manning's very Australianness enabled him to become an English ranker.[16] He possessed a democratic capacity for getting on with people of all kinds. A friend who served in the A.I.F., Carl Kaeppel, who had known him since schooldays, wrote an appreciation of his 'ever gentle and retiring friend' in the *Australian Quarterly* (June 1935). He attributed Manning's small circle of friends to his ill health, for he thought that 'no man . . . by nature was less of a recluse'. He credited him with 'a genius for friendship', a talent that helps explain the way this quiet scholar managed to cope with being a British ranker. Kaeppel found him to be a man who 'charmed all by conversation as humorous as it was acute and profound'. Such diverse characters as Arthur Galton, Ezra Pound, Will Rothenstein, Jim Fairfax, Eva Fowler, Richard Aldington and T. E. Lawrence all responded to Manning's charm. His sense of humour, his sympathy with others, his lack of pretensions and his personal appeal were all factors in his acceptance among the privates. And, perhaps, like Bourne 'he agreed with everything unreservedly, this being one of the secrets of a happy life'. (p. 42) But Kaeppel also saw the other side of Manning's nature, 'the indomitable determination' which enabled him to serve in the Somme campaigns.

He lived a double life as soldier-aesthete. The letters from Rothenstein, discussing aesthetics and carrying greetings from Beerbohm, meant much to him, lifting him 'out of the routine and fatigue of soldiering' back to civilized life. He managed to escape occasionally from the overwhelming physicality of army life to enjoy 'a bath of quiet, one can almost feel its coolness rippling on the flesh' in the local vicarage. At tea with two parsons and the chaplain of the forces a subject which interested Manning came up—gambling. Asked if he thought it right to win money by gambling he shocked his companions by replying: 'Oh, I don't see any harm in it if you attribute your gains not to chance but to providence'.[17]

His good relations with the vicar, 'a civilized man', prefigure Bourne's easy manner with the chaplain, just as his relationships with the NCOs and men in the most testing incident in his training, as recounted in a letter to Rothenstein (26 December 1915), are reminiscent of Bourne's ability to get on with all ranks, to 'muck in.'

> The greater part of the camp are now recovering from three days saturnalia, which culminated last night in something like a gladiatoral show ... The orderly sergeants were both drunk, one of them put his fist thro' a pane of glass, cut an artery, and came in covered with bright blood. We stopped the bleeding and in return for this kindness he threatened to lock up our corporal who came in two minutes late, excusable enough on Xmas Day. Then the corporal went mad and wanted to fight him. I was the first person to interfere, and then with some more stalwart men held our corporal until the 'orderly sergeant' got away.

Manning's qualities and his difference were obvious early to his officers, for his company officer and adjutant asked him, as Manning told Rothenstein (14 November), to apply for a commission as soon as he finished his drill and musketry course. He doubted that he had enough experience, though he does not seem to have shown Bourne's reluctance to accept promotion. He looked forward to a commission in the New Year, and to the small luxuries of the officer, including hot water and more quiet. In May 1916 Manning had his opportunity, being in residence at Exeter College, Oxford, with the No. 6 Officer Cadets Battalion. Sergeants were ruling the quads, Great Tom, the famous bell, was silent, and almost all the young men were in khaki. But Oxford was looking delightful and he was happy in such beautiful surroundings. The course was rigorous, he told Rothenstein (7 May), designed to weed out the unfit. To his disappointment, no doubt, Manning failed it. Intelligence, sensitivity and scholarship were not enough. A good physique, an air of authority and a capacity to command were more important. But as Jonathan Marwil ascertained it was his breaking of a rule about bringing alcohol into college rooms which led finally to his dismissal back to the ranks in June 1916. Two months later he was back with the 7th Shropshires, not as a subaltern, but as plain Private Manning, No. 19022, with the British Army in France, at the Battle of the Somme.

His small part in the worst battle in the worst of wars began in the second week of August, before Guillemont, 'the hottest part of the line', as he wrote to Rothenstein in an undated letter (September 1916). It was high summer. Swarms of blue-bottles feasted on the bloated bodies of the dead. As Corporal O. W. Flowers remembered it: 'Up there at Guillemont it didn't matter where men dropped, they just stayed there with nobody to pick them up. It was days and days before anybody dared to go out to pick them up and bury them. The bodies were piling up all the time, piling up by the roadside'.[18] Then on 24 August came the rains, turning the trenches and the roads into slimey bogs. Only a few weeks before, Manning had had published in the *Spectator* (8 July) his first war poem, 'The Choosers', which dealt with the theme of Chance, and bristled with the rhetoric of war in a vanished chivalrous age.

> Men are but shadows! And prone about me
> I see them hushed and sleeping in the hut,
> Made solemn and holy by the night,
> In the dead light o' the moon:
> Shadowy, swathed in their blankets,
> As sleep, in hewn, sepulchral caves,
> Egypt's and Asia's Kings;
> While between them are the footsteps
> Of glittering presences, who say: Lo, one
> To be a sword, upon my thigh!
> And the sleepers stir restlessly and murmur
> As between them pass
> The bright-mailed choosers of the dead.

But, now, of this modern battle, he wrote (2 October): 'No one can imagine it, my dear Will, it is sound, and sight, and smell, and touch all revolting; and it quietens everyone for two or three days after'. After his failure as a cadet, the good opinion of Rothenstein and Beerbohm comforted him in his ordeal. It was, he wrote in the same letter 'as tho you had patted me on the back'. And he ended with a flourish of bravado: 'everything is going splendidly'.

There are only four letters to Rothenstein from the front, all 'scrawled at odd moments', yet Manning, after rereading them some years later, wrote to Rothenstein (19 August 1931): 'the other letters astonished me rather as proving how accurately in the book I had recaptured the feeling I had while actually in the line. They are a guarantee of its veracity'.

It is a matter of the mood of the letters rather than of the detail of his experience which can be read in his novel, which he described in its Preface as: 'a record of experience on the Somme and Ancre fronts, with an interval behind the lines, during the latter half of the year, 1916; and the events described in it actually happened'. He mentions, however, in his letter of 31 October, the shell-shocked dog (which Martlow, in the novel, brings into their cellar dug-out in a shattered house). Manning also writes of his work as a runner. (Bourne, too, is for a time a runner.) This life-long asthmatic, for whom crossing pre-war Picadilly Circus had been an ordeal, now made long journeys between midnight and dawn, under continual shellfire:

> We are supposed to go in pairs but so far I have always gone alone, and it is a curious sensation. I am not ashamed to say that I have felt fear walking beside me like a live thing: the torn and flooded road, the wreckage, mere bones of what were living houses . . . absolute peace of the landscape and indifferent stars, then the ear catches the purr of a big shell, it changes from a purr to a whine and detonates on concussion. Another comes, then a third. After that a short space of quiet. Sometimes, as I have said, I feel fear, but usually with the fear is mingled indifference which is not pious enough to be termed resignation.[19]

He sketched for his friend the atmosphere of this life of 'dirt, misery and madness . . . the realities of war', writing (10 November 1916): 'Even when out of the line our life is miserable, and one to which no man should be condemned. We sleep on the floors of barns, we are tormented by lice, and we haven't had a bath for weeks'. There was no escape from the noise of the guns, and Manning, who had found it impossible to sleep in peacetime London, must have suffered badly in this 'weary nightmare'.

The letters touch too on the moral and philosophic themes of *Her Privates We*. 'War is in the nature of things', Manning wrote to Rothenstein (10 November). 'People attribute ultimate responsibility for war, with all its insensate brutalities to God; forgetting that it arises from their own brutal instincts'. He reflects, in the proto-existential manner he would use later in the novel, on the mystery of freedom, for, in these circumstances of total control, he could still escape from it all into his mind, into speculation. He contrived to live on two levels. Referring to this experience he wrote later:

> There's a streak of streak of mysticism in my nature, and I found that I felt most free in precisely those conditions when freedom seems to the normal mind least possible—an extraordinary feeling of self-reliance, and of self-assertion. I could feel it then, but I can analyse it now in cold temper as 'the heroic illusion'. In every 'show' one undergoes a kind of Katharsis (as Aristotle described the function of tragedy) or what St Paul called 'an emptying of oneself', and curiously enough it is precisely at such moments that a man becomes most intensely himself.[20]

He alludes also to the heroism and endurance of the ordinary man in the face of suffering and death. He was moved by these Shropshire lads, in their steel helmets and khaki uniforms plastered with grey mud, with their blue eyes and high colour, their weariness and their animal patience: '. . . they are almost entirely physical creatures to whom actuality is everything: that they can suffer as they do and yet respond to every call made upon them is to me, in some measure, a vindication of humanity'. Sharing in something of their humility, he was grateful for Will's cigarettes, letters and expressions of friendship. He was gladdened also by Beerbohm's good opinion of him, passed on by Rothenstein, for 'I have always loved him'.[21]

After the slaughter of the Somme the need for officers was acute. Manning must have performed reasonably well in the field, being a lance-corporal by December 1916. He was once again marked out by his superiors as officer material. He had been shell-shocked and slightly gassed in the Battle of Ancre,[22] so, after five months at the front, was given leave. He arrived in London on Christmas Day 1916, saw Eva and then went back to Edenham, to spend January resting and awaiting orders, including the possibility of a commission. After the noise and terrors of the front the tranquillity of his home must have been more attractive than ever in some ways. But he was no longer the green and gentle novice who had first come to Edenham. He had suffered and he had survived; he was a soldier with the experience of a battle unimaginable to those who had not been in it. Now he reflected on the differing points of view of the private and the general. He had won no military honours; the engagements he had fought in, in August and November, had been mentioned only briefly in Sir Douglas Haig's despatches. Yet, as he wrote:

> they give me the matter for a lifetime. Well, a general takes a scientific and extensive view of effects. Our view is narrower, more detailed and intensive. He is governed by reasons, and we by instincts. I know which have the stronger reality and determining force in war. For even in this age of mechanical murder, war has not become a science, but remains an art.[23]

Another young Australian, serving as an officer with the British Army on the Somme, was less philosophically dispassionate in his impression of Haig: 'To the men involved, it is hell! to the people at home it is a list of casualties, to him it is a line on a map!'[24]

Manning gave vent, however, to his more emotional reactions in some war poems, part of a collection, *Eidola* (meaning Phantasms), which was seen through the press by Eva Fowler in 1916–17. This book contained quite a number of lyrics (written before his war service) laden with flowering plum branches and maddening cymbals; and the *Times Literary Supplement* reviewer (5 April 1917) preferred these 'competently crafted' Edwardian-style verses to his 'gaunt little poems of war'. For Manning, in at least one poem, 'A Shell', becomes a modernist, and something of an Imagist.

Here we are all, naked as Greeks,
Killing the lice in our shirts:
Suddenly the air is torn asunder,
Ripped as coarse silk,
Then a dull thud . . .
We are all squatting.

In 'Grotesque' a bitter black humour replaces the gentle, intellectual irony of *Scenes and Portraits.*

These are the damned circles Dante trod,
Terrible in hopelessness,
But even skulls have their humour,
An eyeless and sardonic mockery:
And we,
Sitting with streaming eyes in the acrid smoke,
That murks our foul, damp billet,
Chant bitterly, with raucous voices
As a choir of frogs
In hideous irony, our patriotic songs.

The exquisite, innocent aesthete of pre-war days could not survive the Somme unchanged. He had faced death, and, even worse for a man of his sensibility, had found, like Bourne, that he could kill. In his poem, 'The Face', he examines the death of a young soldier, reminding us of the pivotal scene in Martin Boyd's *When Blackbirds Sing,* in which the hero, Dominic Langton, kills a German boy and knows he can no longer serve.

A boy's face delicate and blonde,
The very mask of god,
Broken.

Reviewing the collection, Katherine Tynan notes the strange mixture of Arcadia and the horrors and ugliness of war.[25] Not all of Manning's war poems discard his earlier, archaic diction, and some verses, for example 'The Sign', show a philosophic calm, which contrasts with his grimmer style: 'And I know that this passes:/This implacable fury and torment of men'. Richard Aldington, however, in the *Dial* (7 May), in a generous and enthusiastic review praising Manning's realism and beauty, his passion and irony, was delighted that so delicate and sincere a poet had been converted to free verse. However, another review in the *Dial*, this one by Conrad Aiken, dismisses the poems as 'jejunely precise'. But a fellow soldier-poet, Siegfried Sassoon, thought well enough of some quasi-existentialist verse by Manning to copy it into his diary while in convalescent hospital in May 1917.[26]

. . . for these I fight,
For mine own self, that thus in giving self
Prodigally, as a mere breath in the air,

I may possess myself, and spend me so
Mingling with earth, and dreams, and God: and being
In them the master of all these in me,
Perfected thus.

Manning's war poetry has, until recently, been rather overlooked, though Richard Aldington, after rereading *Eidola*, wrote to H.D. in June 1948: 'His war poems are strangely akin to mine, sometimes on identical themes. His are very much better of course. I am glad to have rediscovered them'.[27] Aldington in 1959 protested at the exclusion of his old friend from a volume of war verse. 'I think it feeble . . . to exclude Fred Manning and Roy [Campbell] both real soldiers—and to include such chair-borne warriors of the knife and fork brigade as Auden and Spender.'[28] Recently Kaiser Haq has remedied this neglect with a comprehensive article on the poetry, and Leonie Kramer's *My Country* anthology contains four of the war poems. Two of the poems also appear in *Clubbing of the Gunfire: 101 Australian War Poems*, edited by Chris Wallace-Crabbe and Peter Pierce.

By the time *Eidola* appeared, Manning, while still a soldier, had left the battle front behind. His active service, while real and testing and dangerous, had been brief; and his secondment to a commission may well have saved his life, by taking him out of the trenches. He longed to go back to the front, which fascinated him. Instead he faced rather different antagonists. He was to see out the war, surrounded by British officers, most of whom he found quite incompatible, in the baffling, rebellious land of his forefathers—Ireland.

16

The Officer

FREDERIC MANNING at last won his commission. After training at Lichfield, Staffordshire, he was gazetted as a second lieutenant in the Royal Irish Regiment on 30 May 1917. Whether this regiment was a matter of choice or chance, it probably fitted with his sentiments. His time with the Shropshires had shown him that, in spite of his years of Anglicization, he was not truly English. Like his alter-ego, Bourne, 'he was not of their county, he was not even of their country, or their religion, and he was only partially of their race'. He had spent ten years in an English village, but he lacked the attachment from birth to the village and the squire and the church bell and the landscape. In the land of his ancestors, he might feel more at home.

Before leaving for Ireland, he saw his mother in London at the Stafford Hotel. With three sons in the forces—Charlie and Jack were both training at Aldershot as gunners in the Royal Australian Field Artillery—Lady Manning had settled in England, with her daughters, for a while. Manning hoped to introduce Rothenstein to his mother and also to his friend Aubrey Herbert. At a last dinner with the Binyons he discussed aesthetics and continued the discussion with Rothenstein by letter after he reached Ireland in July.[1] From Richmond Barracks, Tipperary, he wrote to him (17 August), arguing his case that authoritative critics were the curse of literature, that form could not be separated from content, that concepts of aesthetics should be temporal not spatial. Even during training he had written to the painter about his ideas of beauty in art as an aspect of movement and comparing the unity of a work of art to the flight of an arrow; 'beauty results when the words are easily traversed by an idea, when the continuity is unbroken and the movement is complete'.[2]

A British officer preoccupied with such ideas could only be an odd man out in barracks life. He had mentioned casually to Rothenstein (21 July) that he was under arrest for having broken all the rules of the mess 'out of sheer ignorance and no premeditated vice'. He was then in danger of court martial, having quarrelled with all the senior officers and his colonel. Though he found the colonel decently polite, in July 1918 he told Rothenstein that the C.O. had given him a hard time from the beginning. Manning's intellectual aestheticism, his ironic temperament, his diffidence, his puritanism, his general oddness, must have been irritants. Then there was the more clear-cut issue of his poor health, strained further by his war service and the toxins of alcohol.

And being a colonial did not help matters. The daughter of an academic family, Australian-reared Mary Edgeworth David, visiting England in 1913–14, was taken aback by the virulent snobbery of the upper middle class, especially of regular army officers. Martin Boyd, like Manning a lieutenant in a British regiment, had difficulties with fellow officers and he used one such clash as the basis of a scene in his war novel. Australian Dominic Langton, serving in the British Army, is called a bastard by another officer. Langton replies that he does not think one gentleman calls another a bastard. 'Is Langton a gentleman? I thought he was an Australian', says the Englishman.[3] Boyd appears to have had a somewhat prickly temperament, for he left the regimentation of the army for the individuality of the Royal Flying Corps, but was soon denouncing the members of the 'Riff-Raff' as loud Canadians and uneducated Englishmen. It seemed out of character, however, for the quiet, nervous Manning of pre-war days to find himself in trouble with authority. His time at the front must have strengthened his ego, given him the confidence to be his unusual self. Freed from the sway of overbearing Galton, dealing with a frightful reality and a severe discipline in his own way, he had reached maturity.

His war service with average men, from the evidence of his novel, seems to have revived an element of Australian egalitarianism in him. Possibly the heroism at Gallipoli had aroused a latent patriotism, such that Bourne, who is notably chaste in his own speech, can even be proud of Australian proficiency in swearing. Bourne has a great deal in common with his creator, so that his reactions may well reflect those of Manning. They are both of slight build, and, as Captain Malet notes, Bourne is unused to manual labour. The description of Bourne fits Manning's photographs. Bourne has short hair, and a 'beaky nose between the feverishly bright eyes, the salient cheekbones above the drawn cheeks, the thin-lipped mouth, set, but too sensitive not to have a hint of weakness in it, and the obstinate jaw'. (p. 227) Bourne thinks like Manning, in a philosophic reflective mode; he is like him in manner, quiet, educated, detached. Bourne too is an insomniac and a chain-smoker, and fond of his small comforts, including wine and food. A gentleman in style and speech he writes in a tiny script (as Manning did), can use a typewriter and speaks French (of a kind). He is not English, or Anglican. He is rootless, mysterious, without a background, a puzzle to the officers, but with a capacity to make friends with all ranks: privates, officers and even NCOs, whereas Richard Aldington's hero, English George

Winterbourne found that 'the NCO's particularly hated any educated or well-bred man in the ranks, and delighted to impose painful or humiliating tasks on him'.[4] Bourne-Manning, while a Tory in politics, is a democrat in style. He judges everybody, from Major Shadwell to little Martlow, not by their class, but as individuals, by what they are and how they do their job.

When Bourne is infuriated by the stupid and petty regulations dear to the heart of some regular officers, it seems clear that was also Manning's attitude. After a British colonel reprimands a laconic Australian lorry driver for smoking, much to the man's obvious amazement, Bourne explodes: 'You want a few thousand Australians in the British Army', says Bourne angrily. 'They would put the wind up some of these bloody details who think they own the earth.' (p. 191) And, 'Bourne had long ago come to the conclusion that there was too much bloody discipline in the British Army . . .'. (p. 13) Like his compatriots in the A.I.F. he is a shameless scrounger, trying to make life a bit more comfortable for the ordinary soldier, even if a few regulations are broken.

The petty distinctions drawn between men and officers, even out of the line, goad Bourne to a special fury. He hates the sign *reservée pour les officiers* and loses his temper when he is refused service in a British canteen because it is only for officers. His companions, Shem and Martlow, are content to go round the back as instructed, but Bourne, usually so phlegmatic and easy-going, rages:

> If I were a colonel . . . mind you, only a colonel; and a man like that bloody lance-jack, who has never even smelt a dead horse in South Africa, turned one of my men out of a canteen started for the benefit of the troops by public subscription, I would get the battalion together, and I would sack the whole bloody institution from basement to garret, even if I were to be broke for it. [p. 190]

The anger carries a whiff of the violence of A.I.F. rioting in Cairo. Of course the novel must have been influenced also by Manning's experience with the officer class in Ireland.

Affronted pride is no doubt part of Bourne's emotional outbursts but Bourne has cooler criticisms of the rigidities of regular officers of the British army. 'The majority of them, though there were brilliant exceptions, did not understand that the kind of discipline they wished to apply to these improvised armies was only a brake on their impetus.' (p. 71) Manning himself may well have discussed with Jack and Charlie Manning the ways of the improvised army of the A.I.F., with its new-born mystique, and its creative general, John Monash. Clearly, Lieutenant Frederic Manning was a very different type of officer from his new companions in Ireland.

One of Bourne's arguments against taking a commission is that he has taken on the colour of the ranks and would not be able to think as an officer should. Manning, moving from the raw misery of the men in the field to the punctilio of a traditional mess, carrying with him his regard for the strength and endurance of private soldiers, and a revived democratic inheritance, blessed also with an ironic amusement at jacks-in-office, no doubt found himself unable to take the pomp and ceremony of the officer class of the regular army seriously. Some officers saw his actions as alcohol-induced, though given the after-effects of front line service, his insomnia and his generally poor health, his condition may well have been misunderstood. The result was that he came before the court on 6 August and was reprimanded for his behaviour, but fear of other punishment fortunately faded away when a sympathetic doctor diagnosed him as shell-shocked (he was having trouble with his balance on the parade-ground) and, towards the end of July, he was ordered into the military hospital at Fermoy, County Cork, for a month.

His Manning grandparents had come from Cork. His mother was also Irish born. At odds with the stiffness of the senior British officers and with British military rigidity, Manning responded intensely to the 'disorganised and unsystematic Utopia' of Ireland: to its gods, its saints, to Deidre and St Patrick, to the shawled women and the unkempt, half-savage children, to the brogue and the friendliness. He was amused by the disorder, the emotionalism, the disregard for law and regulations, the unlicensed bicycles on the footpath, the illicit whiskey and the general childlikeness. 'Everyone does what is right in his own eyes, except as regards those two curses of humanity, religion and politics'. Such freedom and fecklessness were new to him, for these 'divinely improvident' people lacked the ambitious energy of his parents and were the antithesis of Arthur Galton, with his cerebration, his severity and his industry. Part of Manning's nature revelled in the chaos, although his sympathy did not extend to the Sinn Feiners, for he had heard stories of their cowardly outrages. Manning also kept up his intellectual debate on aesthetics with Rothenstein, even propounding the theory that the genius of the modern age was too restless and vacillating, and that the priestly art of Egypt went to prove that 'men may retain their originality within the limits of the most rigid hieratic convention'.[5]

The brief stay in hospital had robbed him of a possible posting overseas. But he still hoped to be sent to either France or Salonika, for, whatever the horrors of the war, he wanted to be at the front, in action. He moved, instead, to Wellington Barracks, Dublin, where he managed to rub along with his brother officers, in a fashion, without changing his contemptuous estimate of them. He found them all stupid, with neither an intelligent idea nor coherent speech, and he did not except the half-dozen he called 'good fellows'. Tremendously tired of the phrase 'an officer and a gentleman' he maintained it was invented because the two things were incompatible.[6] Sexually reserved himself, he found the 'school-boy chatter' about loose women unbearable.

His pre-war touch of irritability seemed to have firmed into a streak of intolerance. Feeling that he was drowning in 'this sea of imbecilities' he was delighted to meet a friend of Rothenstein, the Irish poet and painter, George Russell. Russell, who used the pen name AE, was at that time editing the

James Fairfax during his student days at Oxford; 'There are only yourself and a few others who are real to me', Manning wrote to him.

Richard Aldington in 1917, before his acrimonious split with Manning

Ezra Pound, c. 1909: 'I like Pound very much, but he will certainly be damned', Manning wrote.

A late self-portrait of William Rothenstein, who remained a friend until Manning's death.

Frederic Manning and Lady Manning at the officer training school in Staffordshire, 1917; 'Perhaps war and glory and liberty are stupidities . . . but they are unavoidable stupidities, like love'.

*T. E. Lawrence, a man well suited
to understanding the double-natured
Manning: 'Lawrence of Arabia',*
above: *in a more anonymous
guise,* below

Frederic Manning in the early 1930s, 'a scholar and a soldier'

Irish Homestead and his Dublin rooms were a meeting place for the artists and intellectuals of the city. He differed with Manning's pre-war attitude on Ireland, for he praised the leaders of the Easter Rising and, though a Protestant himself, scorned the intransigence of Ulster. But he had a breadth of mind and spirit lacking, it would seem, in Manning's fellow officers. Manning later described him as 'a gentle creature, easily amazed at the unreason of life and yet practical in everything but his thought which is all vision'.[7] At the Irish Recruiting Council Manning met another interesting and intelligent Irishman, Stephen Gwynne, politician, man-of-letters and a soldier in France until 1917.

But he was becoming bored with the seeming pointlessness of his barracks existence, and when bored he might turn to alcohol. Early in October 1917 he was hospitalized again in a neurasthenic state. Only 'the Front' now kept a hold on his imagination. When Rothenstein applied for a job as a war artist, Manning hoped he would do some sketches of crowded dugouts to bring out the magnificent desolation, the demonic quality of war, and 'the Miltonic sense of hell'.[8] The labyrinthine trenches reminded him of that artist loved by Galton, Giovanni Piranesi, and his grim drawings of Roman prisons, the *Carceri*. As he had no prospect of returning to active service—for he was crippled by lumbago, a legacy of the wet trenches—and finding it impossible still to get on with his C.O. he tried, in October 1917, to resign his commission on the medical grounds of nervous exhaustion and insomnia. At first the authorities refused, then, since the Adjutant wanted it Manning claimed, they agreed. On 27 February 1918 his resignation was noted in the *London Gazette*.

Manning was free to return to England, but he did not fly back immediately to Galton and Edenham. He remained in Ireland, living at Belfield, Sir Patrick Lynch's large property in the then rustic Stilorgan, about ten kilometres from Dublin. It was a period of mental and physical restoration in the quiet mountain area, helped by the companionship of his host's daughter, Sybil Gowthorpe, and her friend, Polly Barry. Both women kept in touch with him in later years. In this period of peace he was wondering whether to try for a job or to rejoin the army. To consider re-enlistment appears rather an eccentric course for one who, in military eyes, had failed as an officer, who had such problems with his superiors, who had suffered mentally and physically, who was appalled by the waste of human intelligence in the army and who felt that it was often 'the brutal and sly' who reached positions of command.[9] The notion of his own way of life, his own career, and the pleasure of the friendships he had made in Ireland must therefore have held considerable appeal. It was, in contrast with his past, a kind of independence.

To make matters easier, the man he saw as his enemy, the C.O., had gone. The other officers, perhaps a trifle shame-faced, offered to make Manning an honorary member of the mess; and even the Adjutant, Manning said, urged him to return to the regiment. It is perhaps another testimony to his charm that, once the domineering C.O. was off the scene, the others were anxious to make amends. The army was, at the least, some occupation for a man who had never been employed. Even the pacifist Herbert Read considered taking a regular commission at the end of the war. And, for imaginative Manning, behind all the pettiness and stupidities of army life moved 'the great war' where 'one's sacrifice and one's humiliation even, is the measurement of his ultimate worth'.[10]

He had sense enough to realize, whatever the strange attraction, that he would never make a good parade officer, that with his poor health and weak body there was little prospect of reaching the front line again, which was the only place he wished to be. His war was over. His period of active service had been short and he had been spared the testing and retesting under fire which caused even the bravest to doubt their ability to go on. The young Australian writer, Adrian Stephen, winner of the Croix de Guerre on the Somme and the Military Cross at Passchendaele, wrote: 'I have been through some big battles but the biggest of all was with my nerves in the last position. I won—but I wouldn't care to repeat the fight'.[11] That was in August 1917. In March 1918 he was concerned about the effects of the never-ending struggle on the men. 'I think it is all a question now of morale—can we fight as we fought of old on the Somme and elsewhere? We shall see.' Stephen was killed in action three days later. Frederic Manning's service did not lie in this heroic pattern. He was, however, a brave soldier who had been through a shocking, unforgettable experience.

A month before the Armistice he crossed to England. His mother and sisters who had been visiting in Ireland also returned, and the family took a flat at 8 Evelyn Mansions, Carlyle Place, London, in November. On the eighth of that month he regretted that he 'would not be in at the end', but for him it was not a time of mindless celebration. He feared that 'peace may be as dangerous as war'.[12] In the midst of the uproar on Armistice Day other perceptive spirits felt a similar uneasiness. D. H. Lawrence, looking in on a party in Bloomsbury, warned that hate and evil were greater than ever and that war would break out again.[13] Maynard Keynes, at the same party, was also pessimistic.

In contrast, for many people it was a time for new beginnings, for new hopes of happiness. Rather to Manning's horror, his middle-aged friend of many years, Ryllis Hacon, was contemplating marriage again. 'To me marriage has always seemed a desperate adventure, even for the young', Manning wrote, 'but when one's character has ceased to be fluid, and one has lost youth's happy trick of improvisation, it overpasses the boundaries of courage. But I pray that is only a man's notion'.[14] He embarked upon no new ventures, but fell back into the old way of life at Edenham. He took up his friendships again with Eva Fowler and with Pound. Manning worked on an article about Remy de Gourmont, whom he 'did not love over-much',[15] for Pound to publish in the February–March issue of the *Little Review*. As well, Sir George Arthur, a connection of Galton's, sought Manning's collaboration on a life of Kitchener. Manning was to deal with the period 1911–17. He accepted, then illness intervened, and his doctor forbade him to go on with the work.[16]. The guns had fallen silent, but now another kind of death began to terrorize the world.

One of the Mannings' servants at Evelyn Mansions developed the Spanish flu; another went to nurse her daughter and died of it. His brother, Charlie, back from France, was ill with fever yet Fred suffered only a slight attack. He was in drained mood when he wrote to his 'dear aunt' enclosing a copy of his de Gourmont article in December 1918. 'I have a theory that we all died in the Great War, and don't know it.'[17] Sudden death from the flu plague reached to all levels: old men, young men, women and children. Wyndham Lewis's mother and T. E. Lawrence's father succumbed, as did Will Dyson's lovely, talented wife, Ruby Lind, sister of Norman Lindsay, who died at her Chelsea home, aged thirty-one, on the night of an Artists' Ball being held to celebrate peace. The costume she had planned to wear lay unfinished in the room.

Manning suffered another attack of fever in March 1919 and, weakened by his earlier bout, nearly died from flu and pneumonia. His brother was summoned from France, and for two nights Manning was 'so much over the border that the remainder of the way had no terrors'. But sickly Fred survived. After three weeks in a nursing home, he spent the next two months in a sanitorium at Mundesley, on the Norfolk coast.[18] His writing was put aside for a time, though an article on the Irish question, 'An Unionist's Apologia', written before his illness, appeared in *Nation* (23 March 1919). His time in Ireland had altered his outlook. He now thought England should get out of Ireland. As he wrote to *The Times* (7 May): 'We can only create a public and civic spirit in Ireland by making the Irish responsible for their own safety and order'. He also felt that England had never appealed to a large body of conservative opinion there, but set one fanatical section against another and termed it 'keeping the peace'.

Like so many ex-soldiers he had problems in finding his place in the post-war world. A younger generation was moving into positions of literary influence, though Pound, while supportive of the new talents, had remained constant in his respect for his old friend during the war years. Pound had praised Manning's work, indirectly, when he wrote an angry rebuttal of Richard Garnett's reader's report on James Joyce's *Portrait of the Artist as a Young Man*. '"Carelessly written",' quoted Pound, and continued: 'this of the sole or almost sole piece of contemporary prose that one can enjoy sentence by sentence and reread with pleasure. (I except Fred Manning's *Scenes and Portraits*)'.[19] He paid another tribute to that book in the *Little Review* (March 1918), when he included it in 'A List of Books', 'not to be neglected by the intelligent reader'. He still appreciated Manning's humour, telling Iris Barry of Manning's description of Pound as 'more like Khr-r-ist and the late James MacNeil Whistler every day'.[20] Manning may have been thinking of the fact that the American painter was also laughed at for his innovations and was noted for his wranglings, while the 'Khr-r-ist' perhaps summed up bearded Pound's exuberant vanity and his sense of mission. Pound also passed on to James Joyce some indecent lines written by Manning on Joyce's old Jesuit school, Clongowes Wood College. 'Manning again in circulation' was part of his news for William Carlos Williams in January 1919.

It was not the same world. Manning had lost his leading place with the *Spectator*. 'I think [Robert] Graves is the butcher they provide for any stray Orpheus', he told Pound, 'forty are slaughtered in a couple of columns'[21]—a reference to the legend of the pre-Homeric Greek poet, though Orpheus was torn to pieces by enraged women not by a literary reviewer. A similar bitterness was felt by many returned soldiers. One day they were heroes, the next they were shunned. Even pacifist-inclined Martin Boyd bewailed the loss of glamour and gallantry in the post-war world:

> I saw a man, whom I last year had seen
> Fighting most bloodily and gloriously;
> Today I saw him in a Bank between
> Two other clerks, and he laboriously
> Was putting half crowns in a little pile.[22]

Manning, at least, was clear-headed; he had made his choice and still stood by it. But many felt fooled, used by those who had stayed at home, the politicians and conscientious objectors. Aldington was deeply affected, and he raged: 'They have broken up our lives without any effort at compensation'. He had a strong sense of the difference between those who had been to the front, and those who had not. 'As well ask a frigid person to understand passion', he wrote.[23] Manning, similarly, could never forget his experiences, but with his strong mind and reflective temperament he could try to fit this reality into the patterns of mankind.

> All the same I do not envy the men who escaped the experience, and I knew most of the ideals which moved us private soldiers to be an illusion and 'jeturage [*sic*] du vent' before I joined. That is really our reward, not to have gained anything: but to have achieved freedom for ourselves in our will.[24]

It was an unusual summation. Others may have seen it differently, but for Manning that winning of his freedom was a reality. These painful, tragic years had killed off the gentle, hopeful young poet in him and had worsened his health. 'If Manning did not have T.B. before the war, he certainly had it during and after', was Aldington's opinion. But Manning had achieved a stern maturity. Although he turned again to his writing, his old friends, his home at Edenham and his life with Galton, he was no longer merely the biddable disciple.

17

The Losses of Peace

AFTER THREE YEARS as an automaton',[1] after his near fatal brush with the flu, Frederic Manning's energies had declined to an even lower point than in his pre-war poor health. He was short of money after his illness, ('damned hard up', as he put it to Pound a little later in August 1920) for his small income from reviewing had been cut almost to nothing. He accepted, out of sheer necessity, a commission from the family of Sir William White to write a biography of the great naval architect who had invented the mighty dreadnought battleship. It was an unwise decision, as it turned out, for it brought Manning to his nadir in spirits and energy. White had been a friend of Manning's pre-war admirer, Henry Newbolt, and, more importantly perhaps, of Sir Douglas Galton, Arthur Galton's cousin. Pressure to take on a task which was not to Manning's taste may have come from Galton. The book would bring Manning back to writing, and to literary circles, as well as bring extra money into their household, though it may have led later to feelings of resentment. Yet it was necessary task-work, for when inviting Will Rothenstein to stay (29 July 1919), Manning apologized for his very shabby rooms. The stringency of his position had not yet altered his somewhat amused regard for Galton, for he offered him as a lure, as a phenomenon whose eccentricities would entertain Rothenstein.

It was a time of readjustments for a shocked world. Manning's old friend, Ryllis Hacon, happy in her new marriage, had left for Canada. The Pounds and Richard Aldington were involved in making their decisions about where and how to live, how to cope with their emotional reactions to the disaster of the war. Jim Fairfax, who had served as an officer attached to the 15th Indian Division, R.A.S.C., and had been mentioned in despatches four times, visited Edenham to reminisce:

> . . . in your familiar room
> Sitting once more where books climbed ceiling high
> While through the window on that English lawn

Stooped the low branches of the mulberry-tree
Where Kim would crouch for hunting [2]

Fairfax was no longer, however, the carefree poetic undergraduate. Politics interested him and marriage and a settled life. He returned to Sydney and was admitted to the Bar there in 1920, before deciding to make his career in England.

Manning had left youth behind for a saddenned maturity. With Fairfax changing his way of life, the renewed friendship with the stable, kindly Rothensteins and their children became more and more important to him. This lonely and seemingly confirmed bachelor had written during the war: 'children help to make life worthwhile'.[3] Now he took a sympathetic interest in the future of young John Rothenstein, who was preparing for Oxford. He advised Will that he thought history and law were solid, though it was a pity that Greek was in the hands of a 'mountebanke' like Gilbert Murray. Murray, Australian-born son of a president of the Legislative Council of New South Wales, won no indulgence as a fellow countryman. Was there, in Manning's attitude, a touch of envy at the success story of Murray's life in worldly terms, a certain bitterness that he had not had Murray's educational advantages? Gilbert Murray, born in Sydney in 1866, son of Sir Terence Murray, was taken to England when eleven by his widowed mother and capped a brilliant educational career by becoming Professor of Greek at Glasgow at the age of twenty-three. In 1908 he took the chair of Greek at Oxford. He married an English aristocrat, Lady Mary Howard, a cousin of Bertrand Russell, and became a leading figure in the humanitarian liberal establishment. Gently radical, a teetotaller and a pacifist, active in good causes, he was not a sympathetic figure to Manning, who held strong views on the futility and cant of liberalism.

Manning, in his letter to Rothenstein, took an austere view, in general, of the charms of the beautiful university: 'Oxford means an adventure to the Enchanted Isles: a great deal is mirage: and yet I think there is much that is substantial there, if one declines to be led by men, and confounded in movements'. His old friend, Shadwell, the Provost of Oriel, had personified the blend of scholarship and chivalry which meant Oxford to him. 'But the enchantment of the place is a little ennervating and individuality becomes more and more rare.'[4] John Rothenstein was at that stage feeling the pull of Rome and Manning, nominally Catholic, expressed himself strongly on that religion to the boy's father (31 December 1919): 'attractive and externally magnificent, apart from some sordid intrigues, it is a dull and soul-less piece of mechanism. The apparent magic is a cloak for barren syllogisms. It broke Newman's heart and still fears Newman's influence'. The disciple had not completely shaken off the influence of his old teacher. Yet he implied an odd set of circumstances in the vicarage when, in the same letter he again invited Will to stay, with the qualification that 'my part of the house is still desolate and tumbling down'. The partnership of earlier years seemed to have split. To add to the financial tensions, Galton was furious that he was banned from reviewing on the *Spectator*, though Fred received a few books. Galton was now a bitterly disappointed man, and since the war he and Manning had grown apart.

In pre-war Edenham Frederic Manning had been isolated from the pleasures of the outside world. His consolations had been his close relationship with Galton, his work, and his youthful hopes for the future. Now thirty-eight, in worse health than ever, carrying the burden of sorrow of the ex-soldier, he was no longer no longer the unworldly, malleable acolyte and his position had worsened in every way. As well, after spending several years in the company of many men, however unlikely they might have been as companions, he was now thrown back into his old near solitude, with a cranky old man. The tedium was relieved only by the occasional visit to London, as before the war, to stay with Eva Fowler and her husband, to see a few friends, including Binyon, who looked 'tired and overworked',[5] to hear a recital by Myra Hess at Eva's or to meet a minor writer, Evelyn Underhill, an acquaintance of the Pounds. He also met again the girl he described to Will Rothenstein (16 March 1920) as 'the adorable Jelly', to whom he had dedicated the exotic 'Paroles sans Musique' in *Eidola*. Hungarian-born Jelly D'Aranyi was a violinist of note who performed frequently with Myra Hess, sometimes at Eva Fowler's salon.

Comradeship had been the one great consolation of the war for most soldiers. Pacifist-minded Martin Boyd felt its loss acutely, recalling in his autobiography that he had 'missed above all the comradeship, the great good mixed with the great evil of army life'.[6] It must have been a similar break for Frederic Manning. Although he found no real friends, no soul mates like Galton, Fairfax or Pound, he had got on well with the rankers and with some of the subalterns. Service had meant company for someone long cut off from a breadth of experience and a range of friends. The return to the narrow world of his youth, which now lacked the optimism of the earlier years, must have been a wrench. And for all ex-soldiers there were the anguished memories of friends who did not come back.

In this period of stressful readjustment the White book became a nightmare and an obsession to debilitated, depressed Manning. He poured out his unhappiness in a letter to Pound (15 November 1919): that he wished he had lived under Diocletian or perhaps Domitian, that he thought this was a good age in which to be dead. Although his article on Binyon's poetry appeared in his friend Charles Whibley's *Picadilly Review* (23 October 1919), he felt discriminated against by the literary establishment led by J. C. Squire, Edmund Gosse and George Saintsbury. He was producing little for publication. Rothenstein kindly invited him to write a accompanying note to a drawing of the gloomy Dean of St Paul's, W. R. Inge, and it appeared in Rothenstein's *Twenty-four Portraits* (1920). He wrote a review on rhythm in verse for the *Spectator* (20 December 1919) and passed a harsh, and perhaps personally biased, judgement on Lionel

Johnson's 'intellectual dishonesty' in another issue (20 January 1920). Burdened with his own unhappiness, his dark knowledge of war, he was determined to face life squarely, as he had had to do; he saw Johnson's life as a denial of reality, an attempt to escape from the truth which experience imposes on us. But a significant sentence runs: 'The most charitable view to take is that he was an impressionable boy, acting under the incitement of older and stronger minds'. Had Galton, in his disappointment with Manning's failure to make a mark, compared him unfavourably with the earlier protégé?

Most of his depleted energy was taken up now by the White book and, to add to his misery, the people he met while researching it filled him with fury and loathing. He felt they 'stank of money and blood', with their profits paid for by some ploughboy lying in France. Yet, as he admitted to Pound (11 November 1919), he would have taken a share in an armaments firm if he could have had it, and so would the ploughboy. His letters to Pound were an escape valve for emotions possibly not welcomed by the zealously patriotic Galton; and in writing to this other committed writer he could escape from the grinding task of the White biography, into literary argument, into talk about contributions to the *Dial*, including parts of the eternal romance, into terms for the expected publication of it, into squibs about an old enemy, 'Mr Hidebound Goose'. Pound was a friend to whom he could talk about almost everything, although, true to his nature, Manning kept his most private feelings to himself.

He thanked him for an inscribed copy of the impassioned, anti-war *Hugh Selwyn Mauberley*, planned to join with him in another magazine, and suggested publishers, for they both felt they had nothing in common with the 'Squirearchy' and its magazine, the *London Mercury* (established 1919). Manning's main concern remained the 'Golden Coach', and Pound was doing his best to have it published in America in the *Dial*, of which he was European correspondent. Late in August 1920 Manning acknowledged, somewhat facetiously, Pound's praise of the work. In October Manning proposed sending to New York, in some trepidation as to what might befall it there, 'the finest historical romance since Esmond, full of wit, humour, irony, style, Epicureanism, Lucianesque scepticism, Franciscan mysticism, Papal Machiavellianism and the mailed fist of Louis Quartorze (the aforesaid L.Q. to be depicted with a full complement of ministers and mistresses)'. Pound could summon up his friend's pre-war mood of ironic joking, and dispel his depression a little. Manning's hopes revived. The great work was to finished by December 1920; and it was to be sent in sections to the *Dial*—the first chapters to appear perhaps in the January-February 1921 issue —although Manning joked that it might be somewhat *risqué* for that magazine.

More than ten years after their first meeting, Pound remained an admirer. Ever helpful, he sent off 'one hundred delicious pages of Manning'[7] to the American magazine, and puffed his friend's name by including it in a list of future contributors, which began with Marcel Proust, and included Bernadetto Croce, W. B. Yeats, T. S. Eliot, Louis Aragon, James Joyce, Richard Aldington and Aldous Huxley. Yet he himself was finished with England. While Manning was clinging to this important friendship, signing himself: ' *Vale et me ama*' (farewell and love me), and 'out of the flux of indestructible atoms, thine', Pound was planning his escape to Europe, telling Harriet Monroe that England was so dead an American would be wasting time there.[8] Paris was the place to be. Pound had found new solutions: a new city, and a new creed of economics, the anti-Semitic Social Credit of Major C. H. Douglas, also favoured by Orage of the *New Age* and by that passionate socialist, Will Dyson.

The departure of the Pounds for Paris in December 1920 must have been a considerable blow to Frederic Manning. Ezra and Dorothy had been an important part of his youth and were a contact with high spirits and enthusiasms. Now he withdrew a little further into himself, writing that the world of the mind was the only possible Utopia in these sad days; 'in this dance of death of political buffoons, cynical, mean businessmen and stupid, useless workmen'.[9] The new England for him had 'neither honour nor sense', he told Will (3 August 1920) and he was so angry at the British treatment of Feisal of Iraq, the leader of the pro-British Arab revolt during the war—he felt that promises of independence made to the Arabs had been betrayed in the peace settlement—that he thought of applying for a job with him.[9] The romantic image of his second country, which had shone in one of his war poems, was tarnished.

> . . . this England which is mine
> Whereof no man has seen the loveliness
> As with mine eyes . . . [10]

England was looking very dreary now, plagued with slums and close to starvation. 'We cannot continue to be a great producing country when 3/5th of our population are kept on the verge of famine', he wrote to Will (18 September 1920). He feared that the social system was collapsing, but the remedy he appeared to recommend in the same letter was very strange: 'I don't think any really fine civilisation is possible without slavery—the Athenian democracy was only possible because it rested on a slave base'. Manning, the gentle Franciscan, had as his other side this rigid, out-of-touch theorist. It may have been a last breath of the Galtonian influence, which had dominated his thinking for so long.

As the Pounds moved out of his life, Manning was about to face a much greater loss. In January 1921, Arthur Galton suddenly became desperately ill. Borrowing the Ancasters' car, Manning rushed his friend to a Wimpole Street nursing home for an emergency operation for tumour of the prostate. Galton appeared to make a good recovery and Manning, to build the patient's confidence, returned home to Edenham at the end of January. He left 'the poor old man' in bed, like a great baby, with all his toys beside him on a small table: his most cherished books, a small ivory foot-rule, which he has had since he was twelve, and two or three small pebbles picked up in various parts of the world. All small, all toys and all possessing the magic virtues which children give to their belongings.[11]

The pathetic charms did not work. Galton died on 20 February 1921. A plain grey slab, close by the church, was his memorial in the churchyard at Edenham. No cross or inscription marked his tomb. It bore only his name and the dates of his life span. The grave of the doubting Walter Pater, carried, at his own request, a cross and a message of hope: 'In te, Domine, speravi' (In Thee, O Lord, have I hoped). The grave of the Anglican priest of more than twenty years bore no such Christian signs. It may have been another example of Galton's emotional austerity, a hatred of display. Or it may have been, as Pound claimed, that Galton was no longer a Christian, that all his religious struggles for certainty had ended in atheism. Galton left his volumes of Voltaire, that great fighter against the church, to Olivia, his friend since 1885.

Despite the last few unhappy years, the loss of his surrogate father, his teacher, his guide, his companion, left Frederic Manning rudderless. He wrote to Houtin (2 March 1921):

> I feel as though part of my own mind were dead. We were so closely bound together, in our affections, in our ideals and beliefs, spiritually and intellectually, that now I cannot realise his absence.
>
> Each of us was in a sense, an extension of the other's conscience and thought; we could see with each other's eyes, and feel with each other's hands. I think that his fondness for my little book came from the fact that I had made explicit many of the beliefs and desires he held implicitly.
>
> His mind was clear, firm and decided to the end. There was no doubt, no anxiety, no hesitation. I felt that it was not a life being ended but a life being completed. He was full of courage for himself and of tenderness for me. It was our separation that was bitter.

It appears a noble end, but Stoical rather than Christian. And across the abyss of death this stern, masterful man kept his hold on his disciple: 'I want to live as he would wish, and a man's friends are part of the man'.[12] The relationship had been deep and loyal; and for all Galton's tantrums Manning had inherited from him a devotion to exacting standards. The war-time experience had separated them, but the debt remained.

It was a tremendous blow; the end of the major part of Manning's life. To add to his unhappiness he now had to uproot himself now from the vicarage which had been his home for so long. He could not tear himself away from Edenham, and rented half a house in the village while he considered what his future might be and while the domestic and legal problems attendant on the clergyman's death were sorted out. Still shocked by Galton's death, he was stunned five months later when Eva Fowler died suddenly, aged forty-nine, from a heart attack at her London home. Manning was sunk in grief again and wrote to Houtin (10 July): 'She was, after Arthur Galton, the person to whom I owed most in England; they were, in a sense, the two poles of my conscience . . . a woman of delicate sensibility . . . the most loyal and generous friend a man could have'. To Will he wrote (15 August) that all the interests of twenty years were now closed. After a memorial service at Westminster Cathedral, Eva Fowler's funeral took place from St Mary's Catholic Church, Kensal Green. She had toyed, in the fashion of the day, with spiritualism and with modish Biblical criticism but, unlike Galton, she remained a believer in her faith.

The loss of the two people central to his life in England exposed the shallowness of Manning's roots there. He thought of living permanently in Europe, in France or Italy. 'There is little to keep me in England now', he told Houtin (12 August 1921), 'and I am of those who have no country'. So much for the pro-English flourish in 'Autarkia' (quoted above). Twenty years residence in the English countryside and service in an English regiment had produced a state of mind akin to the 'geographical schizophrenia' of Martin Boyd's Anglo-Australian Guy Langton who says: 'Our stay in England aggravated an inherited homelessness. It had Anglicised me but I had not become English'.[13] On the other hand, provincial Australia could not draw Manning back. He was a cultural expatriate, finding a spiritual homeland in this time of desolation in art and the things of the mind. These were what nourished him: 'My final opinion is that what is apparently most transient in life is immortal, the desire of youth which is never satisified here. But that is poetry, art . . . '[14]

Now that Galton, Eva Fowler, Dorothy and Ezra Pound, and Jim Fairfax were all gone from his life, and Olivia was taken up with her new son-in-law, only Richard Aldington remained from his main pre-war group of friends to encourage him in his work. Manning became even more introspective, absorbed in ideas of magic, mysticism and religion. He had published three brief fables about God and the meaning of existence in the Easter 1920 issue of *Coterie*, a somewhat precious, avant-garde magazine. His contributions, in his mannered, Paterian style, looked out of place beside the work of new writers like the Sitwells, Aldous Huxley and Roy Campbell. Aldington, however, defended Manning. 'He attempts to reconcile us to life . . . Novelty is of small importance to a mind like Mr Manning's which expends its highest faculties upon those sentiments and ideas which are the essence of civilisation', he argued in the same issue.

Aldington's own sufferings in the war, his feeling for those who had been through it and his dedication to literature made him especially sympathetic to the lonely older man, so that Manning turned to him in a search for some kind of literary work, asking if Aldington might find him some reviewing (18 June 1921). He also complained to Houtin (4 October 1921) that most of the literary magazines were controlled by Squire and 'his master', Gosse, 'quite an ignorant person who has made his way by adroitly using his friends'. Generous Aldington replied, apparently, with an offer to take Manning into his own country cottage, for T. S. Eliot was concerned lest Aldington's house should become a home for neurasthenics like Manning and himself.[15] Manning had already explained to Aldington that while grateful for his kind offer he had no need of it, as he had a small private income. (His father had left him the income from £5000 held in trust.) He had just had extra expenses since Galton's death. Aldington went to great trouble on behalf of this comrade in war and in writing. He apparently asked T. S. Eliot if he might persuade Desmond MacCarthy of the *New Statesman* to give Manning some reviewing. Although Eliot had not yet met Manning and did not share Aldington's enthusiasm for *Scenes and Portraits*, considering it literary and derivative, he esteemed him as a fine literary journalist, and one of the best prose writers of the day.[16] Eliot's efforts with MacCarthy on Manning's behalf probably resulted in publication in the *New Statesman* (3 September 1921) of Manning's elegant article on 'Libertinism and St Évremond'. Charles Saint-Évremond, a sceptical seventeenth-century gentleman, soldier and writer, Epicurean and exile, was a character to amuse Manning, with his charm and breeding and nicety of style. But such a piece was not really at home in a lively, almost radical political weekly. It did not lead to a new career.

The episode displayed the extent of the co-operation between writers of the period—at least with those who had something in common. All three had contributed an essay on 'Poetry in Prose' to the April 1921 issue of *Chapbook*, a monthly miscellany. All three were unhappy. Eliot, wracked by the problems of an impossible marriage, was approaching a nervous breakdown which occurred over October–November that year. Aldington, passionately distressed about the war, his marriage broken, was entangled in a net of emotional relationships; and Manning, grieving still over his own losses, worried also about Eliot's troubles and asked Aldington (8 October 1921) if there was any way he could help.

Disoriented by his griefs, low in energy and spirits, and finding the task he had undertaken too onerous, Manning had proposed, in confidence, to Aldington in August that they should collaborate in finishing the White book. Aldington went to Edenham for a few days that month and the visit was a success. Manning had proposed also that they should go shares in a book on Lionel Johnson as he had received the poet's letters and papers from Galton and expected the approval of Miss Johnson. (The papers were later returned to the Johnson family by Manning's solicitor, A. V. Moore.) Aldington's visit relieved Manning's depression. After a few days spent at Will Rothenstein's in early October, where he met John Drinkwater and a fellow Australian expatriate and neo-Georgian poet, whom he liked, W. J. Turner, he settled back to his work. Aldington had his own troubles in November and Manning commiserated with him, while expressing his gratitude for his help. Stricken with fever and flu again, he urged Aldington to continue with the project and told him he had obtained Miss Johnson permission to use Johnson's letters. But then he apparently fell into indolence and depression again. Unhappily, what began as an example of co-operation between friends ended in a bitter split. For Manning, 1922 was a bad year, as he was plagued by bouts of ill health, loneliness and boredom. Few of those whom he invited came to Edenham. Only the Rothensteins continued to keep up their friendship. It was at their home that he met the exciting hero of the war in the desert, Lawrence of Arabia. He liked the great man immediately, and invited him to visit Edenham in February 1922; but the elusive Lawrence did not come. Jim Fairfax married that year and was deep in his political ambitions. Edenham was very lonely.

After a severe illness in the middle of 1922, Manning convalesced on the West Coast in June. His mother and two sisters arrived in July, and his eldest brother with his wife and son also visited England that year. Possibly the family reunion emphasized his isolated life. He told Houtin that month that he thought of taking a flat in London. Travel was another solution to his problems: a warmer climate, new faces, possibly new friends. In the 1920s he became nomadic, compared with his pre-war stability. In November he was in Rome, a city he loved, in a very weak state to judge by his scratchy handwriting, so different from his usual beautiful script. He met there, through a letter of introduction from Rothenstein, another poet-aesthete whom he liked, Geoffrey Scott, and he described one of his poems, 'I Locked the Sun', to Rothenstein (26 November), as 'really exquisite'. Scott, scholar, architect, writer, poet and winner of the Newdigate Prize, was Press Attaché at the British Embassy in Rome and Manning dined there with him. A friend of Berenson, an even closer friend of Berenson's wife, Mary, it was said, and closest of all, sexually, in his youth, to John Maynard Keynes, Scott was an extraordinarily handsome man, married to a titled English woman. Apparently something of a Renaissance man he lived the kind of life Manning might admire but had no part in. Manning also observed in Rome the Pope and many blackshirts, *fascisti*, though according to Rothenstein he disliked the extreme political tendencies then making themselves felt. Passing through Paris on the way home, he saw Pound, enjoying his new life, and met his friend, James Joyce.[17] He showed no inclination to join these dedicated modernists in Paris, though he was plannning to leave Edenham at last. Instead, having inherited a few hundred pounds from Galton, as he told Houtin in July 1922, he had purchased a small property in Surrey.

The upsets of 1922 had lost him the friendship of Aldington, who had received no payment for the work he had done. Manning was heavily burdened with medical expenses but Aldington, too, was hard pressed financially. In a stiff little note (16 January 1923), in which 'My dear Richard', his usual salutation, was replaced by 'Dear Aldington', Manning apologized for the delay and promised to send something pending a final settlement with Lady White. That letter was marked 'nothing sent' by Aldington. According to him legal suasion finally brought payment. Only

Aldington's version of the disagreement remains. It may be that Manning found his work unsatisfactory—he claimed to have altered Aldington's chapters a good deal—or that he was so very ill that he could not deal with the problem and set it aside until he should have recovered. It may have been a question of misunderstandings, of external pressures on them both preventing explanations, for Aldington in the early post-war years felt 'as neurasthenic as a kitten'.[18] He was also quite offended in mid-1922 when Eliot ventured a mild criticism of an article he had written, and he was cool to Pound, describing him to Harriet Monroe (August 1922) as 'a semi-lunatic'.

The matter festered within both men. Aldington was indignant, and Manning's pride was hurt. The anger of his former friend was hard to bear. He wrote of Aldington to Houtin (5 January 1924) with an unusual flash of malice, describing him as a fluent scribbler with a very minor position on *The Times* obtained through his wife's influence. It seems a somewhat poor return for Aldington's kindnesses. Aldington was enraged by the affair and he later described Manning as a dipsomaniac. He wrote to H.D.: 'Unluckily Fred became such a dipso, it became very painful to know him'.[19] But Aldington, usually so generous, could also be unkind in his judgements, as his lampoons of Eliot and his wife showed. He could acknowledge, however, that Manning, in his weak health, depended greatly on others and that Galton's death had left him at a loose end, without the stimulation he needed in order to work, and that in the face of the drudgery involved in the White book, he was paralysed.[20] Long after the quarrel, Aldington talked in a generous way of Fred Manning to another Australian literary expatriate, Alister Kershaw, who gathered that while the two had not been close friends, their relationship had been more than a mere literary acquaintance.

That year, 1922, was some kind of turning point. The old life was ended, the old friends, except for Will, lost. Manning left Edenham behind and by January 1923 had settled in his new home in Surrey—Buckstone Farm, Chobham—which put him within reach of London yet retained a rustic peace. It marked an attempt to start a new life, after the years in Lincolnshire. But illness pursued him, and he lay in bed for three months, nursed by his seventy-five-year-old mother. In September he was shocked when Aubrey Herbert died suddenly after being rushed to a nursing home for an emergency operation. '. . . in Aubrey Herbert I mourn one of the most loyal and generous of men, generous even in his prejudices and in his loyalties immoveable . . .' he wrote to Will (21 November 1923), 'some men have the power of experiencing all life in a single day and he was of those who do not grow old'.

He had lost, now, almost every one of the friends of his youth, by death, by breach, or by marriage. His career was making no progress. The biography that had cost him the friendship of Aldington appeared in September, and was received coolly in England, especially by the *Times Literary Supplement* (15 November). Manning dismissed the reviews as hostile and ignorant when writing to Rothenstein (21 November 1923) and comforted himself by maintaining that the sales were excellent. He had seen White as a good man caught up in an unholy business, and at least one perceptive reviewer noted the ironic insight in this apparently straight-forward biography. 'It is on the whole a melancholy tale, one which makes one suddenly realise that the progress of civilisation is not as simple, as one might think, but tortuous, full of mystery and menace.'[21] As Manning had remarked, prophetically, in his piece on Dean Inge: 'Science only extends the field of human error'.

His losses and his sufferings had produced a toughening of the spirit, a strengthening of his defences, yet not a hardening of the heart. He could respond to the pain of others, and was concerned for tubercular young Rachel Rothenstein, whom he visited frequently in her serious illness in 1923; but he had withdrawn from the world. 'I know myself what a stimulus public applause may give', he wrote to Rothenstein in November, 'and I know how dangerous the pleasure of it may be . . . our prayer should be only for our daily bread . . . if it content us we are free'. Proud, ill, sensitive he faced and accepted his loneliness and his unhappiness. For he could still find solace in the world of words. To Houtin he wrote on 11 November 1923: 'Winter has come, and like Galton, I find myself repeating Horace's ode, "Ad Thaliarchum": A fire and a book are my only company'.

18

The *Criterion*, T. S. Eliot and the 1920s

'T<small>OMORROW</small> I shall see the editor of the *Criterion*', wrote Manning to Houtin (4 February 1924). 'He wants me to write for the periodical which is a quarterly review.' On the face of it, it seems unlikely that the revolutionary poet, T. S. Eliot, whose *Waste Land*—first published in the first issue of the *Criterion* in the autumn of 1922—had made him the most talked about modern poet, should seek out a little-known, old-fashioned writer who had more in common with the 1890s than the 1920s, and who appeared to have lost his small pre-war status in the post-war world.

Eliot, however, saw the writers of the 1890s as being closer to the disillusioned moderns than the rationalist progressives of the literary generation of Bernard Shaw, H. G. Wells and Lytton Strachey. Manning, though an Edwardian man-of-letters, displayed a scholarship in European literature, a pessimism about society, a concern with religion and aesthetics and a conservative attitude to politics which matched Eliot's sentiments. He might smile as an ironical doubter at Eliot's search for religious faith but he would understand, while Eliot had previously made an effort to help this writer passed over by the middlebrows. However much they differed as poets, they were dedicated to art; and as nervous, mannered, dandyish expatriates in flight from the provinces they were akin in sensibility. Eliot's own knowledge of suffering made an unspoken bond, for he once told Lady Ottoline Morell that those who enjoyed good health scarcely realized the bravery required from those who did not. Eliot had as well a high regard for Manning's journalistic prose, 'one of the very best prose writers we have'.[1]

The two met; Manning agreed to write an article on a religious subject: a review of Houtin's biography of the dissident priest, Charles Loyson, *Père Hyacinthe*. From their conversation, Manning judged that Eliot might have some clerical bias to overcome in religious questions and summed him up as a curious man, 'rather reactionary in politics and social questions, and revolutionary in literary matters'. He felt Eliot was afraid of many things, particularly liberalism in its many forms.[2] Although the elite *Criterion* had only eight hundred subscribers at its height, and Manning claimed to be only an occasional reader, it must have comforted him to see his name on the cover of the July 1924 issue, alongside those of Marcel Proust, W. B. Yeats, and Virginia Woolf. He was not totally forgotten. The five letters he wrote to Houtin in February on the matter testify to his initial excitement.

The majority of his contributions to the *Criterion* were concerned with religious themes: the existence of Jesus—he did not doubt his historical reality—in 'Christianisme' (January 1925); 'Greek Historical Thought' (April 1925); the religious magic of Sir James Frazer's *The Golden Bough* (September 1927) and Newman (January 1926). Sceptical of organized religions, he was fascinated by questions of belief and doubt and the role of religion in society. Where Eliot was looking for a personal belief, Manning saw religious questions as, tragically, largely political. 'A Church, in so far as it has a worldly and temporal object, represents the compromise which society makes with God', he wrote in his review of Houtin. Agreeing with Renan's epigram 'a philosophy for the wise, a religion for the people', he believed that social morality could not survive the loss of religion for long, and yet he saw no hope for religion as it was constituted in the modern age. He was not an atheist, and remained in the Catholic Church because he liked its rituals, but he thought most religions much of a muchness, asserting he would as soon be a Buddhist as a Quaker.[3] He could believe in God, but not in a Church. 'Life is a mystery and in this mystery perhaps there is a God' was how he put his position to Houtin (12 February 1924). He wrote more frequently to the Frenchman, in his intellectual as well as personal loneliness since Galton's death, seeking criticism of his articles, expressing his views, on the religious question in particular, and concerning himself about Houtin's health.

The mystical streak which had become apparent during the war dominated his post-war thinking, and he was interested increasingly in the unconscious and in the interaction of magic, mysticism and religion. He shared with Eliot a fascination with the work of Sir James Frazer on these themes. Newman, he thought, was a mystic as well as a poet; not only a master of literature but an interpreter of life. For Manning, the great Cardinal was a bridge between what were now his two main concerns, religion and aesthetics; and between the rational and irrational sides of his own nature.

Once we have known the influence of Newman, we do not escape from it easily. It renews itself in us. We return to him; and we return from so many directions, and for so many reasons: for the sake of his dialectical brilliance, his rhetorical power, his devotional fervour, and his imaginative vision. In his prose we hear the last echo of the eighteenth century, before the triumph of democracy, the building of Babel and the confusion of tongues. Its lucidity, its severity of form are an unconscious tribute to the rationalism, which he detested, of that great age.[4]

The other subject which preoccupied Manning in the 1920s was aesthetics. In his first article after his return from the war, he compared de Gourmont's prose unfavourably with what he termed the male and splendidly objective writing of Prosper Mérimée.[5] Galton had always admired Mérimée, and, possibly, the brutality of life as Manning had seen it in war gave him a greater understanding of Mérimée's toughness. He and Pound agreed to differ on aesthetics, for Manning contested de Gourmont's belief that the idea of beauty has its origin in the sexual. Manning wrote: 'man besides being a lover, is a hunter and warrior; he is a creature of action, avid of experience . . . will is manifested in action'. He found de Gourmont too feminine, by which he meant too passive, too reflective. He also thought de Gourmont underestimated the importance of the magical, the divine, the irrational, while practically ignoring the will to live. The experience of the war years had confirmed him in these views: also in the ideas that beauty is movement, that action is as important as reflection, that the role of the will is central in life.

In spite of his acquaintance with Eliot and regard for Pound and some of his work, he showed little interest in modernist theories, and he had been dismissive of Proust's 'interminable "subjectif" epic' to Houtin (5 January 1924). In an article, 'Critic and Aesthetic' in the *Quarterly Review* (July 1924), he opposed the notion of progress in the arts. 'There is no progress in poetry from Homer to Shakespeare, or from Sophocles to Racine, or in music from Bach to Beethoven, or from Beethoven to Debussy; there is difference, that is all.' He criticized again de Gourmont's emphasis on sexuality, saying:

> If the secret of art's fascination is to be traced, say, to the physical attraction of a model's portrait, why should Rembrandt's men and women by the passive dignity of their acquiescence in the melancholy of age exercise upon our minds so irresistible a charm? . . . our emotion in the presence of a Rembrandt portrait arises from the recognition of identity and difference; recognizing a common fate.

He also rejected art for art's sake. To Rothenstein (21 November 1923) he professed himself anti-Pater, Wilde and de Gourmont.

This kind of commonsense lucidity might be out of step with the fidgety 1920s, avid for the new and exotic, but the innovative poet-editor and the old-fashioned contributor kept up a slight acquaintance, lunching together occasionally. Manning met, through Eliot, the critic Bonamy Dobrée, and the gentle, animal-loving poet, Ralph Hodgson, who brought his dog along to such events. But the 'exquisite and listless Eliot'[6] and the exquisite of exquisites did not become close. Eliot, six years younger, an originator, belonged as an artist to the modern world of experiment in language, images, rhythms. *The Waste Land* had shown him confronting the devastation and disillusion of the post-war world (though he had not seen service in the war as he had been rejected as unfit by the United States Navy). As

Stephen Spender put it, Eliot 'lived no shadow aesthetic life haunting fifth-century Athens or pre-Raphaelite or Renaissance Italy, as did Ruskin and Pater, Wilde and Yeats and Pound'[7]—and, one might add, the pre-war Frederic Manning of *Scenes and Portraits.* Manning, however, until the end of the 1920s remained silent about his time in the army, about the great difference between his life and Eliot's during the war years.

He became more isolated and inturned, concerned with more abstract thought than he had been before the war. According to Rothenstein he rarely came up to London. His friendships were fewer, though he kept up the relationship with the Rothensteins, reading parts of his romance to them—which Will found enchanting—and he invited their younger son, Billy, to stay in October 1924. He was pleased to be asked by Siegfried Sassoon to be one of those contributing to the gift of a clavichord to mark the eightieth birthday of the Poet Laureate, Robert Bridges; he delighted in a conversation with Beerbohm, who was visiting Will from his Rapallo home; and he encouraged with his friendship and visits, Will's young daughter, Rachel, who sought a sun cure for tuberculosis at Leysin, Switzerland.

To her father he wrote (17 August 1924):

My dear Will,
Even when you touch a melancholy subject, your letters are written with a golden pen: and that drama of light and shadow played in front of the eternal hills, is a symbol to you of that other drama played before the eternal fates.
Humanity is nobler in its sufferings, than in its victories. But a crowd suffering or victorious is irrelevant beside the individual soul. One ceases to think of a crowd, eventually, as individuals detached from it, each with his own individual gift, and each capable, if it be only for a moment, of beauty and nobility. Each of us, as it were, is a verdict on life, a Judgment if only implied and tacit, scarcely a Judge.
Give my love to Rachel and tell her I love her wise patience, and that I hope she is even now colouring to the golden brown of the wheat ripening opposite my window. You seem to me two people wrapped in love, as in a warm cloak, and I can only send my love to salute you.
Yours always affectl . . .
Fred[8]

He could well understand the supportiveness of family love. In mid-1924 he had been seriously ill after an appendix operation and, after five weeks in hospital, he was nursed back to health by his ever-devoted mother. Then he fell victim to flu again. Rothenstein, with whom he spent two days in October, described his friend as 'having the worn look as of carved ivory due to constant ill-health'.[9] His three sisters were visiting England. He had not been home for more than twenty years. A long, quiet sea-voyage might restore his health; he decided to return with them, planning to rest on the ship. Without warning another tragedy engulfed him. His youngest sister, Trix, aged thirty-six, died in Paris on 14 October, after an illness of only a few days. Again he was deeply saddened. 'The loss to me and to my mother is immeasurable', he told Will (19 October 1924), a month before sailing from Marseilles for the city of his birth.

In the two decades he had been overseas, Sydney had spread to accommodate a population of around one million. A small underground rail system was under construction, work had begun at last on the Harbour Bridge, and trams and cars had replaced most horse-drawn vehicles. The skyline was changing as taller buildings replaced the old, low ones but the spirit of the place remained provincial. D. H. Lawrence invoked the atmosphere of the city in the early 1920s in his novel, *Kangaroo*, contrasting the left-over bitterness of some angry ex-soldiers with the brashness and complacency of most of the citizenry, who were revelling in the prosperity and new freedoms of the 1920s. The pleasures of Sydney were still physical: surfing, yachting, cricket and sport in general, supplemented by the new crazes of motoring, jazz dancing, ice-skating and the moving pictures. An intellectual, aesthetic invalid, observing this sunny, noisy, mindless scene from his mother's comfortable, though now saddened, home—Wynyard, Rose Bay—surely saw little to keep him there. Very little of a cultural nature was happening in Australia in 1925.

A few artists and writers were trying to manufacture an 'Australian Renaissance'. Norman Lindsay, with his son Jack and the poet Kenneth Slessor, had begun promoting a creed of Vitalism in the magazine, *Vision*, but it ceased publication after only one year in 1924. Vance and Nettie Palmer were endeavouring to encourage an indigenous literature, and a few other unquenchable spirits like lyricist John Shaw Neilson were not deterred by the lack of cultural stimulation. But the two novels of some note published in 1925 were both by expatriate Australians: Henry Handel Richardson's *The Way Home*, the middle volume of her Mahony saga, and Martin Boyd's weak but interesting *Love Gods*, a study of a sensitive young ex-soldier in post-war England. Boyd had returned home to Melbourne after the war in August 1919. He had spent eighteen months in partying and idleness, and had found that outside of his family he felt he was in a foreign country. Unable to find a congenial milieu in his homeland, he settled for expatriatism. For Frederic Manning it was surely much the same. He too must have felt the uneasiness of the double alienation that Boyd described: 'I have suffered much through being considered an Englishman in Australia and an Australian in England, and the target of the ill-bred of both countries'.[10]

But the journalist and poet Leon Gellert, who had survived Gallipoli, recalled a great admiration for Manning among the aspiring young poets of Sydney. Gellert, who still suffered from the effects of shell-shock, shared with Manning a capacity to involve himself in the sorrows of his soldier comrades, in the terrible physical legacy borne by many returned men. He shared as well a touch of Manning's mysticism. He remembered Manning, whom he met in a lift at the *Sydney Morning Herald* building, as fragile and uneasy, a frail figure as he limped across Pitt Street.[11] (Gellert later found the time of the visit hard to place although he thought it was in the 1920s.) He was working then for the glossy magazine, *Home*, which represented an interest in sophistication and cosmopolitanism in post-war Sydney. It found room among its society gossip for the art of Margaret Preston, the photographs of Harold Cazneaux and the verse of Hugh McCrae. Manning's interests were more severely intellectual. He might be branded, in today's jargon, as an 'élitist' but he was not the only returned expatriate who found his homeland wanting. In August 1925 *Home* featured an article by Will Dyson who had come back after his brilliant success in England to work for the Melbourne *Herald* group. He answered the compulsory question for all returning Australian artists: 'Why have you returned', with a tongue-in-cheek interview with himself. He explained: 'My work in London was finished . . . There was no further use in continuing to live on the outer fringes of Empire. I resolved to return to the passionate, throbbing life of its centre. I have bought a house in Moonee Ponds'. Dyson, no highbrow, intellectual conservative like Manning, but of a radical, socialist background, returned to Europe in 1930, since he found his native land so dull that he described it as 'a paradise for dull, boring mediocrities, a place where the artist or the man with ideas can only live on sufferance . . . Was it ever to fill its mental spaces and become a country fit for adults?'[12]

The cheerful 1920s in Sydney were no setting for a critical intellectual who needed something more than Gladys Moncrieff in *Maid of the Mountains* at the Theatre Royal and tea dances at the Wentworth Hotel. By May 1925, Manning was back in Surrey, accompanied by his brother, after his melancholy voyage to Sydney. His health was bad, his heart was weak, and he spent most of July and August recovering from flu, lying in a chair in the garden at Buckstone, trying to concentrate his mind on the Newman article he was writing for the *Criterion*. 'One cannot follow the doctrine of Newman and remain a Catholic' was the conclusion he confided to Houtin (15 August 1925).

His Irish friends Sybil Gowthorpe and Polly Barry visited him that year but Buckstone, and country life, now bored him. 'I seem to grow more alone every day of my life', was his sad admission to Will (9 October). 'True, I lunch and dine with my neighbours from time to time, but doubt whether they exist.' By the end of 1925, when he wrote to Houtin, he had sold the farm, had returned to Dublin, to Belfield, and was looking forward to his mother's arrival in March. He found that he no longer wished to write for Eliot's magazine, now called the *New Criterion*. He gave no explanation to Houtin except that he found little to admire in it. It was not a matter of quarrelling with Eliot, whom he liked, and who liked his writing, he claimed.[13] That indolence, that physical weariness he suffered from, may have made such writing more of a burden than he could manage, or he may have felt an odd man out in the magazine—too heavy or too old-fashioned. It was no place for his 'Golden Coach'. Yet he continued to write for it until 1927. He turned also to a biography of Galton, for he had kept his letters, found it difficult, and fell back on his unfinishable book. The small poem, 'Animae Suae', was reprinted from the *Irish Statesman* (edited by his old friend AE) and published in the New York *Literary Digest* (3 April 1926). There it appeared on a page devoted to current poets which also featured Edmund Blunden. But the poem was very much in his well-crafted, musical and languid pre-war manner, as if his war poems had never been written.

The affection he had felt for the land of his ancestors, as a soldier, began to cool under its intellectually chilly climate. AE, though a Protestant, refused to publish in the *Irish Statesman* a review by Manning of Houtin's book, *Un Prêtre Symboliste* on a controversial figure, Marcel Hébert, another dissident priest;[14] and when Manning met Yeats and his wife again in Dublin around the end of 1925, he felt that life in Ireland had chastened and subdued the pair: 'because no man is a prophet in his own country, and least of all a senator'.[15] He welcomed the withdrawal of England from Ireland, saying: 'England masked the disease from which Ireland suffers'.[16] He kept some contacts with his Belfield friends, but his Irish period was almost over.

Back in London in March 1926, at Garland's Hotel, Pall Mall, where he often stayed, he began work on an introduction to a new edition of *Epicurus, His Morals*, edited by Walter Charleton (1619–1707). A new publisher, Peter Davies, had encouraged Manning by commissioning it. Davies was a literary man himself and had been friendly with Manning since the early 1920s. The edition was limited to 750 copies, so it was not likely to bolster Manning's public reputation. He was pleased, therefore, to hear a few years later that an Oxford don, W. D. Ross, had recommended his introduction as 'treating Epicurus from a new point of view'.[17] The chapter showed him still reflecting on the mystery of the processes of the mind.

> The most curious thing in memory is its timelessness, the illusion, if it be one, of our own eternal existence: it is only by some effort, however slight, of reason that we are able to recapture the sequence of events, and then proceed to rationalise our experience and impose some kind of order on its natural incoherence.

Walter Charleton's object, he maintained, was to interpret the doctrines of Epicurus in such a way as to render them tolerable to his own age (the late seventeenth–early eighteenth centuries). There was much in Charleton's interpretation which might have relevance in Manning's own constricted life:

> We regard self-mastery as a great good, not so as in all cases to limit ourselves to little, but so as to be contented with little if we have not much, since we are fully persuaded that they have the smoothest enjoyment of plenty who stand least in need of it, and that all those things which our natures need are easy, and only our idle fancies difficult to gain . . . If you live according to Nature, you shall never be poor, but if according to Opinion, you shall never be rich. Nature desires little, Opinion infinite.

Despite the stresses of living in the city Manning seemed able to write there and could still make the most of its small pleasures. Untouched by the general strike of May 1926 he spent a pleasant enough summer in London with his mother and his friends, including Jim Fairfax, now a conservative M.P. for Norwich.

His life, in the late 1920s, was becoming more restricted on the one hand, with fewer friends (Houtin died in 1926), little writing; yet, on the other, more nomadic, with more casual acquaintances as he moved restlessly from hotel to hotel around England, or stayed with friends, or sought a better climate and 'cures' in Europe. The Rothensteins remained as faithful as ever, and John, who was under instruction and about to join the Catholic church, sought the advice of the old family friend. 'I wouldn't leave the Church', replied Manning, 'but I'm often inclined to doubt whether, were I outside, I would become a Catholic'. When the young man asked him to be a sponsor at his confirmation, Manning agreed: 'if you think my nature sufficiently godly, and sufficiently paternal, I have not the slightest objection'.[18]

In contrast to Manning's ambivalence on religion and nationality at this time was T. S. Eliot's whole-hearted acceptance of Anglicanism and England, for he was baptized and confirmed in the Church of England in 1927, and became a British citizen. He had found the answers to his questions. The slight acquaintanceship faded. Manning's final break with Eliot's magazine may have followed on the pique he felt at an unfavourable review, in October, by philosopher R. G. Collingwood of his *Epicurus* in what had become—for a brief period in 1927—*The Monthly Criterion*. Collingwood said drily: 'the cautious reader will not imagine that Epicurus and Dr Charleton's Epicurus are the same person'. Although Manning and the critic seemed in general agreement, Manning took offence, replying with a stiff letter in January 1928, and he wrote no more for the magazine. His last article for it, on Prosper Mérimée (November 1927), was something of a statement of the position on life that he had reached; an unsentimental, tough-minded acceptance of a hard world.

Mérimée (1803–70), a secretive, cynical, unhappy man of the world and of the salons, a public man of countless love affairs, possessed in his writings the same quality that Manning admired in Newman: 'tense emotion restrained under classic severity of form'. He appreciated too the dramatic nature of Mérimée's stories and their irony. It was an admiration stemming from earlier years, perhaps, for Galton had judged Mérimée the clearest thinker of the nineteenth century because of his hatred of spurious sentimentality, his passion for the truth of life and his acceptance of the energy and violence of the world; all qualities Galton saw himself as sharing, no doubt. Manning, by 1928, appeared to have adopted the same harsh standards. He rejected the notion of Mérimée as a 'man in a mask', hiding his unhappiness and sensibility and a tender, loving heart as a dishonourable weakness. 'His reserve is simply that of the well-bred man towards a world which he knows, for which he has something of contempt. He neither asked for its sympathy nor admitted it to his confidence.' Mérimée appeared an enigma, he maintained, only because he was perfectly sane.

This seems close to the stance Manning sought to adopt himself. Ill, proud, aloof, disappointed in his hopes, saddened by his losses, he did not make excuses for his failures or fall into the trap of self-pity. An apparently cool, guarded cynic had replaced the gentle exquisite, who had been killed in the war, one might say. To some extent in his case, though, it was a mask. The touch of cruelty in Mérimée, his cold hardness, what Pater had seen as pure mind with nothing of the soul, his touch of satisfaction, almost, at the grimness of life, did not accord with Manning's nature. Intellectually he might think himself indifferent to the tragedies of life, might bear his own sufferings quietly, might cut with his sharp wit, but an intense sensibility to the pain of others was one half of his being, however much he might imagine he had suppressed it.

In these stressful years he was more fortunate than many other survivors, for he had a small private income and the care of his loving mother. Together—and sometimes with Edith—they spent a good deal of time in Europe in 1928: in Italy, and at the health resorts in high mountain areas of Austria as his respiratory problems grew worse. When they stayed at the Hotel Edlaherof, near Vienna, Manning found the countryside enchanting and the life very amusing, as he sunbaked watching the beautiful young people in their brief costumes. From Edlach he went to Semmering, then to Vienna early in September; then he planned to spend a few days in England before rejoining his mother in Vienna for Christmas. He had met many charming Austrians; and the music had been delightful.[19] It was the life of the sick dilettante. He seemed to have given up writing. When the weather warmed up he returned to Lincolnshire, where the memories of so many years centred, and spent the summer of 1929 at the Bull Inn, in Bourne.[20] Towards the end of July he went up to London where his sister was staying at the Pioneer Club. It was then that a younger friend, also an ex-soldier, the publisher, Peter Davies, who had first broached the idea in 1927, finally persuaded him to write down his memories of the war, and the emotions and thoughts stifled for so long found release.

19

Reawakening

$\mathbf{F}$REDERIC MANNING dedicated his war novel: 'To Peter Davies Who Made Me Write It'. Davies had suggested the idea, had believed in Manning, and had encouraged, coaxed and chivvied him during the writing. This young publisher, without whom Manning would not have produced his classic book, was a very different Pygmalion figure to middle-aged, intellectual Arthur Galton. For one thing, when they first met he was in his twenties, fifteen years younger than Manning. For another, his romantic, troubled background had suffered from excess of emotion rather than of cerebration in the Galtonian style. His early life had been as full of tragedy and drama as Manning's had been of provincial quiet. Davies's experiences, however, enabled him to make a significant contribution to Manning's work as he was able to understand Manning's nature and situation more fully than most and to bring out his ability. He too was of a sensitive, sympathetic and artistic temperament and an ex-soldier.

He was born in 1897, the third son of a barrister, Arthur Llewelyn Davies and his wife, Sylvia, the daughter of the dramatist and *Punch* cartoonist, George du Maurier. The Llewelyn Davies were a handsome, rather radical, intellectual family of a serious turn of mind. In contrast the du Mauriers were amusing, light-hearted and slightly Bohemian. Being born into a family of such talent seemed a fine start in life; and Peter Davies's earliest years were spent in the model of a loving, happy, upper middle-class Victorian nursery. But both parents died in their early forties after tragic illnesses. They left their five sons aged from six to seventeen in the care of James Barrie, the most popular playwright of the day and a very wealthy, if rather eccentric, foster parent.

'Uncle Jim' had entered the lives of the Davies boys more than a decade before. His most famous character, Peter Pan, had evolved from his encounter in the Kensington Gardens with the family when Peter was still in his perambulator. Barrie, infatuated with the children and their mother, showered gifts and attention on them. Peter Davies, however, came to hate the imaginary boy who dogged him all his life. Only a few weeks after his mother's death he started at Eton where he was ragged cruelly as the 'real' Peter Pan.

When the war broke out seventeen-year-old Peter and his elder brother George, a Cambridge undergraduate, were commissioned as second lieutenants in the 60th Rifles. Brilliant, dashing George, Barrie's special favourite, was killed in action in March 1915, aged twenty-one. Peter fought in the Battle of the Somme. After two months there he was invalided home with shell-shock. He returned to the front, however, and won the Military Cross in 1918; but he had suffered so much that he could not return to family life and the fussy solicitude of Uncle Jim. He was demobilized early in 1919, 'a shattered remnant'[1] of his former self. The fates had not finished, however, with Barrie and his 'lost boys'. In May 1921 the magnetic fourth brother, Michael, who was closest to Barrie and the inspiration of the statue of Peter Pan in Kensington Gardens, drowned in the Thames near Oxford. His fellow undergraduate and close friend, Rupert Buxton, died with him and the circumstances of the tragedy were never explained. Peter and his other two brothers were overwhelmed, but Peter, courageously, overcame his grief and in 1926 formed, with his youngest brother, Nico, his own publishing house. His publishing list reflected his own interest in serious literature. The novelist Compton Mackenzie called him 'an artist among publishers'.[2]

Deeply affected by his personal tragedies, and by the war, Davies had the capacity to understand both sides of Fred Manning, his intellect and his sensibility. They met, it seems, in the early 1920s, for Davies later said (*Daily Mirror*, 26 February 1930) that he had tried for nine years to make his friend write down his war experiences. The friendship, then, came before Davies's emergence as a publisher. But one of the first books he published was the edition of *Epicurus* (1926) for which Manning wrote an introduction. The war book was a very different venture. But Davies, as his idiosyncratic and successful publishing career showed, had the knack of seizing on the unusual.

As a publisher he was aware that in the late 1920s, mysteriously, after a decade of peace, interest in the war had revived. Davies judged that a war novel by Manning might prove a success, financially and from the artistic point of view, and he increased his urging of his friend to record his memories. The poets had written in the midst of battlefields, responding immediately to their situation; and a number of war memoirs had been published during and immediately after the war.[3] But after the first rush there was something of a lull, until in 1928 two classic English war books appeared, Siegfried Sassoon's *Memoirs of a Fox Hunting Man* and Edmund Blunden's *Undertones of War*. It was, however, the enormous success of Erich Remarque's *All Quiet on the Western Front* that marked the new era of war books and led to Peter Davies's determination and his increased pressure on Manning to write of his experiences.

The publication of such books as Robert Graves's *Goodbye to All That* made 1929 a peak year of passionate memories.[4] Eric Partridge's little-known, fine account of Australians in Egypt, Gallipoli and France, *Frank Honywood, Private*, also came out that year. And Peter Davies had a success with Charles Carrington's *A Subaltern's War*, written under the pseudonym Charles Edmonds. Davies had wit enough to see, after the success of Remarque, that the ordeal of the British private had been neglected. The first great German novel about the war, Ernst Jünger's *Storm of Steel*, had been a hymn of praise to the old Prussian officer class. 'Chivalry here took a final farewell', he wrote. 'It was here [the officers' mess] among the spirits of the undaunted dead that the will to conquer was concentrated and made visible in the features of each weather-beaten face.' (p. 100) But *All Quiet on the Western Front* had been such an enormous success, because, radically, the author had broken with such traditions and turned to the agony of the average man, however drunken, cowardly or stupid. Davies saw the opening for a British book on the rankers. He also saw, what other publishers might have doubted, that Manning was the person to write it. Manning's reputation was that of an old-fashioned exquisite who wrote solemn articles for small magazines. But Davies knew him as a friend. He knew his breadth of sympathy and his realism. He and Manning must have talked of their experiences and of how they saw the war. To write of those events, still fresh in mind and charged with emotion, would be a complete escape from the paralysing formalism of the romance.

According to legend, Davies locked Manning into his flat in London, and rushed each chapter to the printer as it was written. He did not give his author any opportunity of rewriting. Everything was done in such a hurry that Manning was receiving the proofs of early chapters before the last ones were written.

> I was a little afraid of it as I wrote it. It was wilful and spontaneous, and took its own way. It came so hurriedly that some things were forgotten. Peter took it from me sheet by sheet, and cast it into adamantine type. But for him I might have rewritten it. What an escape![5]

For decades Manning had laboured over his 'Golden Coach', without reaching an end. Indeed, he seemed to have put it aside in the late 1920s. But he wrote this book without hesitations, almost without alterations, as the microfilm manuscript in the Mitchell Library, in his beautiful, tiny script shows.[6] It almost seems an example of his aesthetic theory of the work of art as one movement, of his view that the process of artistic creation, like the flight of an arrow, is, mysteriously, all of one piece. He had not built it up, sedulously, from separate elements. It had, however, been brewing within him for a long time: 'tho' I wrote it all in a little over six months, it was not hastily conceived: even during the war I thought of writing it'.[7]

It was the encouragement and urging of Peter Davies which freed Manning from his years of restriction so that the words flowed spontaneously. Passionate memory was also involved. Australian novelist Leonard Mann experienced a similar free flow of creation when writing his war book *Flesh in Armour.* He wrote it, he said, 'straight off, straight from memory, it was so vivid. No need for any note'.[8] One of Mann's main characters, who reads Pater in the trenches, has something of the same reserved dignity as Manning's hero Bourne. Mann was an enthusiastic admirer of Manning's writing, of his strength of mind and his scholarship, terming *Scenes and Portraits* 'exquisite but also learned'. He found it curious that British reviewers ignored the Australian element in the war novel: 'perhaps because they have not wanted to make anything of it'.[9]

To write of the ordinary soldier as Manning did was something new in England, as Davies had realized. Kipling's soldiers were brave and resourceful men though scarcely thoughtful; but they were exotics, professionals fighting in far away lands. The Great War, however, was the war of the common man, the inexperienced civilian, the average man. Kitchener's volunteer army encompassed clerks and schoolteachers, farmhands and miners, shop assistants and schoolboys, writers and philosophers, all innocent of warfare and killing until this cataclysm.

The mystique of the soldier now enveloped all manner of men. Manning chanced to have been one of them and with his special talents, his lucid prose style, his sharp eye for detail, his sympathetic understanding, his intellectual balance and grasp, was perfectly suited to record the experience. Peter Davies chanced to turn to publishing and in his turn was well-fitted to understand Manning and his talent. This child of the upper middle class had been thrown by fate into a less cosy world and could appreciate Manning's fatalistic tone and the universality of his subject. As a young officer of fine sensibility, Davies had seen the sufferings of the ordinary soldiers. He was determined that their story should be told, and his enthusiasm and energy were exactly what were needed to overcome Manning's ennui and indolence. He was the perfect publisher for this hesitant perfectionist, so that he could draw out of him what no one else could—a masterpiece on war.

Davies, having drawn the book out his author now had another difficulty to face, for Manning insisted that there be no censorship of the language of his soldiers. This, in 1929, when one four-letter word was sufficient to deter any publisher! Davies compromised by publishing an expensive, private and unexpurgated, anonymous edition of 520 copies, entitled *The Middle Parts of Fortune*, under the imprint of the Piazza Press. Today the language, while straightforward and obviously what the men would have used, has less impact than it would have had sixty years ago. The words are now heard on the lips of small school children, and one

American reviewer thought that, paradoxically, the taboo words sound bland because now they are everywhere, and that the euphemisms were more suggestive.[10] The title used for the first version, *The Middle Parts of Fortune*, was coined from the quotation from *Hamlet* II.ii. quoted thus on the title page:

> On fortune's cap we are not the very button . . . Then you live about her waist or in the middle of her favours? . . . Faith, her privates we.

American editions have favoured this title over the better known British one, *Her Privates We* which perhaps held overtones of old Queen Victoria. It was the unexpurgated Piazza Press version which Arnold Bennett, the leading reviewer for mass sales, treated so favourably in the mass circulation *Evening Standard* (23 January 1930), the most important paper for reaching the man-in-the-street, who was, after all, the real hero of the book.

Bennett, no war-monger, called it: 'an inspiring and beautiful book . . . a quiet and utterly convincing glorification of the common soldier . . . It compels in the reader a reluctant belief that war is glorious after all'. And he commented on the fact of the limited edition, explaining that it was 'because all the language of the common soldier is displayed in full. You understand: all. You will find in it nothing whatever to which even a Home Secretary could object; but the vocabulary renders general publication impossible. There is an edition partially expurgated for popular use'. He paid further tribute saying: 'The tale is full of horrors . . . but it is also full of nobility'. Davies had prepared, also, an expurgated edition, using for the first time the title *Her Privates We*, making the point that it was the story of the ordinary men, the unsung heroes, the unknown soldiers. Out of its context the punning innuendo of the title caused no stir, though the ghost of that closet devotee of Rabelais, Arthur Galton, may have smiled. As a further piece of marketing possibly, or simply from his typical modesty, Manning hid his identity behind his army number, the author being simply Private 19022. Aubrey Herbert, whom he had so admired, had published his little book on the campaigns of Gallipoli and Kut anonymously. Manning, with his delicate sensibilities, may well have agreed with such avoidance of public exposure. He was also, he confessed, a little terrified of publicity. It was not until 1943, in the midst of another war, that the book appeared under his own name—after his death.

The novel, with its motifs of chance and inevitable mortality, echoed the theme of his pre-war poem, 'Kore', and its notion of 'The yearly slain'. Each chapter is headed with a Shakespearian quotation. Many deal with the question of man's mortality, from the vigour and bluntness of that heading Chapter 1: 'By my troth I care not; a man can die but once; we owe God a death . . . and let it go which way it will he that dies this year is quit for the next'[11] to the fatalism of the final epigraph: 'Fortune? O, most true; she is a strumpet'.[12]

Oddly enough, this sombre work and Evelyn Waugh's *Vile Bodies*, an evocation of the frenetic world of the Bright Young Things of the 1920s, to whom the worst crime was to be too intense, were both on the best-seller list for February 1930. Worlds apart, one might say, yet Waugh ends his hilarious satire of that brittle era in the midst of another battlefield, an invented one, in another war, in a chapter entitled 'Happy Ending'. It was only a decade from 1929 to 1939. 'The war to end war' had not succeeded in its aim. Many could see that though the battles had stopped, the war was not finished. The experience of the generation of 1914 was becoming more frighteningly relevant to the youth of the 1930s. This may have been a reason for the renewed interest in the war. To the survivors of the first carnage, ignored and shunned so often if they tried to explain what they had endured, it was a bitter victory that their sons might face the same fate. Manning emphasized the ingratitude awaiting unfortunate ex-soldiers with the quotation he used, of Falstaff, on the title page of the second volume of the original unexpurgated edition. 'I have led my ragamuffins where they are peppered; there's not three of my hundred and fifty left alive, and they are for the town's end, to beg during life.'[13] Such sights could be seen any day in the streets of London in the post-war world. After all the parties, all the drinking, all the careless love affairs, as depression settled over the world an uneasiness about the future took hold as prosperity disappeared suddenly. Will Dyson wrote bitterly of the poverty and economic problems of the 1930s: 'They are mean, they are debasing, to thousands of my generation they are making the rat-haunted dug-outs of the Somme seem palaces in which the soul could at least breathe the air of manhood'.[14]

The times seemed fitted for a thoughtful book on modern war. Seeming victory could end in another kind of defeat. Prosperity was not necessarily a progress; and war might erupt out of the most hard-won peace. It was not that the new spate of war books as a whole enthused about war. Most were passionate expressions of rage and pain. But Manning's novel, so realistic, yet so deeply reflective and philosophical, was unusual in that it raised the problem of the enduring nature of war, and the response of ordinary men to tragic circumstance. It contained no bombast, however, no talk of honour and glory, no tub-thumping patriotism, no German-hating chauvinism. He had shaken off that aspect at least of the influence of Arthur Galton. He had shaken off, too, in his lucid, plain prose, the exquisite cloak of Paterian style, which had carried some traces of art for art's sake even in *Scenes and Portraits*. His particularly sharp sensibility and his sympathetic admiration for the nobility to be found in ordinary people, blended with his individual, if pessimistic vision, to produce a work which was totally his own, in style and substance, however much it owed to the judgement, will and understanding of his publisher. It may not have been the kind of success that Arthur Galton had hoped his pupil might achieve, for it was a work that the masses might read and was not restricted to a scholarly, highbrow group; and it belonged to an experience in which

Galton had had no part, which he could not have understood. The master triumphed, however, in one aspect. The plain, clear prose was a return to the models admired by Galton.

There was no doubt, however, that Manning owed a major debt to Peter Davies, the young man who had taken him in hand, and encouraged and prodded this indolent, tired being into producing this individual book. Unlike Galton, Davies had not overwhelmed Manning with a stronger personality. He had left him free, if under the constraint of producing, to express himself as a creative artist. But more importantly Davies had understood Manning as a friend. Nico Davies, writing to Henry Manning (14 January 1963) said that he could not think of any author who had meant more personally to Peter than Manning. *Her Privates We* was important to Davies as a best-seller. It was, no doubt, important to him in a more personal way. As an ex-soldier Davies had similar memories to Manning. For him, as well as for the author, the book was something of a catharsis.

Peter Davies's business venture succeeded, and he became a leading figure in the publishing world, his imprint being a guarantee of an unusual kind of book. He published and encouraged other Australian writers including Christina Stead and Herbert Moran. The shadows hanging over him never cleared, however. His melancholy family history haunted him, and on 5 April 1960 he threw himself under a train at Sloane Square underground station. The Coroner's Jury returned a verdict of 'suicide while the balance of his mind was disturbed'.[15] His death made world-wide headlines as the suicide of Peter Pan, but *The Times* paid a proper tribute: 'an irreparable loss to the publishing trade, for here was a personality, witty, astringent, with a brilliant and remarkable knowledge of literature, and withal he possessed a deep and kindly understanding of his fellow men'. He was of the same stamp, in many ways, as his friend Frederic Manning; and without his perception, his energy and his sympathetic encouragement as friend and editor it is likely that *Her Privates We* would never have been written.

20

A World of Its Own

THE SPECIAL quality of *Her Privates We* is its total concentration on the experience of war: 'the war had made it a world'. (p. 25) Most other great books of that war relate the experience to civilian life, to the world before or after. Robert Graves is as vehement in his rage about his public school, Charterhouse, as he is about the stupidities and absurdities of army life. Siegfried Sassoon's golden Edwardian idyll of hunting fields and cricket pitches sharpens the brutality and tragedy of the scenes of suffering and despair that follow; and Ford Madox Ford and Richard Aldington use their accounts largely as vehicles for passionate personal tragedies and individual visions of England. Among Australian war novels, Martin Boyd's *When Blackbirds Sing* is best in its scenes of bitter social comedy, set in the panorama of his series of novels dealing with Anglo-Australian upper-class life; and Leonard Mann's *Flesh in Armour* and J. P. McKinney's *The Crucible* are partly studies in Australian lower middle-class Puritanism.

To these writers war is some dreadful aberration, some impossibility, some absurdity, which occurs and gets in the way of real life. Dreadful, yes, says Manning, but obviously not impossible, and in itself part of reality. For he accepts that war is in the nature of things, and proceeds to examine its actuality on a number of levels. He focuses attention on the experience of a group of British soldiers in a regiment termed the Westshires, on the Somme–Ancre front in the second half of 1916. As Mary McCarthy has said, this is not a political book: it is not concerned with either glorifying or condemning war.[1] It is not the story of a sensitive young man, embittered and outraged by an horrific ordeal. It is least of all a paean of praise for death and blood and glory and violence in the manner of Ernst Jünger, who wrote: 'The war was our dream of greatness, power and glory'.[2] By setting his limits of time and space, by concentrating on what he himself had observed and known, by abjuring, in his characters, any ties with the past and hopes for the future, Manning creates a world in itself, narrow but honest. He confronts, at the stretch of his perception, the physical, psychological and philosophical aspects of what he sees, with ironic pessimism, as a human-engineered disaster.

On its most accessible level the book is a slice of documentary. Lyn Macdonald, who has written in detail of the battles of that war, praises Manning's topography and events as 'astonishingly accurate'[3] and speculates as to whether he may have revisited the battle area. She concludes that this was unlikely. Military historians Michael Howard and John Terraine commend the novel's authenticity; and the critic, Paul Fussell, says that the language is 'the right idiom, at once coarse and fastidious'.[4] In his Preface Manning wrote that 'in recording the conversations of the men' he 'seemed to hear the voices of ghosts', and that the events described actually happened. It is, however, documentary raised to a highly imaginative level. As Terraine writes: 'Great War novels step constantly into and out of the fact and fiction worlds'.[5] While Manning maintains that the characters are fictitious, his protagonist Bourne is such a reflection of his own speculative, detached self that the book is in some sense a journal of Manning's war, and his reponses to it.

It opens in the aftermath of an attack, 'a show', with the enigmatic Private Bourne stumbling into a dug-out, 'beaten to the wide'. He is joined by an officer, Mr Clinton, who shares with him his whisky flask and his terror of 'breaking'. '"Don't talk so bloody wet", Bourne said to him through the darkness, "You'll never break".' One theme is set, that of enduring, of a stoic pride in sticking it out. That night, as his fellows lie in nightmarish slumber, Bourne relives the storm and fury of the battle. Next day he and his group move away from the immediate threat of death to a rest period behind the lines, and this long hiatus of comparative quiet forms the main section of the book.

Here the troops are concerned, not with fighting, but with the day-to-day matters of life out of the line; with marching, singing, gossiping, drinking, quarrelling and occasionally flirting with the French peasant girls. Burdened with parades, fatigues and inspections, they also face the degrading physical discomforts of lice, fleas, cold, mud, sordid billets, few baths, dreary food and petty discipline. Manning details all the trivia of their daily life against a background of continuous conversations, of soldiers with soldiers, with officers, with NCOs, with peasants. Characters come and go in the desultory manner of life. Yet all the concentrated detail is gathered together, to symbolize the eternal fate of the soldier through the ages. H. M. Klein, in analysing the structure of the novel, shows Manning's artistry in moving all the seemingly disparate elements towards the climax of Bourne's fate,[6] what Edmund Blunden calls in his Preface to the 1964 edition the 'current of destiny'.

The men, while concerned with small matters, know they will return all too soon to fear and danger, perhaps death. Manning stresses the patient endurance of their life: 'The strange thing was, that the greater the hardships they had to endure, for wet and cold bring all kind of attendant miseries in their train, the less they grumbled'. The peasants, whom Bourne also admires, still working in the ravaged fields around their shattered houses, share this gritty pessimism.

> 'C'est la guerre', they would say, with resignation that was almost apathy: for all sensible people know that war is one of the blind forces of nature, which can neither be foreseen nor controlled. Their attitude, in all its simplicity, was sane. There is nothing in war which is not in human nature; but the violence and passions of men become, in the aggregate, an impersonal and incalculable source, a blind and irrational movement of the collective will, which one cannot control, which one cannot understand, which one can only endure as these peasants, in their bitterness and resignation, endured it. *C'est la guerre.* [pp. 108-9]

Bourne, not of the county or religion of these soldiers, not even English, is something of a loner. He shares his leisure time in this interval of comparative peace with two other outsiders, Shem, the Jew, probably a townsman among all these miners and ploughboys, and sixteen-year-old Martlow, the kid, marked off by his youth. Whether these two are based on actual people or are imaginary, they present facets of Manning's feelings. He had shown in his letters, at times, touches of the anti-Semitism common among Englishmen and Australians in his formative years. He had grown up with the unpleasant *Bulletin* prejudices in the air, and since the Jewish community in Sydney, while industrious and active, was very small, he may well not have met anyone like 'tough, sturdy and generous Shem' before his army service. Bourne and practical Shem 'scrounge' together. Shem is independent, unsentimental, tireless, a good soldier and a survivor. Possibly he represents, in part, Manning's tribute to the Jewish heritage of that sturdy, reliable friend, Will Rothenstein.

'The kid' arouses different emotions. With him Bourne is paternal, protective, affectionate; amused by 'his rosy-cheeked impudence' (p. 38) yet aware that for someone like Martlow, life had probably always been a kind of warfare. Manning, for so long cosseted—first by his mother and sisters, then by Galton and Eva and other women friends—could now project himself in the unusual role of a father-figure, by making Bourne show concern for boys like Martlow, 'blubbering like the child he really was, as they went over the top'. There were many such boys in that war, Australian as well as English, who put their age up in the cause of adventure. When Bourne, 'a reticent and undemonstrative man' throws his arm around Martlow's neck, it is a statement of deep affection.

The trio become close companions, working together, enjoying their simple 'bon times' together, sharing Bourne's delicacies from home, endeavouring to make life more bearable, sticking together in various escapades. They are soldiers-in-arms together rather than conventional friends. As Bourne explains it to the chaplain: 'good comradeship takes the place of friendship. It is different: it has its own loyalties and affections; and I am not sure that it does not rise on occasion to an intensity of feeling which friendship never touches . . .' (p. 79) The bond in the face of death is unique:

> At one moment a particular man may be nothing at all to you and the next you will go through hell for him. No, it is not friendship. The man doesn't matter so much, it's a kind of impersonal emotion, a kind of enthusiasm, in the old sense of the word. Of course one is keyed-up, a bit over-wrought. We help each other. What is one man's fate today, may be another's tomorrow. We are all in it up to the neck together, and we know it. [p. 80]

This middle section of the book involves some scenes of comic relief—contacts with peasants, a spell in the orderly room for Bourne (much to his disgust at its 'cushiness'), the luxury of a bath, drinks in an estaminet, suppers in the town—and a seemingly slight relationship with a French girl. Bourne, inhibited and nervous, always treats women with ceremony, and angrily repulses the too crude advances of a girl in an estaminet. But the demure girl at Bruay, 'with the incomparable sleekness of her black hair' who asks for his help in translating letters from her English soldier lover touches him to an acute jealousy of the other man. Bourne's feeling for the girl blends into a feeling for the shadowy man. The diffuseness of the feeling, the 'aching sensibilities' may cast some light on Manning's own complicated sexuality. Five of the eight Manning siblings did not marry, suggesting a background of problems in sexual life. A sense of a 'past irrevocably lost' pervades the chapter, and when Bourne discusses with Martlow the drunken unhappiness of the boy's gamekeeper father, he offers an unexpected explanation of it: '"I should say, Martlow, that your father had been crossed in love", he said gently'. After the girl rejects his kiss and his declaration of love, the feather-weight affair is over. Yet it remains significant to Bourne, for he reflects about it that: 'In all action a man seeks to realize himself'. (p. 120)

The three friends are transferred to a signals division and the novel begins to move back to the front. As the men prepare for a night march they are swept by excitement, 'even those who feared made the pretence of bravery'. The tragedy of their situation, no longer obscured by the machinery of life behind the lines, becomes plainer. Manning's soldiers on this night, as they march towards the front, so touching in their down-to-earth manner, carry our sympathies back to one of those far-distant nights on the Somme.

> The rhythm of all those tramping feet, slurring the stresses slightly, held him in its curious hypnosis. He was aware of it all only as one might be aware of a dream. The men sang, sang to keep up cheerful hearts:
>> 'ere we are, 'ere we are, 'ere we are, again,
>> Pat and Mac, and Tommy and Jack, and Joe!
>> Never mind the weather! Now then all together!

> Are we down 'eártéd? NO! ('ave a banana!)
> 'ere we are, 'ere we are . . .

> It might have gone on indefinitely, but the men suddenly switched into Cock Robin, into which some voices would interject 'another poor mother 'as lost 'er son,' as though to affront the sinister fate against which they were determined to march with a swagger. As they marched through one little village, at about ten o'clock, doors suddenly opened and light fell through the doorways, and voices asked them where they were going.

> 'Somme! Somme!' they shouted, as though it were a challenge.

> 'Ah, no bon!' came the kindly, pitying voices in reply; and even after the doors closed again, and they had left that village behind, the kindly voices seemed to drift across the darkness, like the voices of ghosts: 'Somme! Ah, no bon!'

> And that was an enemy to them, that little touch of gentleness and kindness; it struck them with a hand harsher than death's, and they sang louder, seeing only the white road before them, and the vague shadows of the trees on either hand. At last the singing died away; there was nothing but the tramping of myriad feet; or they would halt for ten minutes, and the darkness along the roadside became alive as with fireflies from the glow of cigarettes through a low mist. [p. 140]

It is dreamlike, yet it is a nightmare. In such scenes Manning shows his great strength, his combination of realism and sympathy.

The pace becomes swifter as the book moves to its end in the action of another attack. Martlow is killed, and mild Bourne goes berserk, firing at three men running towards him with their hands up:

> the ache in him became a consuming hate that filled him with exultant cruelty, and he fired again, and again . . . 'Kill the buggers!' . . . All the filth and ordure he had ever heard came from between his clenched teeth; but his speech was thick and difficult. In a scuffle immediately afterwards a Hun went for Minton, and Bourne got him with the bayonet, under the ribs near the liver, and then, unable to wrench the bayonet out again, pulled the trigger, and it came away easily enough. 'Kill the buggers!' he muttered thickly. [p. 217)

The special comradeship has been broken. 'They had been three people without a single thing in common; and yet there was no bond stronger than the necessity that had bound them together.' (p. 232) Shem, who has suffered a minor wound, is moved on; but Martlow, lingering in Bourne's memory, 'seemed to be only out of sight, behind the hut as it were, or even just on the point of coming through the doorway'. Bourne must now go on alone. His Colonel promotes him to lance-corporal and recommends him for a commission, but an aggressive officer sends Bourne on a night-raid soon after and he is killed. Private Weeper Smart, ugly, uncouth, melancholy and previously so antagonistic to gentlemanly Bourne, insists on carrying back the dead body, and the book ends with a return to this mysterious comradeship of soldiers. Phlegmatic, fatalistic Sergeant Tozer provides the final epitaph:

[He] moved away with a quiet acceptance of the fact. It was finished. He was sorry about Bourne, more sorry than he could say. He was a queer chap, he said to himself, as he felt for the dug-out steps. There was a bit of a mystery about him; but then, when you come to think of it there's a bit of a mystery about all of us. He pushed aside the blanket screening the entrance and in the murky light he saw all the men lift their faces and look at him with patient, almost animal eyes.

Then they all bowed over their own thoughts again, listening to the shells thumping heavily outside, as Fritz began to send a lot of stuff over in retaliation for the raid. They sat there silently, each man keeping his own secret. [p. 247]

By returning to the troops for his ending Manning moves the focus back from the personal to the general tragedy, and to the mysterious individuality within that generality. His hero is not so much Bourne, as the ordinary man as soldier. As he wrote in his Preface: '. . . my concern has been mainly with the anonymous ranks . . .' Manning's use of Shakespearian epigraphs emphasizes his point that the soldier, for good or bad, is an eternal figure. The men of the Westshires, civilian volunteers, are as much soldiers as those who fought in the Wars of the Roses, as much part of English history. Soldiers' concerns and emotions do not change much over the centuries; there is the loving nostalgia for home and family in the heading of Chapter 2:

> But I had not so much man in me,
> And all my mother came into mine eyes
> And gave me up to tears.[7]

There is the dislike of petty authority, of 'an idle and fond bondage in the oppression of aged tyranny'[8] represented by the orderly room; and there is the great, ever present fear: 'We see yonder the beginning of day, but I think we shall never see the end of it . . . I am afeard there are few die well that die in a battle'.[9]

To the civilian in day-to-day life, death is far off, something that happens to 'them', to be read about in the obituary columns. To the soldier facing battle the prospect is immediate, and continual. War underlines the fact that young men are as mortal as old. As Manning writes: 'There is an extraordinary veracity in war which strips man of every conventional covering he has, and leaves him to face a fact as naked and inexorable as himself'. In civilian life, after a death, after a funeral and the grieving, the bereaved move back into the seeming immortality of daily life. The soldier, on active service, continues to confront the inevitable reality. Paul Fussell says that Manning recognized death in war as 'a figure for the death sentence which is life'.[10] Remarque was reaching towards Manning's view when he wrote, in *All Quiet on the Western Front*: 'war is a cause of death like cancer and tuberculosis, like influenza and dysentery, the deaths are merely more frequent, more varied and more terrible'. (p. 229).

Fussell dubs Manning a proto-existentialist. It is possible to see some resemblances between the attitudes of the Australian writer and the Algerian existentialist novelist, Albert Camus (1913–60), in *The Plague*. The writers have a similar sensibility, blending tough-mindedness with solicitude, and have a similar concern with ultimate realities. Both were provincials drawn to the metropolis who, despite their talents, felt not quite accepted there and remained somewhat at the edge of their mainstream culture. Camus always felt himself one of the poor *pieds-noirs*, a French Algerian; Manning thought of himself as without a country. Both writers are deeply concerned with the problem of the sufferings of the innocent in an apparently cruel and senseless existence. Camus, an atheist and totally different in personality, is more despairing of the absurd world than Manning, who held a kind of mystical belief in the possibility of God. Both find the answer to the terrors and sorrows of existence in the sympathy of one human being for another, and in an admiration for the nobility and endurance of humanity, the heroism of ordinary people. Dr Rieux, when the terrible ordeal of *The Plague* is over,

> resolved to compile this chronicle, so that he should not be one of those who hold their peace but should bear witness in favour of those plague-stricken people; so that some memorial of the injustice and outrage done them might endure; and to state quite simply what we learn in a time of pestilence: that there are more things to admire in men than to despise. [p. 251]

The words might be applied as fittingly to Manning's book.

Bernard Bergonzi also sees in some of Manning's reflective passages 'something of the tragic vision of some existentialist philosophers'.[11] Manning, absorbed in the mystery of war, as well its horror and sadness, reflects on the nature of freedom and self and will. Astonishingly, for a soldier, he finds in the midst of battle a resurgence of individualism, a heightened awareness of being. 'Life was a hazard enveloped in mystery and war quickened the sense of both in men.' (p. 76) The clear-sightedness of his psychological perception is on a par with his accurate reflection of physical reality.

> The mystery of his own being increased for him enormously and he had to explore that doubtful darkness alone, a foothold here, a handhold there, grasping one support after another and relinquishing it when it yielded, crumbling; the sudden menace of ruin, as it slid into the insubstantial past, calling forth another effort, to gain another precarious respite. If a man could not be certain of himself, he could be certain of nothing. The problem which confronted them all equally, though some were unable or unwilling to define it, did not concern death so much as affirmation of their own will in the face of death; and once the nature of the problem was clearly stated, they realised that its solution was continuous and could never be final. [p. 184]

As a philosopher, Bourne-Manning can retreat into his mind and find some comfort there. He moves, however, between the philosophic and human planes, and is mindful of the agonizing plight of his more physical companions.

> Whether it were justified or not, however, the sense of being at the disposal of some inscrutable power, using them for its own ends and utterly indifferent to them as individuals was perhaps the most tragic element in the men's present situation. It was not much use telling them that war was only the ultimate problem of all human life stated barely, and pressing for an immediate solution. [pp. 181-2]

Nevertheless, Manning remained convinced that 'war is in the nature of things', as he had written to Will Rothenstein from the midst of the battlefield (10 November 1916), while admitting that if he were an orthodox Christian this war would have shattered his belief in Christianity. He repeated the belief in his Preface to the novel: 'War is waged by men, not by beasts or by gods. It is a peculiarly human activity. To call it a crime against humanity is to miss at least half its significance; it is also the punishment of a crime'. Richard Aldington reacted against this view in typically passionate fashion:

> That sounds like a reminiscence of a wartime sermon by the Rev. Arthur Galton. What conceivable crime needing so fearful an expiation could have been committed by millions of young men of different nations who suffered and were slain in a struggle for prestige so futile that its apologists are forced into defending it because it Europeanised Turkey.[12]

Manning is not concerned, however, with justifying that war. He felt as deeply as anybody about the tragedy involved. His point is the pessimistic one that human nature is such that we fall into catastrophe, because we are imperfect in reason and emotion. As he wrote in his note on Dean Inge: 'The future is not determined by reason; but reason and those obscure reactions to circumstances which we call instincts, are molten together, precipitated into the incoherent effects of action, by a sudden passion of the will'.[13] That he was pessimistic about humanity's ability to avoid war did not mean that he did not abhor it. E. M. Forster's view, that Manning had no faith in civilization and regarded peace as an interlude and war as the only reality through which alone humanity's deeper nature is involved, is a misunderstanding of the man, a turning on their head of all values by which he lived. Manning was by no means the nihilist that Forster accused him of being. Indeed Forster, with the fixation on sudden death in his novels, could be said to be the one more fascinated by destruction. Even in a post-war story, 'The Purple Envelope', Forster wrote: 'And Howard loved to take life, as all those do who are really in touch with nature'. The life involved is animal, but the touches of cruelty and blood-lust, as a kind of life-giving force, are there.

To Manning the destruction of nature and culture, youth and beauty, the death of the simplest soldier, was as much an abomination as it was to

Forster. He was not, however, a progressive. He did not believe that civilization inevitably became better and better. As an intellectual and an aesthete
he believed that Prussian militarism would damage European civilization
and freedom. Like Hulme he believed that there were causes worth fighting
for, and, if hindsight disagreed with his judgement of the situation that did
not alter the fact that, like so many other idealistic, adventurous young
men of that time, he was willing to hazard his life for his belief. The
realities of service, however, soon destroyed any romantic notions of heroism. Bourne watches with a sardonic grin as an army carpenter makes
wooden crosses, inscribed with the motto of the regiment, 'Where glory
leads'. And, as Manning writes of his fellow soldiers:

> It was useless to contrast the first challenging enthusiasm which had swept
> them into the army, with the long and bitter agony they endured afterwards. It
> was the unknown which they had challenged; and when the searching flames
> took hold of their very flesh, the test was whether or not they should flinch
> under them . . . We can stick it, they said. [p. 201]

When, from time to time the men discuss their attitudes to the war, despite
their disillusionment they are united in their contempt for conscientious
objectors and deserters, especially one of their own, the slippery Corporal
Miller. Why should he evade the fight when they have to go through it?
They distrust civilians, journalists and politicians, and abominate most
staff officers and brass hats; 'magnificent people on horses glancing
superciliously at the less fortunate members of their species whom necessity compelled to walk'. (p. 164) Yet they admire most of the officers of the
line, who share their peril; and for all their resentment and despair tend to
agree that 'The Fritzies had to be stopped'.

There is no talk of honour and glory and patriotism among them. Private Madely, who had a fight with a miner when home on leave, is fighting
for himself and his own folk, 'not a lot of bloody civvies . . . Say they be
ready to make any sacrifice but we're the bloody sacrifice . . . You'd think
your best friends wouldn't be satisfied till they seed your name on the roll
of honour'. A few, like Sergeant Tozer and Private Pacey are fatalistic: 'If
we die, we die an' it won't trouble nobody, leastways not for long it won't;
an' if we don't die now, we'd 'ave to die some other time'.

This sort of philosophizing does not appeal to the younger soldiers.
'"What d'you want to talk about dyin' for?" said Martlow resentfully. "I'd
rather kill some other fucker first. I want to have my fling before I die, I
do".' Friendless, unhappy Weeper Smart has the simplest approach to their
predicament: 'Ah tell thee, that all a want to do is to save me own skin'.
Weeper despises the brass hats for their lack of imagination, their lack of
understanding of the men, and accepts that he is in a situation that has no
solution: 'All that a says is, if a man's dead it don't matter no more to 'im
'oo wins the bloody war . . . We're 'ere, there's no gettin' away from that,
Corporal. 'Ere we are, an' since we're 'ere we're just fightin' for ourselves,

we're just fightin' for ourselves an' for each other'. And when Weeper, the antithesis of the romantic hero, brings back Bourne's body, he becomes the final symbol of the comradeship which binds them all.

The comradeship of soldiers, their special feeling for one another, raises the question of homosexuality in their relationships. The English officer, Charles Carrington, looking back over forty years could not remember any scandal or misconduct among the troops he knew in the Great War. Martin Boyd recalled much talk of 'lovely boys' but no actual homosexuality as far as he was aware.[14] But, cut off from the company of women, living in intimate circumstances in a situation of dire extremity, there was obviously a good deal of what Paul Fussell has called 'homoeroticism', a generalized feeling of man for man. And the tragedy of the young soldier touched older men especially. But *Her Privates We*, for all its soldiers' language, is a chaste book. Bourne's aching tenderness for the French girl, his affection for 'the kid', are matters of the most delicate sensitivity. Manning's reserve and fastidiousness—perhaps a heritage of Irish puritanism—mean that he refers to sexual problems in only a generalized way.

He observes that the men swing between a sticky sentimentality and a rank obscenity and he registers, with some distaste, an awareness of the desperate, carnal mood in an estaminet. He makes the point that 'In the shuddering revulsion from death one turns instinctively to love as an act which seems to affirm the completeness of being. In the trenches the sense of this privation vanished . . .' (p. 50) There, the great imperative is survival.

And survival, for soldiers, resolves into kill or be killed. For Martin Boyd's Dominic Langton killing becomes the impossible thing. Manning analyses reactions to the dilemna with his usual scrupulous honesty. Among Bourne's fellow soldiers some are more callous than others.

> Glazier was the kind of person who killed automatically, without premeditation or remorse, but Weeper was a very different type. He dreaded the thought of killing and was haunted by the memory of it; and yet there was a kind of fatalism in him now as though he were the instrument of justice . . . He knew that the others, including perhaps Bourne himself, did not face the reality of war squarely. They refused to think of it, except when actually involved in battle, and such thought as they had then did not extend beyond the instant action, being scarcely more than a spontaneous and irreflective impulse; but most of them had made their decision once and for all, and were willing to abide by the consequences, without reviewing it. [p. 201]

Manning does not shirk the fact that even in seemingly civilized men there may be strange reactions in the heat of battle, as in Bourne's passion after the death of Martlow. In the fear, the tension, the fury of an attack, an extraordinary emotion approaching exultation can emerge mysteriously, in 'a tempest of excitement'.

The effort and rage in him, the sense that others had left them to it, made him pant and sob, but there was some strange intoxication of joy in it, and again all his mind seemed focused into one hard bright point of action. The extremities of pain and pleasure had met and coincided too. [p. 215]

Even so, such psychologically centred passages are very different from the pleasure Jünger, for example, takes in describing fighting, or the passion for blood and violence permeating some of non-combatant William Baylebridge's stories in *An Anzac Muster.*

But while Manning does not shirk the moral problem and the suffering and the horror of war, he is aware of its 'myriad faces', of the nobility to be seen as well as the evil in the worst of situations, of 'the spiritual thing which lived and seemed even to grow stronger in the midst of beastliness'. (p. 141) *Her Privates We* is, in a sense, a statement of faith in humanity, which is one reason for Peter Davies's description of it in the Foreword to the 1943 edition as 'profoundly democratic'. It is democratic beyond the aspects of Australian egalitarianism already noted, which are similar to those in the war novels of Australians Leonard Mann and J. P. McKinney. Most great English war books gain their strength from the deeply felt experience of sensitive officers who saw the men largely as their responsibility, not as comrades. Ford Madox Ford's Tietjens views them with a dash of *noblesse oblige.* Sassoon and Graves, a captain at twenty, were both young, brave officers, so conscious of their responsibilities to the ordinary soldiers that they decided not to make public their protest at the horrors of war, so that their men should have a friend in command rather than 'a petty tyrant in an officer's uniform'.[15] Even Aldington's hero, middle-class George Winterbourne, who feels a deep admiration for the rankers, is shocked by the fact that a Canadian officer shares a latrine with his men and is censorious about 'scrounging'. But Manning took on the true colour of the ranks, made friends there, shared their life, however odd a private he might have been. And his real hero is the common man, free of class and even of nationality:

These apparently rude and brutal natures, comforted, encouraged and reconciled each other to fate, with a tenderness and tact which was more moving than anything in life. They had nothing; not even their own bodies, which had become mere implements of warfare. They turned from the wreckage and misery of life to an empty heaven, and from an empty heaven to the silence of their own hearts. They had been brought to the last extremity of hope and yet they put their hands on each other's shoulders and said with a passionate conviction that it would be all right, though they had faith in nothing, but in themselves and in each other. [p. 205]

To sharp observation, psychological realism, intellectual depth and artistic form Manning added this genuine feeling for his fellows, so that his novel has earned acclaim as a classic. As the critic Andrew Rutherford wrote:

Honesty, inclusiveness, psychological and moral insight, and the accurate notation of experience are all desiderata in war literature, but they are not sufficient in themselves: they must be combined with the search for an appropriate form and the struggle to articulate through this the author's complex vision of the truth. Such a combination is achieved most notably by Frederic Manning in *The Middle Parts of Fortune*, a novel which must rank as one of the masterpieces of war literature in English.[16]

21

Crowned With Laurels

After thirty years of devotion and effort, Frederic Manning, at the age of forty-seven, had produced a popular success, which was also a great work of literature. Most of the reviews were extremely favourable. Arnold Bennett said he thought this inspiring and beautiful book would be remembered when *All Quiet on the Western Front*, with all its excellences, was forgotten. The ex-officer reviewer of the *Times Literary Supplement*, despite his 'jolly good show chaps' tone, was percipient enough, as war books poured from the presses, to seize on this one as special. 'So many books have been written about the Great War that it were rash to prophesy undying fame for this; we can at least say that any similar book on a former war would have taken its place as a classic of its kind.' He called it 'probably the best and honestest description of life in the ranks during the war that has appeared in English' (16 January 1930).

Australian expatriate Eric Partridge, a veteran of Gallipoli and the Western Front, hedged his bets less. To him it was considerably better than Remarque's work and uncontradictably the best English war novel. 'If Manning never writes another book his fame is secure'.[1] *The Times* (17 January 1930), the *Spectator* (25 January 1930) and *John o' London's* (8 March 1930) all thought it the best thing so far, and the latter described it as 'the work of a rare mind, a mind big enough to see it all dispassionately as a historian and yet able to describe human character with admiration and sympathy'. *The London Mercury* (February 1930) said two things would be certain about what would make the great war book: 'it will be a work of fiction and it will be written by a soldier in the trenches'. Manning's book qualified under those rules. The oddest comment appeared in the *Bookman* (February 1930) which saw in the novel 'a suggestion of Jane Austen'.

Peter Davies's device of anonymity for the author made an extra talking point. There was much speculation. Who was this mysterious private? Was he Mr A. E. Coppard, Mr Siegfried Sassoon, Mr J. B. Priestley, Mr H. M.

Tomlinson, or even the great Colonel Lawrence himself? (This last was an unlikely solution, one would have thought, seeing the book was set on the Somme.) According to the *New Statesman* (22 February 1930) he must be 'a cultured, sophisticated, observant gentleman'; while the *Nation* (16 July 1930) could see plainly that he was a product of the English public schools. Richard Aldington, who had received a copy for review, later said he had no difficulty in interpreting the clues: the name Bourne, and the habit of chain-smoking. But he kept silent on the matter. Will Rothenstein, who knew Manning's army number, was not sent a copy in case he might let the secret out. In the publicity surrounding the work the authorship could not be kept hidden for long. *John o' London's* (March 1930) ripped away the mask and ran an interview with the shy author, given on one of his infrequent visits to London, which earned a small report in his home town (*Sydney Morning Herald* 18 March 1930, p. 11).

Manning, who had been in Austria and who had been very ill again in February, retreated to the Bull Inn in quiet Bourne. In March 1930, while taking pleasure in all the praise he was at last receiving, he could also have amused himself there reading the controversy that had erupted in *John o' London's.rom* on the topic of war books. In an article headed 'These Abominable War Books' (22 February) Lady Ingram had complained that too much accurate detail was 'rather bad form'. An irate ex-serviceman replied: 'I have never heard of any old soldier who had a word to say against either *Undertones [of War]* or *Her Privates We*'; but Sir J. C. Reith (15 March) shared Lady Ingram's indignation. 'Why libel the soldier?' he asked. In this context soldier meant officer; and a set of letters supported him. After a year of enthusiasm the public had become somewhat sated. Manning had been a little unlucky in the timing, for, while sales were satisfactory, a year earlier the book would have been a sensation, as the *Spectator* remarked.

A boredom with all the fuss about soldiers was clear in the review in the *Nation and Athenaeum* (25 January 1930), which chose to treat the whole subject facetiously, saying that *Her Privates We* and *All Our Yesterdays* seemed to be the best war novels published since Christmas. The others must have been execrable for the reviewer continued:

> It reminds one of the Bairnsfather cartoons of the *entente cordiale* type of stories that used to circulate about French peasants and French cats, and it also reminds one strongly of Marryat, Reade and Ballantyne. Bourne, the private, is the modest, pleasant, resourceful hero of all boys' adventure stories, just as at home on the Somme as he used to be among the South Sea Islands or the Canadian prairies . . . As a whole the book attempts very little and achieves rather less than it attempts.

On reading this airy dismissal (had the reviewer really read the book, one wonders, or just flipped over the pages?) an angry Private Kimber fired a counterblast. He found the remarks of the reviewer 'simply astonishing'.

Bourne, he wrote, resembled the hero of boys' adventure stories about as much as the bullring at Étaples resembled a high school for young ladies. He found the book exactly true in tone. 'The remark about Bairnsfather, for instance, is ludicrous—in spirit the book is about as far removed from the barbaric yawpings of the Bairnsfather cartoons as Shaw's wit is from the wit of a die-hard admiral.' The reviewer replied but was routed by another puzzled reader, who had been wary of the review of *Her Privates We* because he had been put off Ernest Hemingway's *A Farewell to Arms* by the same reviewer. Having subsequently come across the Hemingway novel and read it, he was now determined to get his hands on a copy of Manning's book. The Bairnsfather comparison was enough to arouse one's suspicions about the reviewer. Dubbed 'The Man who Made the Empire Laugh' Bairnsfather made a reputation, in the early years of the war, with low comedy cartoons about the trenches which assured the civilian population that the lads were having a laughter-laden time: 'shut that blinkin' door, there's a 'ell of a draught in 'ere' says the Tommy occupant of a bombed out, roofless building on the western front.[2]

Bourne is, indeed, a little too good to be true, a little too wise, too idealized, too sententious at times; his manner of speech is often stilted and his good temper may be a bit unbelievable. His reflections, however, are not those of a *Boy's Own Paper* adventurer. It was true, also, that the public appetite had become jaded. In an effort to refresh it and to make more sales, Peter Davies issued a free pamphlet containing extracts from reviews. His trump card was an endorsement by the greatest hero of the war in the popular mind. In 1918–19 American Lowell Thomas had given a brilliant series of lectures—which became the book *With Lawrence in Arabia* (1925)—which enshrined Lawrence as a public idol.

T. E. Lawrence, while reading Manning's book standing up in Bumpus bookshop, had intuited the authorship, and had rung Davies. 'I want to congratulate you as strongly as possible on *Her Privates We*', he had said. 'It's magnificent, a book in a thousand. You've published a masterpiece. But tell me this. How did you get Frederic Manning to write it?' Davies, impressed by the fame of the caller, replied: 'Of course, you're right. Only do please keep the secret or I'm lost'.[3] Lawrence promised not to tell a soul, and he offered to write a puff for it, which ran: 'No praise could be too sheer for this book. I am sure it is the book of books so far as the British Army-in-the-War is concerned'. He had read *Scenes and Portraits* at least fifty times, he claimed, and was sure that the man who wrote that book was the only man who could possibly have written *Her Privates We*.[4] Davies called Lawrence's deduction 'the most remarkable piece of literary detective work'[5] he had ever known. Manning showed himself a little shrewder when he asked Lawrence if he had the information about the authorship from Rothenstein.[6] It is possible, though, that Lawrence may have remembered some details from an earlier meeting with Manning which put him on the track.

He and Manning had met soon after the war at Rothenstein's London house, where, according to the host, although often reticent about the Arabian campaign, the great hero was preparing to open up on it, when the usually shy Manning broke in to talk about his own war experiences. His intervention may have owed something to the widespread feeling among those who had fought in France that the real war had been neglected by the public in favour of the glamour of the desert campaign. Young John Rothenstein (who was present) thought Manning showed only a perfunctory interest in the great man. On the other hand, Manning acknowledged later that he had felt in rapport with Lawrence very quickly.[7] Perhaps he had been trying to impress this famous figure whose career had been so different. Manning returned to the obscurity of Edenham after the meeting, to his struggle with declining health and lack of money, and other problems; Lawrence continued his strange and unpredictable life.

In his unhappiness after the death of Galton, Manning had tried to turn the acquaintanceship into a friendship. In March 1922 he had written from Edenham, mentioning Rothenstein's name, inviting Lawrence to a quiet weekend. He had held out the inducement of his books and a comfortable room, well-furnished with his own possessions, though he admitted he was in temporary quarters and the rest of the house was rather primitive. Lawrence did not come for he was about to visit Baghdad, and Manning asked for '*anything* from Uruk'.[8] Lawrence was still in the great world at that stage. Manning had tried again later in March, promising to send the romance which he was sure Lawrence would like as much as *Scenes and Portraits*. Again he was disappointed, and the elusive Lawrence disappeared from his life until the success of the war book in 1930.

Manning may have been hurt that his overtures had been ignored. He had obtained Lawrence's address from a mutual friend, Apsley Cherry-Garrard, a rich, short-sighted adventurer and explorer, who had survived Captain Scott's tragic polar expedition when Scott sent him back to base because of his youth. But Manning did not try to make contact again in the 1920s. Lawrence, throughout the upheavals in his own life during that decade, nevertheless retained an admiration for Manning's work and praised *Scenes and Portaits* to E. M. Forster.[9] In the same letter he mentioned another piece of Manning's work that he had seen, on life seen through the eyes of an organ-grinder's monkey.

About the time of Manning's first overtures of friendship Lawrence was approaching the nervous breakdown which led to his seeking obscurity in the ranks. After all the publicity, all the praises heaped upon him, quite a few survivors of the trenches, though not at this time Aldington—a future debunker of the heroic legend—were not impressed by the showiness of Lawrence's war: the Arab dress, the golden dagger, the intriguing with princes and sheiks in exotic surroundings, the brigandish individuality which contrasted so much with the mass slaughter on the western front. His first period in the ranks was brief. His identity was exposed soon by

missed from the R.A.F. in a blaze of publicity. Later that year he joined the
Tank corps, again as a ranker, under the name of Shaw. Ascetic, masochistic, non-drinking, non-smoking, basically power-focused Lawrence—an
extraordinary achiever in worldly terms—was an unlikely friend for retiring, Epicurean Manning, so fond of the small pleasures of life.

Whether in hiding or not, Lawrence remained the country's idol, and a
friend of the great. He kept in touch with Winston Churchill, Lady Astor
and Austen Chamberlain, and was given still to stories of high political
intrigue. He was friendly with famous writers, with Thomas Hardy and
John Buchan; and especially with the George Bernard Shaws, and E. M.
Forster. But Richard Aldington, who disliked Lawrence and his legend
intensely and who thought he had some cause to be angry with Manning,
later wrote: 'Yes, Manning was a friend of TEL but after I ceased to know
him'. Having given an angry outline of the troubles over the White book he
concluded: 'I look on him as a suitable Friend for T.E.L.'.[10] Aldington was
disillusioned with both men, but the letters exchanged later by Lawrence
and Manning show respect for each other's work, and personal liking and
understanding. Will Rothenstein thought Lady Manning was very hurt at
Lawrence's initial silence after Fred's death, 'for she knew of the friendship
between the two'.[11] Such friendship was, however, obviously more important to Manning than to Lawrence.

After Lawrence's piece of detective work on the authorship the two took
up an acquaintance again, being reintroduced by Peter Davies. Manning
thanked Lawrence for his praise and Lawrence replied (21 March 1930):

Dear Manning,

The worst thing about fame, I think, is that in a few years steady experience
of it the victim begins to believe it, against the sure and certain knowledge of his
own heart. And then he's a living lie.

But cheer up. Your next book if it is an introduction to Epicurus or Epictetus
or Epaminondas will not sell fourteen editions or increase your fame. You are
happy: you can dodge it by going on being yourself. The fame was won
altogether honestly and on the square, too, by an anonymous book. I envy you
the cleanliness of your scoop.

The praises are very nice, even when you don't believe them, as you obviously
don't! One would, I think like them to be true! It was always an ambition of
mine to write a good book—only one as if anyone could write only one unless
he died instantly after his first—and I've had try after try at it. The stuff is like
a bar of washing soap: cut it through anywhere and it's just soap.

I think your book, because of its hastiness of form and maturity of design will
live a very long time. One gets impatient with the signs of too much working
e.g. George Moore, and says: 'If the blighter was any good he'd get on with
something else and stop fidgeting with this.' Whereas your book couldn't have
had 10 minutes less spent on it without losing. And your dialogue and sense of
character is very fine. It's by what your people say that they live.

I have read it once more since last time, and everybody in the hut seems to
have read it. Bad for royalties, that: but I enjoy lending a good thing.

Are you staying in England? It would be rather fun if we could meet: only

Plymouth is so far and so dreary a hole, and my lesiure's too slight to let me far away from it. If you are here till the summer we might manage it. I shall think more of your Epicurus then, and less of your privates. You see, I live cheek by jowl with the privates. They are very honest and cleanly people, I fancy. If I can get my copy of it back, I'll try to persuade you to look at some notes I made in 1922 upon life in the R.A.F. as a recruit. I wasn't cheerful like Bourne, but had a rotten time, and so my story is dismal: only I think it is true as far as it goes.

Yours

T. E. Shaw

This generous, friendly letter from the great man of the age was the highest accolade that Manning could receive. He had missed much in friendship since Galton's death, and this understanding from a fellow intellectual who was a peerless man-of-action was a compensation for the hard, lonely years of the 1920s, for his sense of being neglected and out-moded. He had also regained some status as a writer and now aimed to crown the triumph of the war book with the completion of the romance, which Peter Davies was anxious to publish. But the book which had taken so many years of effort and life was never to be finished. Pound called what he saw of it 'delicious', and there were even rumours that he might edit the fragments. T. S. Eliot, while unable to accept it for Faber, wrote in a letter to A. V. Moore (27 March 1949) that it was delightful and worth publishing, and wondered if someone might do a memoir of Manning. Alister Kershaw, writing to Moore (27 March 1949) found what he had read of it 'bewitching'. He was working at the time as secretary to Aldington, and on a bibliography of Aldington's work. He did what he could to get Manning's 'Gilded [or as Manning called it 'Golden'] Coach' published by the publisher of the bibliography. There were other attempts to bring the unfinished manuscript to publication. The fragments that remain of it show it to be closer in style, however, to *Scenes and Portraits* than to the war novel.[12] The extant pages are somewhat too mannered, too subtle, too lacking in pace, too precious, for modern tastes despite their wit and irony. They also lack development and remain a tantalizing curiosity. In 1930, however, Manning, happy in his success, was determined to carry this unfinished work through. He was in very poor health, but the faith that both Peter Davies and T. E. Lawrence had in him acted as an extra spur.

22

Persephone's Realm

THERE SEEMED little reason, superficially, for the swash-buckling, mysterious adventurer and the reticent aesthete to become friends. On the part of obscure Manning there must have been pleasure at being praised and befriended by one of the great; Lawrence, darling of the public and of great names, had apparently less to gain. Yet he wrote: 'I think Frederic Manning and an Armenian called Altounyan and E. M. Forster are the three I most care for since Hogarth died'.[1] They responded to each other, were in sympathy in a rootless loneliness. Both were outside the mainstream of English society: Manning because of his colonial and Irish origins; Lawrence, also of Irish descent, because of his illegitimacy. Lawrence had felt an odd man out at Oxford, and, like Manning, in the officers' mess.[2] Both owed much to an older mentor. The archaeologist D. C. Hogarth had noticed Lawrence's promise as a schoolboy, then had encouraged him to study Arabic and given him his first job on the British Museum dig at Charchemis on the Euphrates in 1911. Both Manning and Lawrence were scholarly bachelors with a marked dependence also on a mother-figure, though elderly Charlotte Shaw and charming Eva Fowler had little in common. Dominating, terrifying, strong-willed Sarah Lawrence was also of a different stamp to loving Honora Manning. Jeffrey Meyers has grouped both men with E. M. Forster and James Hanley as homosexual writers, apparently because of Lawrence's friendship with E. M Forster and Hanley, and Manning's quite separate friendship with Lawrence. There is no evidence for assuming this to be part of their relationship. 'By repute,' wrote Manning (26 March 1930) to Lawrence, or Shaw, as he now called him, 'I am supposed to be many things which I know I am not . . .' He may have been referring to Aldington's charges, including dipsomania, or to some speculation about his relationship with Galton, or just to some political views. In his own way he could be as secretive and elusive as Lawrence.

What strengthened their acquaintance, initially, was their common experience of being intellectuals who had served in the ranks. Both were intent on examining the mystery lying beneath action: Lawrence trying to come to terms with himself, with his demanding ego; Manning, even more hopelessly, was trying to come to terms with the puzzle of existence. The meeting of minds was the theme of Lawrence's letters and he was content with the friendship on that basis. When Manning wrote from Semmering, Austria (11 February 1930), to thank Lawrence for 'the magnificent generosity' of his praise of the war book, and suggested they should meet, Lawrence replied (25 February): 'As for the authorship of the book—the preface gives it away. It is pure *Scenes and Portraits*', but he regretted that he could not get to London to see Manning. So strange himself, he found quiet Manning 'so queer'. Reserved, aloof Manning so modest and so totally devoted to the arts, was a puzzle to the posturing, physical man of action, who wrote of him to the historian B. H. Liddell Hart: 'an exquisite and an exquisite writer. I wonder how he really got on in the ranks. Too fine a mind, I think, for real contact'.[3] Yet Lawrence was agreeable that Peter Davies should use his 'dregs of reputation' to promote sales of the 'love poem', the tribute to the men, which, he claimed, he had read twice already. The contrast between the aesthete and the common soldier intrigued him, and he wrote to Will Rothenstein: 'Wasn't it delightful to find Manning coming out so suddenly as a real flesh-and-blood figure. Beautiful as are "Scenes" and "Epicurus", ever so much more worth while is "Her Privates We"'.[4] Did Lawrence find it more worth while, one wonders, because it was more successful? He admired some popular war books which have not survived at all. He did, however, allot first place to Sassoon in the genre and had pithily summed up the strength of Manning's book: 'hastiness of form and maturity of design'.

Manning sent Lawrence a copy of his *Epicurus*, and again suggested they should meet. Lawrence, however, remained elusive, and although the pair corresponded for about five years meetings were few. Lawrence agreed that it would be fun to meet, but then found reasons for not doing so. Manning looked forward to seeing his new friend in the summer. Meanwhile, having read and enjoyed *Revolt in the Desert* he was anxious to read the full version. Lawrence lent him one of the very heavy, and very few, copies of the *Seven Pillars of Wisdom*, 'rather like the biggest and most expensive family bible'. Manning's verdict (9 May 1930) was: 'magnificent'. He saw Lawrence's book both as a dramatic narrative and as a riddle. It was more than a great book, he wrote, it was a great experience.

Lawrence's reply (15 May), analysing his actions in the war, was as frank as he ever could be, and he was pleased with the praise from 'one whose writing I so vainly admire'. In late June he offered to send the record of his first service in the R.A.F., *The Mint* (published in 1936), to Manning but he had second thoughts, saying that his notes might be scrappy and arty and incompetent. For whatever reason, he did not send his new friend the account of his unhappy time in the ranks, describing the rage he felt against NCOs and officers, the masochistic testing of his will in physical pain. His emotions were volcanic in contrast to Bourne-Manning's generally calm temperament.

Manning was living in London hotels that summer—his possessions were stored in Harrods—revising *Scenes and Portraits* and adding another chapter, 'Apologia Dei', for a new edition to be published by his friend Peter Davies, for he had quarrelled with the publisher of the first edition, Murray. He found it moved very slowly but by October it was ready for the press.[5] After a bad bout of bronchitis he went to Rome with his mother and from there reported to Will (19 December 1930) that Harper's were to publish an American edition and that sales were satisfactory. He returned to England in early January, spending only a day London because of his health, going instead to Bourne. He assumed that since he had not heard from Lawrence he must be disappointed with the new chapter, which was dedicated to him. E. M. Forster and Bonamy Dobrée gave the new *Scenes and Portraits* good notices;[6] and Manning was especially pleased with Forster's praise, saying he had always liked Forster's work.

The new chapter may well have puzzled Lawrence. In the early stories Manning had been fascinated by the intellectual as a man of action: St Paul, Machiavelli, Thomas Cromwell, Innocent III, Leo XIII; by the combination of mind, will, courage and action. Yet when he paid tribute to Lawrence, he retreated completely into thought. The new chapter had not even the pretence of a story or a setting. God addresses Satan in a monologue on time, the moral grandeur of Job, selfhood and freedom. The existential tone which underlies Manning's war novel is also marked: 'For man's desire is to be free, and freedom implies a choice, which lies between two or more alternatives. In that instant of choice, at the first meeting of the act with the objective world, is the creation of self.'

Manning had turned philosopher; and Bonamy Dobrée used a passage from this 'Apologia Dei' in his *Modern Prose Style* as an illustration of fine style in philosophic writing, comparing Manning's swift, metaphorical style with George Moore's trenchant, unemotive writing in *Principia Ethica*. Having found himself as a novelist of record in *Her Privates We*, Manning now gave rein to the mystical side of his nature:

> In every instant, then, man makes his choice, standing like Adam in a new-created earth; for toward that instant the whole of an illimitable past converges to be changed, and from it stretches the changing creation of an illimitable future. He stands there, and in his heart memory gives birth to desire, and he makes his choice, and the world is changed under his eyes.[7]

There was the occasional flash of the old irony. God remarks: 'I am not greatly interested in theology', and 'it is very necessary that God should be an optimist', but this story was all a little dense and abstract, perhaps, for Lawrence, and the correspondence lapsed for a time. Manning was ill frequently in 1931 and, being unable to work, went to Europe early in July, after a brief stop in London, where, as always, he planned to see the Rothensteins.

In late August he broke the silence with Lawrence on the pretext of having met the war hero's old companion of the desert campaign, now King Feisal of Iraq, at a dinner in St Moritz, given by Sir Francis Humphrys, High Commissioner and Commandant-in-Chief in Iraq. With a King and two Italian royalties present the dinner had the touch of decorative ceremony which delighted him, for where Lawrence had withdrawn from the great world, Manning enjoyed any small contact with it. In St Moritz he met also Emil Ludwig, the German novelist and biographer, and Jakob Wasserman, another German novelist, and took pleasure in arguing with them about Bernard Shaw, whom he had once met.[8]

His health had improved at first in Switzerland for, writing from there (19 August 1931), he told Will that where he had been unable to walk a hundred yards along the flat in England he could now walk two miles, mostly uphill, without difficulty. He returned to England in the late summer, but it was still essential that he avoid London for more than short periods, though he hoped to see Lawrence in town that September. Unhappily for his peace of mind, now that he had made a notable success, he had very little strength for writing. After spending some days with his mother in Surrey, he made his headquarters at the Bull Inn, Bourne. In quiet Lincolnshire, it seemed, he felt most at home and at peace, physically and mentally. While tormented by his inability to finish the romance, he still had fortitude enough to accept the harsh nature of reality. Commenting on the death of the 1890s aesthete Charles Ricketts, he wrote to Rothenstein with a note of criticism: 'Ricketts' aim was to create for himself an illusion which would be more tolerable for him to live in than the real world'.[9]

Apart from the desultory correspondence with Lawrence, a few contacts with other friends, and the supportive presence of his mother, he relied on the Rothenstein family for friendship: lunching with them occasionally, taking an interest in what their children were doing, especially in John's painting. His other good friend, Peter Davies, was taken up with his approaching marriage. Manning's mood was sombre. He shared with Will the feeling that the old world was vanishing in the madness of modern times. He had angered Emil Ludwig by saying 'civilization was being devoured by its rats' and he thought that internationalism was no answer. His war experiences had not made him a pacifist, for he remained sceptical about disarmament: 'A true equilibrium is brought about by every nation developing its utmost strength: weakness leads only to dissolution and chaos'.[10] He also remained conservative in politics, although he maintained there was no longer a Tory party. Ironically enough, he saw some hope in Neville Chamberlain.

Lawrence, having heard from Peter Davies that Manning was ill and trying, unhappily, to write, took up the correspondence again in September 1931. He again praised his friend's works, including 'Apologia Dei':

'Some queer differences in mind between you and me makes you as satisfying a writer, to me, as anyone who has written'. A month later Manning thanked Lawrence for a reference to his poems, 'Kindly even in its implied rebukes'. Sending Christmas and New Year greetings from the Bull Hotel he told Lawrence that poor health and lassitude had prevented him from doing any satisfactory work that year, and that Peter Davies was disappointed. Two more attempts to arrange a meeting came to nothing and it was eighteen months before the correspondence was revived. For Manning, 1932 was another bad year of poor health, loneliness and inability to work. 'They say Manning is unhappy', wrote Lawrence to Rothenstein (20 October 1932) but by this time the object of his belated concern was setting out on his last journey home.

Frederic Manning arrived in Sydney on the *Narkunda* on 30 December 1932, and was pictured in 'Men of the Month'—social pages of the *Home* (1 February 1933)—looking strained and lined. 'Homesickness', he wrote in 'The Golden Coach', 'is one of the frailties of age'. The homecoming should have had a touch of the triumphal, the acclaimed best-selling novelist returning to his native land after many years; but his name, because of his use of the pseudonym, was not known and there was little interest. The *Sydney Morning Herald* interviewed him on the day of his arrival, however, saying he was home on 'a health trip', and enquired as to his literary views on war books. He singled out for praise Jünger's *Storm of Steel* and Edmund Blunden's *Undertones of War*, a perfect choice to illustrate the duality of his own nature; the pride and toughness of the German book, the lyricism and gentleness of the English. As for Australian literature he said he was always disappointed with novels written on Australian life, especially those by non-Australians. He nominated Henry Handel Richardson's *The Fortunes of Richard Mahony* as the best Australian novel. If, to his country's loss, he did not record his own interpretation of Australian life, at least he kept up an interest.

It had been a turbulent year in New South Wales politics. The Labor Premier had opened the Sydney Harbour Bridge in March 1932, but such highlights were few. It had been the year of peak unemployment and depression, and of political dissension over the defaulting by the Labor Government on payments to British bondholders. The political crisis came to a dramatic conclusion when the English Governor dismissed Premier Lang from office in May for breaches of the federal law in the handling of public money. An election followed in June 1932. The government changed and one of the results was that Henry Manning, Fred's elder brother, became Attorney-General of the state. Henry had married Nora Martin, daughter of a distinguished former Premier and Chief Justice, in 1905 and had taken silk in 1929. From being somewhat on the fringe of the Anglo-Saxon establishment in earlier years, the Mannings were now well within it. Young William Charles Wentworth IV, of the distinguished pioneer family, was working as an aide to Henry Manning, and was living beside him and his family in Wentworth Road, Point Piper. This robust young man of twenty-four, with an athlete blue as well as an honours classics degree, found 'Freddy' Manning to be a rather 'funny little man' and elderly. Studious, in bad health, uninterested in the practical and the energetic, Fred lived quietly with his mother in a six storey block of flats, Buckingham, on the corner of Wolseley and Wentworth Roads, Point Piper, opposite his brother's house.

Being a firm Tory and with his brother playing a leading part in New South Wales politics, he had no sympathy for the ousted Premier. When Lang still rode high, before the dismissal, Manning had written to Lawrence (4 January 1932): 'Lang . . . has given us an example of what the application of Shavian theories in political practice may produce. It is a comedy for everyone not involved in it'. But his illness during his long stay in Sydney meant that his interest in both the political drama, and in the sporting drama of the body-line bowling by England in the 1932–33 cricket Test series, which obsessed other citizens, was probably languid, although he talked politics a little with Henry. He saw his family: his mother, his sisters and brothers, his nieces across the way. He studied the form guides, kept careful records of his bets, went to the Randwick races with his mother and Edith and tried his hand at play-writing. (Some manuscripts of plays are in his papers in the Mitchell Library.)

A few friends visited his flat, probably including Carl Kaeppel, the classicist and ex-soldier, who wrote about him later with such affection; and there were a few writers, like Leon Gellert, who knew and admired his work. Patrick White in *Flaws in the Glass* describes the Sydney of the 1930s as a village; he felt alienated in its materialist climate even years later. Manning, who had made his life and friends overseas, who was alone, who had lived for so long in an intellectual milieu, must have felt very isolated in this 'village'. In England he still had some contacts with the life of thought and writing. Here he was an exile in his native city. A studio portrait of around this time shows a haunted, brooding face, as if listening to inner voices. In addition there were personal pressures. It was a difficult and distressing time, with his mother, according to her niece, forever in floods of tears lamenting her sorrows. Lady Manning could see, no doubt, that her favourite child was gravely ill, while Fred was determined to return to England to complete his work.

Sydney, for him, must have remained provincial and intellectually dull, although at the University the radical Professor of Philosophy, John Anderson, was spreading the daring pre-war ideas of Marx and Sorel and Shaw and Joyce. P. R. Stephensen was trying to set up an Australian publishing house, and in Melbourne the Palmers continued their efforts to promote Australian literature. Kenneth Slessor's *Darlinghurst Nights* was published in 1933, as was Frank Dalby Davison's short prose epic about the horses of the desert cavalry charges, *The Wells of Beersheba*. Manning, as a horse lover, should have appreciated that loving *tour de force*. It was very little sustenance for a European-style intellectual. The main charm of Sydney remained its climate and the beauties of its waters and sky. As Manning wrote:

> Yesterday evening was wonderful, quite incredible in fact: the east all delicate mauves and greys and in the west clouds, like burnished copper, barring a sky, that passed through imperceptible shades of difference from palest yellow, and greens, through turquoise, to an absolute peacock blue. I watched it until the moon had changed everything to lead and quicksilver.[11]

Perhaps, unhappily, Frederic Manning felt rejected in his own land—especially after the article in the *Bulletin* (22 March 1933) by Nettie Palmer, which refused to accept Manning as an Australian writer because he had not written on Australian subjects. It was part of the nervous narrowness of the nationalism of the day, for Palmer pays tribute to the quality of his prose writing: 'There's one we'd put in the front rank, if we could really claim him'. She praises the originality and maturity of *Scenes and Portraits*, and the humour, comradeship and courage as well as the ambitious nature of the war book. Although she is aware that Bourne is not really English—'Bourne is given no race, no roots at all, no accent in his voice'—and draws a resemblance in attitude to Leonard Mann's 'almost symbolic' Australian, Jim Blount, she cannot accept Manning as an Australian because in one of his war poems he dwells on the English countryside and the English past. Palmer's wish to be severely honest is admirable but a little pedantic and insular. Success abroad, where one dealt with taboo non-Australian subjects, set in a foreign milieu, did not really count at home.

He left Sydney for the last time early in April 1934. Athough he had been very ill while in Australia, and also on the return voyage and on his arrival in England, by July 1934 Manning was once again in his second home, Lincolnshire, living in Gleneden, Burleigh Road, Bourne. He lodged with Mrs Gladys Gelsthorpe, the married daughter of a former landlord of the Bull Inn, in humble but comfortable circumstances, for, with the expenses of his illness, he was again short of money. It was a simple house, set in a small garden in a dull, provincial street. Nothing here of the beauty of the houses of his childhood, or the charm of the vicarage at Edenham. But his landlady was kind, his wants were simple. His health was now so poor, emphysema complicating his asthma, that he was forced to sleep sitting up. In mid-July he sent out a cry for help, throwing off his cloak of reserve:

> Dear T.E.,
>   Where are you?

Lawrence, who had heard from Peter Davies that Manning had been very ill, was disturbed by his friend's pain and replied saying that he was glad Manning was back. 'Your return makes England feel, somehow, better furnished'—and he promised to pay a visit to Bourne.[12] Manning wrote again in September, but it was not until 16 November that Lawrence wrote:

> Alas, you see it never came off. My visits to Cranwell and Nottingham were postponed—and then came a sudden transfer to this unfashionable winter resort. I wander about a large garage and watch ten R.A.F. boats being reconditioned. A tricksy, unsatisfying job, for however done, they could be done better. My motor bike remains in far-off Dorsetshire as Homer would say. Peter Davies wrote to me that you were still consumed with a longing to write that old book which has so often refused to come to you. I beg of you, don't. Copy the poise and equal mind of E. M. Forster, whose every book is acclaimed by the highbrows as a masterpiece, and yet who refrains successfully from ever deliberately achieving another. There are so many books and you have written two of the best of them. To covet a third is greedy. Don't be a book-hog. Read something instead . . . please don't do violence to yourself for some fancied reader's sake. You have your spacious and upholstered niche in our literature. Rest in it.

However well-meaning and sensible such advice was, it could only have added to Manning's misery. Forster was so famous, with the acclaim accorded *A Passage to India* added to that for his earlier novels; Manning was still unknown. A month later Manning wished his friend a merry Christmas and a happy new year with a smile at his own narrow life, and its low-key style: 'Personally I enjoy more an unpremeditated feast and perhaps feel more at home with a bun on Good Friday'. He hoped to be in London early in January. 'I shall be there alone', he wrote, with the implied invitation. It was a last opportunity for the friends to meet. Manning was now extremely ill with respiratory troubles. An oxygen cylinder became part of the furniture of his room and he was under the continuous care of a local doctor, Dr Alistair Galletly. Yet he still struggled to write, to finish the old romance. Endurance and determination were still his, however close the end.

In early February he was suffering from flu and spent some days in a Bourne hospital. He returned home, but then pneumonia struck and his condition became so critical that he was rushed by car to a London nursing home, at 12 Merton Road, Hampstead. He died there of bronchopneumonia and bronchial asthma on Friday 22 February 1935, aged fifty-two. His mother and his sister Edith who had been in England since October were deeply distressed. Perhaps because he had been so ill for so long his death came unexpectedly to his friends. Will Rothenstein, who had been in the country for the weekend, was shocked to hear from his wife on his return that Manning had died. No notice had appeared in the press so he telephoned *The Times* and dictated an obituary. He also telegraphed Lawrence, urging him to supplement it. But Lawrence was then out of contact, travelling by motor cycle after his discharge from the R.A.F. and planning, so he said, to visit Manning in Bourne.

Writing to Peter Davies on 28 February Lawrence explained what had

happened and mourned his friend quietly: 'Some friends of mine in dying
have robbed me . . . Doughty, Hardy and Manning had earned their release.
Yet his going takes away a person of great kindness, exquisite and
pathetic. It means one rare thing the less in our setting. You will be very
sad'.

He was sorry for poor, sick, fastidious Manning, slaving away stringing
words together. 'That's what being a born writer means, I suppose. And
today it is all over and nobody ever heard of him'. Yet he had been fond of
Manning in his own way.

> I suppose his being not really English, and so generally ill, barred him from his
> fellows. Only not in *Her Privates We* which is hot-blooded and familiar. It is puz-
> zling. How I wish, for my own sake, that he hadn't slipped away in this fashion;
> but how like him. He was too shy to let anyone tell him how good he was.

Lawrence was depressed after his discharge, feeling at a loss, and
Manning's death accentuated his gloom. 'I cannot say how sad the news
made me,' he wrote, 'he was a lovely person and it is hateful to see him go
out unfinished, but gone he very definitely is. It makes one feel as though
nothing can matter very much'.[13]

Only three months later Lawrence had a fall from his motor cycle which
resulted in his death on 19 May 1935. Mourners at his funeral in the village of Moreton included Winston Churchill, Siegfried Sassoon, Mrs
Thomas Hardy, General Wavell, Lady Astor and Augustus John, who had
painted him so vividly. King George V told Arnold Lawrence: 'Your
brother's name will live in history'. The fortuitous death meant the national
hero, the great man of action, shared with his obscure, intellectual friend
the roll call of the 'yearly slain' of 1935.

The simplicity of Manning's funeral highlighted the difference between
the two friends. It had taken place on 26 February 1935 and he had been
buried in the Catholic section of Kensal Green Cemetery, grave 939 XNE,
near his dear Eva Fowler. His Requiem Mass was held at the Jesuit church
in Farm Street, London, the same church to which Galton had made his
way in 1875; the church from which Lionel Johnson had been buried. It
had been a quiet family service. Lady Manning had been distressed that the
man her son had seen as one of his best friends, T. E. Lawrence, had not
been there. The only figure from the artistic world present had been Will
Rothenstein, accompanied by his wife Alice, until the appearance of T. S.
Eliot. The sight of the greatest poet of the day paying tribute to a man he
knew only slightly must have been of some comfort to Nora Manning. Will
Rothenstein, with his deep affection for Fred and his boundless kindness,
was the most likely person to have engineered this apparition. But for
Eliot, to whom religious belief was so deeply important, sharing in these
last rites was no formal duty, but an expression of regard.

The tributes paid to Manning were more modest that that which the King accorded Lawrence, but they were nonetheless impressive. Eliot and Manning had been, at best, literary acquaintances, linked by their individual friendships with Charles Whibley, Richard Aldington and Ezra Pound. Yet that the dazzling innovator respected the minor Edwardian versifier as a man and as a writer was clear in his sympathetic obituary, which referred to Manning's poor health, nomadic life and small ouput:

> he was an exceedingly, indeed excessively fastidious writer; and spent as much energy in rewriting and destroying what he had written as would suffice to account for a number of ordinary books . . . His passion for perfection became almost indistinguishable from a passion for destruction of his own work . . . he was without ambition for notoriety, and had a style of writing, and a frame of mind, suited to a more cultured and better educated age than our own.[14]

Other obituary writers registered their regard. The *New York Times* (25 February 1935) noted that his book had been the sensation of the 1930 literary season. Christopher Morley in the *Saturday Review of Literature* (18 May 1935) quoted Peter Davies on his friend:

> Those privileged to know him will agree that he had no living intellectual superior; constant ill-health, combined with an extreme fastidiousness, curtailed the literary output which might have been expected from so fine and penetrating a mind and the modesty and aloofness which prevented him from putting his name to the most successful of his books robbed him of the personal fame which would have been his had he cared to claim it. But both *Her Privates We*, a best-seller immediately on publication and in constant demand ever since and the exquisite *Scenes and Portraits* are as clearly marked out for immortality as anything written in the present century.

This is the tribute of a friend and publisher, but others who were aware of Manning as a writer were also laudatory and sympathetic.

Harriet Monroe farewelled this reserved and retiring poet, this 'Narcissus of the trenches',[15] as one who was without ambitions for fame but of exquisite sensibilities.[16] And Will Rothenstein wrote lovingly in *The Times* (28 February 1935) of his friend's irony, wit, understanding and quick observation. He also wrote of Manning's ill health, lack of ambition and passionate aversion to finishing what he had begun, 'to the despair of those to whom he had read his beginnings . . . His frail person seemed unfitted to cope with a rough world, but how welcome his rare visits, and how lovable his vivid and playful spirits, and when he gave of his friendship he gave with unstinted generosity'. But the obituary disappeared from later editions. As always Frederic Manning was elusive. *John o' London's* (9 March), a journal which had always treated him well, made the point that he was lacking in ambition and little known to his contemporaries.

In his native city, the *Sydney Morning Herald* (25 February), ran a brief appreciation very like *The Times* notice. His fellow ex-servicemen also recorded his going in their magazine, *Reveille* (1 April), accompanied by a small portrait of him in uniform. The high, lined forehead, the large, sad eyes, the unsmiling face conveyed strain and unhappiness; and the article said that at the time of his death he had been planning to come back to Australia because his health had been causing him concern. On May 1 it also reprinted *The Times* obituary.

James Fairfax, now a smooth, solid, prosperous English citizen, who had been absent from the funeral through illness, recalled nostalgically the days of their shared youth in his poem, 'In Memoriam'.

> . . . [I] gladly remember
> How we were young together, talked, drank wine.
> Wrote verse by reams, and talked the late stars pale
> Into the dawn with question and surmise.[17]

Fairfax, with all the joys and distractions of undergraduate Oxford, the company of the students, the scholarship of the dons, had found Fred as important as any of them. Manning, so quiet and so gentle in life, lurked oddly in memory. Pound also did not forget his early friend, despite being confined in the Washington Federal Asylum for the Insane from 1946 until 1958. Richard Aldington remembered Manning too, and wrote of him with some sympathy. But it was fellow Australian Carl Kaeppel, who appeared to admire and feel for Manning, as writer and as man, more than anyone but Will Rothenstein. He would have known Fred's younger brother Charlie at Sydney Grammar and probably had known Manning in the earliest days in Sydney. Kaeppel became one of the finest classicists Australia ever produced, though he found little place for his talents in post-war Australia. He had served as a captain in the A.I.F. and had won the Military Cross. A scholar and a soldier, saddened by his own war memories and later failures, he was well fitted to understand Manning, whom he called 'a writer of genius'.[18]

Kaeppel wrote of him in terms which form a fitting epitaph, recalling the themes of division in Manning's life, and Manning's own pet notion of the double-natured: 'the scholar (not the pedant or the sponge) and the man of action are the obverse and reverse of the same thing'.[19]

23

Kore's Harvest

THE ONLY FAME Manning received was posthumous. Although there were five impressions of his novel in 1930 and it was reprinted in 1935 and 1937, it was not until the reset edition of 1943 appeared that he featured on the title page as the author and received in the introduction by Peter Davies the overt tribute he had evaded in life. In the early 1960s, when the Vietnam conflict began to raise again the moral problems of the deaths and sufferings of war, interest revived in the tragedy of the Great War. Bernard Bergonzi's *Heroes' Twilight*, published in 1965, raised again all the unanswerable questions about the puzzle of war. Three years earlier, in Australia, Professor L. T. Hergenhan, by bringing to notice Manning's work, was a forerunner of what Stephen Murray-Smith called, in 1964, 'the Manning revival'.[1] A new edition of *Her Privates We* appeared that year, with an introduction by Edmund Blunden, and this was reprinted in 1970. Pan put out a paperback version in 1967. John Douglas Pringle's perceptive essay on *Her Privates We* was published in 1971. Finally, in 1977, the original and unexpurgated version, under its original title *The Middle Parts of Fortune*, was acclaimed by critics in England and the United States. It was reprinted in 1986 as a Hogarth paperback, under the title *Her Privates We*. The book had become, according to M. R. D. Foot in *Encounter* (February 1987), 'a classic'. The long journey from the provinces of the Victorian era to international recognition had been completed.

And in his native land, Manning's work is now recognized. *The Oxford Companion to Australian Literature* calls his novel the most important Australian work on World War I for the universality of its approach. Stephen Murray-Smith has classed it with *The Fortunes of Richard Mahony* as one the two works of Australian literature valid for all mankind.[2] In documenting a reality faced by people of all countries Manning transcended nationality. Did his situation as an expatriate, freeing him from national ties, isolating him, enable him to take this pure yet general approach?

193

His expatriatism was of a special kind. He was not one of those who leave behind their provincial beginnings and attempt to take on completely the colour of their adopted as land as was the case with T. S. Eliot. Manning was not as whole-hearted about the country of his semi-adoption. He did not become an Englishman. Nor was he one of those expatriates who live and work abroad while belonging essentially, if mysteriously, to the country of their birth. Manning, though he kept traces of his origins, lacked the definition, the national flavour exuded by such types. (Aldington did not think of him as Australian.) Some writers may spend years abroad, wear the tag 'expatriate', but belong naturally to the culture of their homeland. Ernest Hemingway and Scott Fitzgerald, in Mary McCarthy's distinction between expatriates and exiles, belong to this category.[3] But Manning, intellectual and aesthetic, was alienated from his provincial homeland; he could not live there.

He was not, however, obviously an exile. Andrew Gurr has argued the exile seeks to recreate a vision of a lost society, that exile can be a constructive creative force; and he cites the work of Katherine Mansfield and V. S. Naipaul.[4] Detached, often insecure, such writers create a home in memory. While separated willingly from the birthplace they rebuild in their imagination the country of the past. Cosmopolitan expatriate and exile may, at times, overlap. Katherine Mansfield, for instance, lived and observed literary Bohemian life in England and Europe as well as turning back to the New Zealand of her childhood for some of her finest work. Henry Handel Richardson wrote of the passions of European music students in *Maurice Guest*, before recreating her Melbourne schooldays in *The Getting of Wisdom* and part of the history of her native land, and the story of her migrant father, in her trilogy.

The exiled writer is often obsessed with the theme of childhood, but reticent Frederic Manning, though well aware of the 'irrecoverable past', kept his secrets. He may have lacked the creative impulse of such exiles, or, secretive and fastidious always, have suppressed such impulses as too personal, too revealing, and likely to bring pain to members of his family. Although he lived abroad, following his own life style, his family ties seem to have been strong and important to him. There were letters, visits by his siblings and parents, trips home, long periods spent together with much affection between family members, and, in particular, his special closeness to his mother; he remained 'Uncle Fred' to younger family members. If there were any nostalgia, any longing for an idyllic past, or any pain in memory, it was his nature to keep such feelings to himself, except for an occasional flash. 'His eyes strained after the vessel, for he was like an exile there, who sees a ship bound to his own country and his heart goes with it.' (*Scenes and Portraits*, p. 40)

Removed to England by Arthur Galton, confined by that severe man's dislike of sentimentality and romanticism and by his grandiose aims, young Manning was set early in life on the path of high-minded scholarship and philosophic thought, of censorious fastidiousness about emotion. The intuitive responses of the novelist to memory and experience were largely suppressed in the cause of intellect. On the other hand, in his constrained circumstances—physical and emotional—he was unable to make a vital connection with the society in which he had chosen to live. As Lawrence had observed, his 'not being English . . . barred him from his fellows'. And he was not an originator, startling an old society with something new like Eliot.

While he charmed those who understood and appreciated his gifts, he was, in his youth, nervous, dependent and lacking in force in dealing with domineering, power-centred natures. As a protection he certainly wore, like Bourne, 'the pose of detachment', which Gurr calls 'the clearest hallmark of the exile',[5] but this diffidence separated him also from his new country, and from experience. Not quite an Englishman, not quite an Australian, not quite a philosopher, not quite a novelist, and not really a poet, the country of the mind became his home. He might adopt an Anglicized manner, but he was in reality a form of the ultimate expatriate, cut off from the past, yet out of contact with the life of the country of the present. Dominated by his strong-willed tutor, restricted by his heritage of Irish puritanism and denied that which was elemental in life, to which he was attracted, his creativity was confined, at first, to artificial verses, philosophical 'stories' and the conventions of the old-fashioned, mannered historical romance.

Then the philosopher-versifier became the soldier and the novelist. The concentrated experience of life, death and suffering that he faced in those months on the Somme was poured into one stripped and coherent book, written quickly and with passion. But it was rooted in his philosophical speculations and his particular past. His kind of expatriatism meant that he was free of the emotional ties with a special English past of writers such as Graves and Aldington, while he retained some of the democratic heritage of his birthplace. As an observant, philosophical, ironic outsider, absorbed in the myth of loss and return, of death and regeneration, he could look at his personal experience of war as an aspect of an eternal reality, and at his companions as symbolic of the potential for stoical heroism in ordinary human beings. It is this standing-back, this capacity to look, clear-eyed, at the whole picture, to see both the horror of war and the nobility to be found in the worst of situations, exemplified in concrete detail, which gives Manning's novel its special distinction of theme and form.

If Arthur Galton had not been led, by chance, to Sydney would *Her Privates We* have remained unwritten? Would Sydney have gained, instead, some ironic saga of bourgeois life akin to Boyd's Langton series about Melbourne? Given the dynamism of the exodus of the first decade of the century, it is likely that Frederic Manning would have made his way abroad, though, without the pressures of the tie with Galton, he may well have returned. But it was Galton who largely formed his mind, who both encour-

aged and restricted his talents. And the separation from family and homeland, the rootlessness, formed part of Manning's particular sensibility.
While it is a matter of some regret that Manning never wrote on an Australian subject, *Scenes and Portraits* and his war novel are universal in
scope. With their essentially philosophic bases, they belong as much to
Australia as to the rest of the world. And if his claim to a literary reputation rests largely upon one book, he is not alone in that.

Manning wrote from training camp to Will Rothenstein on 19 November
1915: 'We have a right to be judged by the best things we have done: as
indeed we judge such men as Coleridge for instance, so weak and such a
failure, and yet so sure-footed and secure in the little he did achieve'. It is a
summation that might well be applied to Frederic Manning himself.

Notes

Abbreviations

F.M.	Frederic Manning
R.A.	Richard Aldington
J.G.F.	James Griffyth Fairfax
A.G.	Arthur Galton
A.H.	Albert Houtin
L.J.	Lionel Johnson
T.E.L.	T. E. Lawrence
H.M.	Harriet Monroe
E.P.	Ezra Pound
W.R.	Sir William Rothenstein
D.S.	Dorothy Shakespear
S.S.	Sappho Smith
J.A.S.	John Addington Symonds.
H.R.H.R.C.	Harry Ransom Humanities Research Center
M.L.	Mitchell Library
N.L.A.	National Library of Australia
S.M.H.	*Sydney Morning Herald*

Quotations from *Her Privates We* are from the Hogarth press, 1986 edition.
Quotations from *Scenes and Portraits* are from the 2nd ed., Peter Davies, 1930.

Introduction: The Man in Question

1 From Desmond O'Grady in conversation with the author.
2 E.P. to D.S., 8 January 1913, Pound, *Ezra Pound and Dorothy Shakespeare*, ed. Pound and Litz, p. 180.
3 Aldington, 'Australian Revaluations', p. 27.
4 A reminiscence from Richard Aldington communicated to the author by Alister Kershaw.
5 Haq, 'Forgotten Fred,' p. 56.
6 The Hergenhan articles are listed in the Bibliography.
7 'Almost Ours', The Red Page.
8 'The War Continues', p. 77.
9 *Heroes' Twilight*, pp. 190, 193.
10 *The Literature of War,* p. 99.

[11] 'Politics and the Novel', *Occasional Prose*, p. 208.

[12] F.M. to W.R., 10 November 1916, Rothenstein collection.

[13] *The Plague*, p. 34.

[14] Manning, 'The Jesters of the Lord', *Scenes and Portraits*, p. 183.

[15] T.E.L. to F.M., 16 November 1934, Frederic Manning papers.

[16] T. S. Eliot quoted in Bergonzi, *T. S. Eliot*, p. 2.

[17] 'The Prodigal Son', p. 38.

[18] Jonathan Marwil's *Frederic Manning: An Unfinished Life* appeared while this book was in production. It contains some new detail on Manning's army record, Irish friendships and dealings with John Murray, his first publisher, but no large deposits of source material have as yet been located.

1 Young Fred and Family

[1] Quoted in John E. Mack, *A Prince of our Disorder*, p. 383.

[2] Peter Davies's *Summer Catalogue*, 1935, quoted in Christopher Morley's obituary on Manning, *Saturday Review of Literature*, 18 May 1935, p. 15.

[3] *Australian Dictionary of Biography*, vol. 10, Melbourne, 1986, p. 397.

[4] Henry Parkes, *An Emigrant's Home Letters*, London, 1897, p. 115.

[5] Twopeny, *Town Life in Australia*, p. 36.

[6] Adams, *The Australians*, p. 31.

[7] Randolph Bedford, *Naught to Thirty-three*, Sydney, 1944, p. 48.

[8] Manning, 'Past', *Eidola*.

[9] Kaeppel, 'Frederic Manning', p. 48; W. Hudson Shaw, 'Lawrence Hargave', MS 5661, N.L.A., does not mention the friendship.

[10] 'At Even'.

[11] *Viewless Winds*, p. 29.

[12] To A.H., 1 November 1908, Albert Houtin correspondence.

[13] *S.M.H.*, 8 January 1898.

[14] *Bulletin*, 13 January 1894, p. 4.

[15] *A Single Flame*, p. 35.

[16] Ibid, p. 8.

[17] Boyd, 'Dubious Cartography', p. 8.

[18] *Bulletin*, 9 June 1894, S.S. column.

[19] Twopeny, op. cit., p. 217.

[20] Ibid., p. 106.

[21] Kaeppel, op. cit., p. 47.

[22] Aldington, 'Australian Revaluations', p. 26.

[23] 'The Friend of Paul', *Scenes and Portraits*, p. 124.

2 Mr Galton

[1] *S.M.H.*, 30 May 1893.

[2] Galton, 'Government House', p. 540.

[3] Manning, 'The King of Uruk', *Scenes and Portraits*, p. 12.

[4] Obituary by Laurence Binyon, *The Times*, 7 March 1921, p. 14.

[5] F.M. to A.H., 21 March 1926, Albert Houtin correspondence.

[6] Galton, *Rome and Romanizing*, p. 11.

[7] Ibid., p. 18.

[8] Ibid., pp. 53-4.

[9] *The Memoirs of John Addington Symonds*, p. 94.

[10] Forster, *Goldsworthy Lowes Dickinson*, p. 20.

[11] *Rome and Romanizing*, p. 53. Also letter to *The Times*, 5 January 1903, p. 9.

[12] *Rome and Romanizing*, p. 38.

[13] 'To the Century Guild'.

[14] 'An Examination of Certain Schools and Tendencies in Contemporary Literature,' p. 98.

[15] Secrest, *Being Bernard Berenson*, p. 175.

[16] 'Matthew Arnold. April 15, 1888.'

[17] Galton, 'Walter Pater', p. 52.

[18] Ibid.

[19] A.G. to L.J., 12 May 1889, manuscript belonging to Mrs E. T. Dugdale, quoted in *The Letters of Walter Pater*, p. xi note.

[20] 'Winchester', *The Complete Poems of Lionel Johnson*, pp. 1-5.

[21] Johnson, *Some Winchester Letters*, p. 11.

[22] 'Oxford', *The Complete Poems of Lionel Johnson*, pp. 145-7.

[23] Samuels, *Bernard Berenson*, p. 61.

[24] L.J. to A.G., 18 February 1890, Wilde, *The Letters of Oscar Wilde*, p. 255 note.

[25] J.A.S. to A.G., 18 October 1889, Letters of John Addington Symonds, H.R.H.R.C.

[26] J.A.S. to A.G., 13 May 1890, Letters of John Addington Symonds, H.R.H.R.C.

[27] Hunt, *The Pre-Raphaelite Imagination*, p. 8.

[28] J.A.S. to A.G., 9 October 1890, Letters of John Addington Symonds, H.R.H.R.C.

[29] To J.G.F., 5 October 1909, Fairfax papers.

3 Philistia

[1] 'Government House', p. 540.

[2] Twopeny, *Town Life in Australia*, p. 105.

[3] Galton, 'Government House', p. 540.

[4] Ibid., p. 541.

[5] A. B. Piddington, *Worshipful Masters*, Sydney, 1929, p. 131.

[6] Wise papers. M.L., MSS 1327/2.

[7] *The Webbs' Australian Diary*, p. 27.

[8] J. A. La Nauze, *Alfred Deakin: A Biography*, Melbourne, 1965, pp. 238-9, 303, 595-6.

[9] Parkes correspondence, vol. 52, 435-50, M.L.

[10] *Oceana*, ed. Blainey, p. 96.

[11] 10 June 1893, S.S. column.

[12] *Bulletin*, 1 September 1894, p. 10.

[13] *Bulletin*, 19 May 1894, S.S. column.

[14] Parkes correspondence, vol. 52, 435-50, M.L. The Catholic press in Sydney was particularly critical of Galton.

[15] Vance Palmer, *Intimate Portraits*, pp. 35-6.

[16] *Crockford's Clerical Directory*, London, 1904, p. 514.

[17] Aldington, 'Australian Revaluations', p. 26

[18] *The Australians*, p. 39.

[19] Galton, 'Some Modern Literature', p. 28.

4 When London Calls

[1] *Our Attitude towards English Roman Catholics and the Papal Court*, p. viii.

[2] *Australian Dictionary of Biography*, vol. 10, Melbourne, 1986, p. 397.

[3] Alan Roberts, 'Planning Sydney's Transport, 1875-1900', in Kelly, *Nineteenth-century Sydney*, p. 33.

[4] *Bulletin*, 30 March 1895, p. 8.

[5] *Sand's Directory of Sydney*, Sydney, 1897, p. 91; 1898, p. 99.

[6] To W.R., 31 October 1916, Rothenstein collection.

[7] *Her Privates We*, p. 8

8 *Bulletin*, 14 April 1894, p. 8.
9 *Sand's Directory of Sydney*, 1897, p. 114; 1898, p. 124.
10 Albert Houtin correspondence, item 477.
11 Information from Sydney Grammar.
12 Eleanor Manning to Mr Phillips, 19 August 1968, MSS 2594/2, Frederic Manning papers.
13 J.A.S. to A.G., 9 October 1890, Letters of John Addington Symonds, H.R.H.R.C.
14 *The Clarion Call to the voters of Woollahra, King, and Waverley*, Sydney, 26 July 1898, M.L.
15 *The Getting of Wisdom*, London, 1910, p. 233.
16 In conversation with the author.
17 Creeve Roe (pseud.), 'When London Calls', *Bulletin*, 1900, in *Creeve Roe*, ed. M. Pizer and M. Holburn, Sydney, 1947, pp. 35-6.
18 Zora Cross, *Elegy on an Australian Schoolboy*, Sydney, 1921, p. 8.
19 *The Transit of Venus*, London, 1981, p. 37.
20 Furphy, *Such is Life*, p. 207
21 *Collected Verse*, Sydney, 1967, p. 15.
22 *A Single Flame*, p. 4.
23 *S.M.H.*, 23 March 1898, p. 6.
24 *Her Privates We*, p. 61.
25 Manning, 'Helgi of Lithend', *Poems*, p. 62.
26 'French Poetry', p. 1123.

5 Abroad

1 F.M. to T.E.L., 4 January 1932, *Letters to T. E. Lawrence*, ed. A. Lawrence, p. 144.
2 F.M. to J.G.F., 23 November 1908, Fairfax papers.
3 Samuels, *Bernard Berenson*, p. 31.
4 F.M. to J.G.F., 29 June 1908, Fairfax papers.
5 F.M. to D.S, quoted in Hergenhan, 'Two Expatriates', p. 94.
6 'Some Winchester Letters', p. 51.
7 Quoted in Murphy, *Prodigal Father*, p. 183.
8 Hone, *W. B. Yeats, 1865-1939*, p. 73.
9 *The Life and Letters of J. H. Shorthouse*.
10 *Dictionary of Australian Biography*, ed. P. Serle, vol. 2, Sydney, 1949, p. 111.
11 *Men and Memories*, vol. 2, pp. 26-7.
12 To J.G.F., 2 September 1911, Fairfax papers.
13 To W.R., 14 November 1915, Rothenstein collection.
14 To J.G.F., 26 November 1908, Fairfax papers.
15 *Intimate Portraits*, p. 63.
16 Galton, *Two Essays upon Matthew Arnold*, p. 35.
17 To A.H., 1 November 1908, Albert Houtin correspondence.
18 'Australian Revaluations', p. 28.
19 *S.M.H.*, 20 September 1900, p. 6.

6 Exodus

1 *The Commonwealth of Australia*, p. 24.
2 *Betty Wayside*, London, 1915, (first published *Lone Hand*, July 1913–August 1914.)
3 *The Awful Australian*, pp. 15, 91.
4 Louise Mack, *An Australian Girl in London*, p. 282.
5 *Sand's Directory of Sydney*, Sydney, 1901, p. 95.
6 *S.M.H.*, 18 March 1903.
7 *Child of the Hurricane*, Sydney, 1936, p. 196.
8 *The Australian Nationalists*, Melbourne, 1971, p. x.

9 Signed 'B.B.', 'To My Country', *Bulletin*, 15 March 1902, p. 3.
10 'The Wanderer', *Hermes* (Sydney), Jubilee Number, 1902, p. 65.
11 *Drawn from Life*, p. 11.
12 *A Single Flame*, p. 12.
13 *An Australian Girl in London*, pp. 239-40, 279.
14 A.G. to the editor, *S.M.H.*, 24 August 1902, MS A g 6, M.L.
15 *Bulletin*, 15 October 1903, p. 46.
16 'The King of Uruk', *Scenes and Portraits*, pp. 9-10.

7 Edenham

1 F.M to W.R., 16 January 1917, William Rothenstein collection.
2 *Crockford's Clerical Directory*, London, 1908, pp. 530-1.
3 Nowell-Smith, ed., *Edwardian England*, pp. 142, 170.
4 'The Poetical Works of Matthew Arnold', p. 47.
5 Albert Houtin correspondence, item 477, n.d.
6 Ibid.
7 To D.S., 17 July 1905, Document 1598, M.L.
8 To D.S., 13 September 1905, Document 1598, M.L.
9 To D.S., 2 December 1905, Document 1598, M.L.
10 Hergenhan, 'Two Expatriates', p. 93.
11 F.M. to J.G.F., 9 June 1907, Fairfax papers.
12 To D.S., December 1907, Document 706, M.L.
13 F.M. to J.G.F., 15 October 1908, Fairfax papers.
14 F.M. to J.G.F., 26 September 1908, Fairfax papers.
15 Manning, 'The Crystal Dreamer', *Poems*.
16 To J.G.F., 12 September 1908, Fairfax papers.
17 D.S. to E.P., 30 August 1911, Pound, *Ezra Pound and Dorothy Shakespeare*, ed. Pound and Litz, p. 41.
18 *Edwardian Life and Leisure*, p. 76.
19 Manning, Introduction to *The Vigil of Brunhild*, p. iii.
20 Manning, 'Ibsen', p. 11.
21 'Soleil Couchant', *Poems*.
22 F.M. to J.G.F., 23 November 1908, Fairfax papers.
23 'Australian Revaluations', p. 28.
24 To J.G.F., 13 January 1914, Fairfax papers.

8 Best Friends

1 *Outlook*, 15 April 1905, p. 524.
2 Ibid., also letter to *Outlook*, 6 May 1905, p. 639.
3 F.M. to J.G.F., 15 April 1907, 10 April 1909, 9 June 1907, Fairfax papers.
4 F.M. to J.G.F., 2 June 1907, 9 May 1908, Fairfax papers.
5 F.M. to J.G.F., 26 June 1907, 30 June 1907, 12 July 1907, Fairfax papers.
6 1 November 1908, Albert Houtin correspondence.
7 'Birthday Ode', *Poems*, p. 229.
8 Manning, 'After Night', *Poems*.
9 Ibid.
10 Vance Palmer, *Intimate Portraits*, pp. 18, 86.
11 *Myself When Young*, London, 1948, p. 20.
12 *Day of my Delight*, pp. 26, 43.
13 'The Bon Times and the Bad', *Times Literary Supplement*, 19 August 1977, p. 997.
14 To J.G.F., 26 September 1908, Fairfax papers.

[15] F.M. to J.G.F., 16 April 1909, 19 April 1909, Fairfax papers.
[16] To J.G.F., 19 April 1909, Fairfax papers.
[17] F.M. to Henry Newbolt, 12 December 1908, Henry Newbolt collection; F.M. to J.G.F., 30 October 1908, 17 November 1908, Fairfax papers.

9 *Scenes and Portraits*

[1] To A.G., 16 October 1890, Letters of John Addington Symonds, H.R.H.R.C.
[2] F.M. to A.H., 16 June 1908, Albert Houtin correspondence.
[3] Review of 2nd ed., *Daily Telegraph*, 16 December 1930.
[4] F. R. Lamennais, 1782-1854, French writer on religion, who left the Catholic church; J. B. Lacordaire, his disciple, a priest who remained within the church.
[5] Letter to the *Times Literary Supplement*, 9 September 1977, p. 1081.
[6] To R.A., 6 July 1921, T. S. Eliot Letters, H.R.H.R.C.
[7] 'The Prose of Frederic Manning', p. 375. Also letter to F. S. Flint, 8 July 1920, by courtesy of Norman Gates, from his forthcoming *Selected Letters of Richard Aldington*.
[8] To T.E.L., 20 June 1930, *Letters to T. E. Lawrence*, ed. A. Lawrence, p. 137.
[9] *Two Memoirs*, pp. 98-9.

10 The Last Exquisite

[1] T.E.L. to Peter Davies, 28 February 1935, Lawrence, *Letters of T. E. Lawrence*, ed. Garnett, p. 860.
[2] T.E.L. to Liddell Hart, 5 March 1930, Lawrence, *T. E. Lawrence to his Biographers*, ed. Graves and Hart, part 2, p. 40.
[3] R.A. to Amy Lowell, January 1919, by courtesy of Norman Gates, from his forthcoming *Selected Letters of Richard Aldington*.
[4] 'The Friend of Paul', *Scenes and Portraits*, pp. 112-13.
[5] Horder, ed., *Ronald Firbank*, pp. 183, 197, 207.
[6] Ibid., pp. 150-1.
[7] 'Imaginary Conversations', p. 21.
[8] F.M. to J.G.F., 9 June 1907, Fairfax papers.

11 Ezra Pound

[1] *Life for Life's Sake*, p. 96.
[2] *Letters of Ezra Pound*, ed. Paige, p. 42.
[3] Preface, *A Lume Spento*, in *Selected Prose*, ed. Cookson, p. 431.
[4] Rome broadcast, 5 May 1942, quoted in Hutchins, *Ezra Pound's Kensington*, p. 47.
[5] E.P. to his mother, 31 January 1909, in Pound, *Ezra Pound and Dorothy Shakespear*, ed. Pound and Litz, p. xi.
[6] To J.G.F., 10 April 1909, Fairfax papers.
[7] Vance Palmer, *Intimate Portraits*, pp. 55, 57.
[8] *Guide to Kulchur*, p. 228.
[9] To J.G.F., 10 April 1909, Fairfax papers.
[10] F.M. to Henry Newbolt, 22 February 1909, Henry Newbolt collection.
[11] To J.G.F., 10 April 1909, Fairfax papers.
[12] To Henry Newbolt, 1 June 1909, Henry Newbolt collection.
[13] F.M. to J.G.F., 30 June 1909, Fairfax papers.
[14] Rothenstein, *Men and Memories*, vol. 2, p. 26.
[15] 'A List of Books', p. 55.
[16] T.E.L. to F.M., 24 June 1930, Frederic Manning papers.
[17] F.M. to A.H., 1 June 1909, Albert Houtin correspondence.

18 E.P. to H. H. Shakespear (father of Dorothy), 13 February 1914, in Pound, *Ezra Pound and Dorothy Shakespear*, ed. Pound and Litz, p. 307.
19 F.M. to O.S., quoted in notebook of D.S., 4-5 November 1909, in Pound, *Ezra Pound and Dorothy Shakespear*, ed. Pound and Litz, p. 9.
20 19 November 1954, in Pound, *The Letters of Ezra Pound and Wyndham Lewis*, ed. Materer, p. 280; March 1952, in Pound, *Some Letters of Ezra Pound*, ed. Dudek, p. 84.
21 A fragment of the 'Gilded Coach', MS 1989, N.L.A. Peter Davies, writing to Shakespear and Pankey, solicitors, 7 January 1955, (MSS 2594/2, M.L.), said Manning always called this work the 'Golden Coach'.
22 Manning, 'Milton', p. 625.
23 'Ave Imperatrix', *Hobby Horse*, vol. 5, 1890, p. 1.
24 F.M. to W.R., 24 January 1916, William Rothenstein collection.
25 Donald Gallup, *A Bibliography of Ezra Pound*, London, 1963, p. 30.
26 F.M. to Henry Newbolt, 2 November 1909, Henry Newbolt collection.
27 *Bookman*, September 1910, p. 258.
28 F.M. to J.G.F., 14 June 1910, Fairfax papers.
29 Notebook of D.S., 16 February 1909, Pound, *Ezra Pound and Dorothy Shakespear*, ed. Pound and Litz, p. 3.
30 *Crockford's Clerical Directory*, London, 1911, p. 1811.
31 F.M. to J.G.F., 16 June 1911, Fairfax papers.

12 Disappointments

1 Pound, Obituary on F. M. Ford, in Pound, *Selected Prose*, ed. Cookson, pp. 431-2.
2 R.A. to Peter Russell, 5 January 1950, quoted in Aldington, *A Passionate Prodigality*, ed. Benkovitz, p. 9.
3 Pound, 'Credo', in *Literary Essays*, p. 12.
4 To E.P., 25 November 1911, Ezra Pound papers.
5 F.M. to J.G.F., 16 June 1911, Fairfax papers.
6 F.M. to J.G.F., 11 September 1911, Fairfax papers.
7 F.M. to Henry Newbolt, 24 October 1911, Henry Newbolt collection.
8 To Henry Newbolt, 30 November 1911, Henry Newbolt collection.
9 F.M. to W.R., 26 December 1915, William Rothenstein collection.
10 E.P. to D.S., 13 July 1912, Pound, *Ezra Pound and Dorothy Shakespear*, ed. Pound and Litz, p. 131.
11 F.M. to J.G.F., 17 February 1912, Fairfax papers.
12 'George Sand', p. 560.
13 'The Literature of Power', p. 991.
14 'The Memoirs of the Countess Golovine', p. 930.
15 A fragment of the 'Gilded Coach', MS 1989, N.L.A.

13 Restless Days

1 *The Storm of Steel*, p. 21.
2 *The Unbearable Bassington* in *The Complete Works of Saki*, p. 681.
3 *National Notes*, p. 73
4 Galton, *Acer in Hostem*, pp. 10, 25.
5 Ibid., Dedication.
6 To J.G.F., 22 October 1912, Fairfax papers.
7 To A.H., 13 March 1913, translated by the author, Albert Houtin correspondence.
8 D.S. to E.P., 14 March 1913, Pound, *Ezra Pound and Dorothy Shakespear*, ed. Pound and Litz, p. 191.
9 9 E.P. to H.M., 17 March 1913, June 1913, Harriet Monroe *Poetry* correspondence.

10 Ford Madox Ford, 'Thus to Revisit', *Dial*, vol. 69, September 1920, p. 242.
11 F.M. to J.G.F., 18 June 1912, Fairfax papers.
12 'The Correspondence of Swift', p. 402.
13 'Shakespearean Criticism', p. 1055.
14 Lewis, *Letters*, ed. Rose, p. 2.

14 Another Friend

1 From Alister Kershaw in conversation with the author.
2 To Charles C. Bubb, 9 August 1917, *Letters of Richard Aldington to Charles Clinch Bubb*, ed. Keller.
3 'Remy de Gourmont', p. 32-4.
4 'The Prose of Frederic Manning', p. 376.
5 William Going, 'The Peacock Dinner', *Journal of Modern Literature*, March 1971, pp. 303-10.
6 M.L. document 1598.
7 F.M. to J.G.F., 26 February 1914, Fairfax papers.
8 Ibid.
9 *J. B. Yeats: Letters to His Son W. B. Yeats and Others*, ed. Joseph Hone, London, 1944, p. 175.
10 Bowen, *Drawn from Life*, p. 49.
11 *Richard Aldington: Selected Critical Writings*, pp. 9-10.

15 The Soldier

1 To H.M., 7 August 1914, Harriet Monroe *Poetry* correspondence.
2 Stromberg, 'The Intellectuals and the Coming of War in 1914', pp. 109-22.
3 'War Notes' by 'North Staffs', *New Age*, 2 March 1916, p. 413.
4 *A Woman's Experiences in the Great War*, p. 39.
5 To A.H., 29 December 1920, Albert Houtin correspondence.
6 To A.H., 28 December 1914, Albert Houtin correspondence.
7 Prologue to Loisy, *War and Religion*.
8 *Acer in Hostem*, p. 59.
9 To A.H., 28 December 1914, Albert Houtin correspondence.
10 'Epigram. R.B.', *Eidola*. This poem also appeared in *Literary Digest*, New York, 27 April 1917.
11 To E.P., 27 May 1915, Ezra Pound papers.
12 F.M. to W.R., 14 November 1915, William Rothenstein collection.
13 E.P. to H.M., May 1915, Harriet Monroe *Poetry* correspondence.
14 To E.P., 19 November 1920, Ezra Pound papers.
15 To T.E.L., 14 March 1930, *Letters to T. E. Lawrence*, ed. A. Lawrence, p. 134.
16 Mann, Review of *Her Privates We*, p. 47.
17 F.M to W.R., 24 January 1916, 19 November 1915, William Rothenstein collection.
18 Quoted in Macdonald, *Somme*, p. 216.
19 F.M. to W.R., 31 October 1916, William Rothenstein collection.
20 To W.R., 1 July 1918, William Rothenstein collection.
21 F.M. to W.R., undated (August 1916), 2 October 1916, William Rothenstein collection.
22 F.M. to W.R., 31 August 1917, William Rothenstein collection.
23 To W.R., 2 January 1917, William Rothenstein collection.
24 Stephen, *An Australian in the R.F.A.*, p. 134.
25 '*Eidola*', *Bookman*, vol. 52, June 1917, p. 97.
26 *Diaries. 1915-1918*, ed. Hart-Davis, p. 169.
27 To H.D., June 1948, by courtesy of Norman Gates, from his forthcoming *Selected Letters of Richard Aldington*.
28 *Literary Lifelines*, ed. MacNiven and Moore, p. 110.

16 The Officer

[1] F.M. to W.R, 1 January 1917, 17 August 1917, William Rothenstein collection.
[2] F.M. to W.R., 24 January 1916, William Rothenstein collection.
[3] *When Blackbirds Sing*, p. 111.
[4] *Death of a Hero*, p. 273.
[5] To W.R., 25 August 1917, 31 August 1917, William Rothenstein collection.
[6] To W.R., 12 November 1917, William Rothenstein collection
[7] To T.E.L., 14 April 1930, *Letters to T. E. Lawrence*, ed. A. Lawrence, p. 134.
[8] To W.R., 6 December 1917, William Rothenstein collection.
[9] F.M. to W.R., 1 July 1918, William Rothenstein collection.
[10] Ibid.
[11] *An Australian in the R.F.A.*, pp. 187, 199.
[12] To W.R., 9 November 1918, William Rothenstein collection.
[13] Garnett, *The Flowers of the Forest*, p. 190.
[14] To W.R., 9 October 1918, William Rothenstein collection.
[15] F.M. to W.R., 9 November 1918, William Rothenstein collection.
[16] F.M. to W.R., 22 March 1919, William Rothenstein collection.
[17] To 'My dear Aunt' (O.S.), 9 December 1918, Ezra Pound papers.
[18] F.M. to W.R., 22 March 1919, 29 July 1919, William Rothenstein collection.
[19] E.P. to J. B. Pinker, 30 January 1916, *Pound-Joyce Letters*, ed. Reid, p. 65.
[20] 13 July 1916, *Letters of Ezra Pound*, ed. Paige, p. 135.
[21] To E.P., 29 January 1919, Ezra Pound papers.
[22] 'Temperament', *Retrospect*.
[23] To H.M., 21 July 1919, 14 October 1919, Harriet Monroe *Poetry* correspondence.
[24] F.M. to H.M., 18 May 1919, Harriet Monroe *Poetry* correspondence.

17 The Losses of Peace

[1] F.M. to 'My dear Aunt' (O.S.), 9 December 1918, Ezra Pound papers.
[2] 'In Memoriam', *The Fifth Element*.
[3] To W.R., 26 December 1915, William Rothenstein collection.
[4] To W.R., 12 August 1919, William Rothenstein collection.
[5] F.M. to W.R., 30 March 1920, William Rothenstein collection.
[6] *Day of my Delight*, p. 112.
[7] E.P. to T.E.L., (August) 1920, *Letters of Ezra Pound*, ed. Paige, p. 219.
[8] E.P. to H.M., 16 December 1920, Harriet Monroe *Poetry* correspondence.
[9] To A.H., 29 December 1920, Albert Houtin correspondence.
[10] 'Autarkia', *Eidola*.
[11] To W.R., 15 January 1921, William Rothenstein collection.
[12] To A.H., 2 March 1921, Albert Houtin correspondence.
[13] *A Difficult Young Man*, p. 177.
[14] To A.H., 12 August 1921, Albert Houtin correspondence.
[15] T. S. Eliot to R.A., 16 September 1921, T. S. Eliot Letters, H.R.H.R.C.
[16] T. S. Eliot to R.A., 6 July 1921, T. S. Eliot Letters, H.R.H.R.C.
[17] Marwil, 'Combative Companions', p. 15.
[18] R.A. to H.M., 7 May 1920, Harriet Monroe *Poetry* correspondence.
[19] 14 February 1949, by courtesy of Norman Gates, from his forthcoming *Selected Letters of Richard Aldington*.
[20] Aldington, 'Australian Revaluations', pp. 15-16.
[21] *Isis: International Review* (Brussels), vol. 6, 1924, p. 423.

18 The *Criterion*, T. S. Eliot and the 1920s

1 T. S. Eliot to R.A., 6 July 1921, T. S. Eliot Letters, H.R.H.R.C.
2 F.M. to A.H., 11 May 1924, 6 February 1924, Albert Houtin correspondence.
3 F.M. to A.H., 29 May 1924, Albert Houtin correspondence.
4 'A French Criticism of Newman', p. 19.
5 'M. de Gourmont and the Problem of Beauty', p. 26.
6 Bertrand Russell, *Autobiography*, London, 1967-69, p. 278.
7 Spender, *Eliot*, p. 215.
8 William Rothenstein, *Since Fifty. Men and Memories, 1922-1938*, vol. 3, p. 29.
9 Ibid., p. 83.
10 *Day of my Delight*, p. 112.
11 Gellert, 'Case of Private 19022'.
12 Quoted in Nettie Palmer, *Fourteen Years*, p. 54.
13 F.M. to A.H., 3 August 1926, Albert Houtin correspondence.
14 F.M. to A.H., 21 March 1926, Albert Houtin correspondence.
15 To W.R., 5 January 1926, William Rothenstein collection.
16 To A.H., 21 March 1926, Albert Houtin correspondence.
17 F.M. to T.E.L., 14 April 1930, *Letters to T. E. Lawrence*, ed. A. Lawrence, p. 133.
18 John Rothenstein, *Summer's Lease*, pp. 37, 124.
19 F.M. to W.R., 18 August 1928, 2 September 1928, William Rothenstein collection.
20 F.M. to Alice Rothenstein, 6 June 1929, William Rothenstein collection.

19 Reawakening

1 Birkin, *J. M. Barrie and the Lost Boys*, p. 283.
2 Ibid., p. 15.
3 Henri Barbusse wrote *Under Fire* in the trenches, and it appeared in book form in 1917. A. P. Herbert's *The Secret Battle* and Roland Dorgoles's *Les Croix de Bois* were published in 1919, Ernst Jünger's *Storm of Steel* and John Dos Passos's *First Encounter* in 1920, and Filippo Marinetti's *The Steel Alcove* and Dos Passos's *Three Soldiers* in 1921.
4 Also published that year were Ernest Hemingway's *A Farewell to Arms*, Richard Aldington's *Death of a Hero*, William Faulkner's *The Sound and the Fury*, George Blake's *The Path to Glory* and R. C. Sheriff's enormously popular play of 1928, *Journey's End*.
5 To T.E.L., 11 February 1930, *Letters to T. E. Lawrence*, ed. A. Lawrence, p. 129.
6 MSS 2594/1, Microfilm reel CY 555, Frederic Manning papers.
7 To T.E.L., 14 March 1930, *Letters to T. E. Lawrence*, ed. A. Lawrence, p. 130.
8 Graeme Kinross-Smith, 'Leonard Mann-A Profile', *Australian Literary Studies*, vol. 7, 1975-76, p. 324.
9 Review of *Her Privates We*, p. 47.
10 Taylor, 'Bourne again', p. 26.
11 *Her Privates We*, p. 1; the quotation comes from *2 King Henry IV*, III. ii. 253-8.
12 *Her Privates We*, p. 234; the quotation comes from *Hamlet*, II. ii. 244.
13 From *1 King Henry IV*, V. iii. 36–40.
14 *Artist among the Bankers*, p. 239.
15 Birkin, op. cit., p. 15.

20 A World of Its Own

1 'Politics and the Novel', *Occasional Prose*, p. 208.
2 *The Storm of Steel*, p. 1.
3 Introduction to *Her Privates We*, 1986, p. [5]
4 Review of *The Middle Parts of Fortune*, p. 26.
5 Introduction to Herbert, *The Secret Battle*, p. x.

⁶ 'The Structure of Frederic Manning's War Novel', pp. 407-17.

⁷ *Her Privates We*, p. 12; the quotation comes from *King Henry V*, IV. vi. 30–2.

⁸ *Her Privates We*, p. 47; the quotation comes from *King Lear*, I. ii. 53–4.

⁹ *Her Privates We*, p. 211; the quotation comes from *King Henry V*, IV, i. 92–149.

¹⁰ Review of *The Middle Parts of Fortune*, p. 26.

¹¹ *Heroes' Twilight*, p. 191.

¹² 'Australian Revaluations', p. 27.

¹³ 'The Dean of St Paul's', (unsigned) in Rothenstein, *Twenty-four Portraits*, (unpaged).

¹⁴ Carrington, *Soldier from the Wars Returning*, pp. 167-8; Boyd, *Day of my Delight*, p. 85.

¹⁵ Graves, *Goodbye to All That*, p. 192.

¹⁶ *The Literature of War*, p. 99.

21 Crowned with Laurels

¹ 'The War Continues', p. 77.

² Bairnsfather, *Bullets and Billets*, p. 130.

³ Peter Davies, *Colonel Lawrence and others on* Her Privates We, [pamphlet], 1930, Derek Patmore Collection, H.R.H.R.C.

⁴ Ibid.

⁵ *Sun*, (Sydney), 21 May 1937.

⁶ F.M. to T.E.L., 11 March 1930, *Letters to T. E. Lawrence*, ed. A. Lawrence, p. 128.

⁷ F.M. to T.E.L., 26 March 1930, *Letters to T. E. Lawrence*, ed. A. Lawrence, p. 131.

⁸ F.M. to T.E.L., 21 March 1922, *Letters to T. E. Lawrence*, ed. A. Lawrence, pp. 127-8.

⁹ T.E.L. to E. M. Forster, 8 September 1927, Lawrence, *The Letters of T. E. Lawrence*, ed. Garnett, p. 536.

¹⁰ To Alan Bird, 23 October 1953, *A Passionate Prodigality*, p. 96.

¹¹ *Since Fifty*, p. 83.

¹² 'The Gilded Coach', MSS 2594/2, item 3, Frederic Manning papers.

22 Persephone's Realm

¹ To Robert Graves, 23 January 1933, Lawrence, *T. E. Lawrence to his Biographers*, ed. Graves and Hart, p. 760. Ernest Altounyan, a minor poet, was also a friend of E. M. Forster.

² Lawrence, *The Mint*, p. 150.

³ 5 March 1930, Lawrence, *T. E. Lawrence to his Biographers*, ed. Graves and Hart, part 2, p. 40.

⁴ 18 October 1930, in Lawrence, *Letters of T. E. Lawrence*, ed. Garnett. p. 704.

⁵ F.M. to T.E.L., 29 October 1930, *Letters to T. E. Lawrence*, ed. A. Lawrence, p. 139.

⁶ Dobrée, 'Imaginary Conversations' and Review of *Scenes and Portraits*; Forster, Review of *Scenes and Portraits* and Her Privates We, *Daily Telegraph* (London), 16 December 1930.

⁷ 'Apologia Dei', *Scenes and Portraits*, 2nd ed., p. 287.

⁸ F.M. to T.E.L., 28 August 1931, 21 December 1931, *Letters to T. E. Lawrence*, ed. A. Lawrence, p. 142.

⁹ To W.R., 14 October 1931, William Rothenstein collection.

¹⁰ Ibid.

¹¹ To T.E.L., 23 March 1934, *Letters to T. E. Lawrence*, ed. A. Lawrence, p. 145.

¹² T.E.L. to F.M., 25 July 1934, Frederic Manning papers.

¹³ To W.R., 5 May 1935, Lawrence, *The Letters of T. E. Lawrence*, ed. Garnett, p. 870.

¹⁴ Obituary, *Criterion*, April 1935, p. 436.

¹⁵ Review of *Eidola*, p. 281.

¹⁶ 'Farewell to Two Poets', p. 219.

¹⁷ Fairfax, *The Fifth Element*.

¹⁸ 'Soldier and Artist'.

¹⁹ Ibid.

23 Kore's Harvest

[1] 'The Manning Revival', p. 229.

[2] Ibid.

[3] McCarthy, 'Exiles, Expatriates and Internal Emigres', *Listener,* vol. 86, 1971, pp. 705-8.

[4] *Writers in Exile*, p. 9.

[5] Ibid., p. 145.

Select Bibliography

Works by Frederic Manning

Books

The Vigil of Brunhild. London, Murray, 1910.
Scenes and Portraits. London, Murray, 1909; 2nd ed. London, Peter Davies, 1930.
Poems. London, Murray, 1910.
Eidola. London, Murray, 1917.
The Life of Sir William White. London, Murray, 1923.
The Middle Parts of Fortune. London, Peter Davies Piazza Press, 1929.
Her Privates We. London, Peter Davies, 1930.
Introduction to Walter Charleton's translation of *Epicurus, His Morals.* London, Peter Davies, 1926.

Articles and Reviews

'Carmen, et quelques autres nouvelles de Prosper Mérimée'. *Monthly Criterion*, vol. 6, November 1927, pp. 448-55.
'Catullus: The Complete Poems'. *Criterion*, vol. 4, June 1926, pp. 603-5
'Christianisme'. *Criterion*, vol. 3, January 1925, pp. 320-1
'Critic and Aesthetic'. *Quarterly Review*, July 1924, pp. 123-44.
'The Dean of St Paul's' in William Rothenstein. *Twenty-four Portraits.* London, 1920 [unpaged.]
'Faith and Discipline'. *New Criterion*, vol. 4, June 1926, pp. 590-3.
'A French Criticism of Newman'. *New Criterion*, vol. 4, January 1926, pp. 19-31.
'Greek Historical Thought'. *Criterion*, vol. 3, April 1925, pp. 134-7.
'Ibsen'. *Daily Telegraph* (Sydney), 3 November 1900, p. 11.
'Le Père Hyacinthe'. *Criterion*, vol. 2, July 1924, pp. 460-7.
'Libertinism and St Évremond'. *New Statesman*, 3 September 1921, pp. 593-4.

'M. de Gourmont and the Problem of Beauty'. *Little Review,* vol. 5, February-March 1919, pp. 19-26.

'A Note on Sir James Frazer'. *The Monthly Criterion,* vol. 6, September 1927, pp. 198-205.

'Poetry in Prose'. *Chapbook* (London), no. 22, 1921, pp. 10-15.

'The Poetry of Mr Binyon'. *Piccadilly Review,* 23 October 1919, p. 7.

'Some Contemporary Poets'. *Cornish Brothers Illustrated Christmas Catalogue of Books,* 1911, pp. 58-9.

'Three fables'. *Coterie,* no. 4, Easter 1920, pp. 17-19.

'An Unionist's *Apologia'. Nation,* 23 March 1919, pp. 773-4.

Reviews in the Spectator

This list is by courtesy of the Librarian of the *Spectator,* Charles Seaton.

1909

| 18 December | 'Shakespearean Criticism', pp. 1055-56. |

1910

16 April	'Milton', pp. 625-6
2 July	'Southey's Poems', pp. 22-3.
23 July	'The Genius of Swift', pp. 134-5.
10 September	'A French Critic on Lyly', pp. 391-2.
8 October	'George Sand', pp. 560-1.
22 October	'The Etruscans', pp. 651-2.
29 October	'Balzac and the "Comédie Humaine"', pp. 694-5.

1911

28 January	'Two Books of Italian Verse', p. 119.
18 March	'The Correspondence of Swift', pp. 402-3.
1 April	'The Work of J. M. Synge', pp. 482-3.
22 April	'The Influence of Greece', pp. 602-3.
20 May	'Mr Zangwill's Fantasies', p. 72.
17 June	'The Memoirs of the Countess Golovine', pp. 930-1.
24 June	'Molière malgré lui', pp. 969-70.
8 July	'William Morris', pp. 69-71.
19 August	'Samuel Rogers', pp. 283-4.
2 September	'Lafcadio Hearn in Japan', pp. 346-7.
23 September	'Coleridge', pp. 458-9.
7 October	'Robert Louis Stevenson', pp. 549-50.
14 October	'On Translating Dante', pp. 599-600.
23 December	'French Poetry', p. 1123.
30 December	'Shelley', pp. 1154-5.

1912

27 January	'The Symposiarch', pp. 153-4.
16 March	'French Literature', pp. 444-5.
30 March	'The Elizabethans', pp. 514-15.
13 April	'Gray', pp. 586-7.
27 April	'De Contemptu Mundi', pp. 647-8.

1 June	'John Andrew Doyle', pp. 874-5.
22 June	'The Literature of Power', pp. 991-2.
13 July	'Travel and Pilgrimage', pp. 59-60.
27 July	William Langland, pp. 130-1.
7 September	'Novels of Character and Environment', pp. 335-7.
28 September	'English Prose Rhythm', pp. 543-54.
19 October	'The Borgia Family', pp. 601-2.
9 November	'Tales of Autolycus', pp. 752-3.
23 November	'Letters of William Allingham', pp. 861-2.
7 December	'Meredith's Poems', pp. 931-2.
21 December	'The Poetry of Coleridge', pp. 1063-4.
1913	
11 January	'Richelieu', pp. 64-5.
15 March	'The Crock of Gold', pp. 453-4.
12 April	'Swift's Friendships', pp. 618-9.
1 November	'Lyric Poetry', p. 683.
1 November	'Frederick Tennyson', p. 721.
1914	
10 January	'Formal Poetry', pp. 58-9.
4 April	'The Poetry of Blake', p. 567.
25 April	'Cesare Borgia', pp. 702-3.
16 May	'Spenser's Sonnets in French', p. 835.
27 June	'The Age of Johnson', pp. 1091-2.
4 July	'A Life of Francis Thompson', pp. 18-19.
1915	
24 July	'The Poet as Virtuoso', pp. 114-15.
1919	
20 December	'Rhythm in Verse', p. 864.
1920	
10 January	'Some Winchester Letters', pp. 51-2.
3 April	'Prosody and Shakespeare', pp. 459-60.

Poems

Not reprinted in collections

'Animae Suae'. *Literary Digest* (New York), 3 April 1926 (first published in *Irish Statesman*, 20 February 1926, p. 736).

'At Even'. *Poetry* (Chicago), June 1913, p. 100.

'Bal Masque'. *Living Age* (Boston), 1 September 1906 (first published in *Outlook.rom*, 19 May 1906, p. 686).

'Hera Parthenia'. *English Review*, vol. 5, May 1910, p. 196.

'The Secret'. *Living Age* (Boston), 20 October 1906 (first published in *Outlook*, vol. 17, 16 June 1906, p. 814.)

'To Artemis the Destroyer'. *English Review*, vol. 5, May 1910, p. 197.

'The Vision of Demeter'. *English Review*, vol. 8, April 1911, p. 7.

Reprinted in collections under changed titles.

In *Eidola*
'Anacreontic'. *Poetry*, January 1917, revised as 'The Cup'.
'Danae's Song'. *Forum*, February 1911, as 'Danae'.
'The Faun's Call'. *Poetry* (Chicago), June 1913, revised as 'The Faun'.
'Passe-pied'. *Spectator*, 26 April 1913, as 'Hurleywayne'.
In *Poems*
'Hecate'. *Spectator*, 12 March 1910, as 'Canzone'.
'Persephone'. *English Review*, December 1909, as 'Kore'.

Manuscript Sources

Frederic Manning papers. Mitchell Library, Sydney. Includes letters from T. E. Lawrence to Manning, 25 February 1930–16 November 1934.
James G. Fairfax papers. National Library of Australia, Canberra. MS 1750. 1-505. Contains 64 letters from Frederic Manning.
Albert Houtin correspondence. Bibliothèque Nationale, Paris. Contains 60 letters from Frederic Manning.
Harriet Monroe *Poetry* correspondence. Regenstein Library, University of Chicago. Contains letters from Frederic Manning, Ezra Pound and Richard Aldington.
Henry Newbolt collection. Beinecke Rare Book and Manuscript Library, Yale University, New Haven, Connecticut. Contains 19 letters from Frederic Manning.
Derek Patmore collection. Harry Ransom Humanities Research Center, The University of Texas at Austin. Contains 10 letters from Frederic Manning to Richard Aldington.
Ezra Pound papers. Beinecke Rare Book and Manuscript Library, Yale University, New Haven, Connecticut. Contains 35 letters from Frederic Manning.
William Rothenstein collection. Houghton Library, Harvard University, Cambridge, Massachusetts. Contains 73 letters from Frederic Manning.
Letters of John Addington Symonds. Harry Ransom Humanities Research Center, University of Texas at Austin.
Other manuscripts as cited in the text.

Newspapers

Bulletin (Sydney). 1890–1935.
Sydney Morning Herald. 1888–1935.

Books

Ackroyd, Peter. *T. S. Eliot*. London, 1984.
Adams, Francis. *The Australians: A Social Sketch*. London, 1893.

Aiken, C. P. *Scepticisms.* New York, 1919.

Aldington, Richard. *Death of a Hero.* London, 1929.

———. *Lawrence of Arabia: A Biographical Enquiry.* London, 1969 (first published 1955).

———. *Letters of Richard Aldington to Charles Clinch Bubb*, ed. Dean H. Keller. Francestown, New Hampshire, 1988.

———. *Life for Life's Sake.* London, 1968.

———. *Literary Lifelines. Richard Aldington–Lawrence Durrell Correspondence*, ed. Ian MacNiven and Harry T. Moore. New York, 1981.

———. *A Passionate Prodigality: Letters to Alan Bird from Richard Aldington 1949–1962*, ed. M. J. Benkovitz. New York, 1975.

———. *The Religion of Beauty: Selections from the Aesthetes.* London, 1950.

———. *Richard Aldington: Selected Critical Writings 1928-1960*, ed. Alister Kershaw. Carbondale, Illinois, 1970.

Bairnsfather, Bruce. *Bullets and Billets.* London, 1916.

Barnard, Marjorie. *The Story of a City.* Melbourne, 1956.

Baylebridge, William [William Blocksidge]. *An Anzac Muster.* Sydney, 1962 (first published 1921).

Bean, C. E. W. *Anzac to Amiens.* Canberra, 1946.

Beerbohm, Max. *A Catalogue of the Caricatures*, comp. Rupert Hart-Davis. London, 1972.

———. *The Happy Hypocrite.* London, 1897.

———. *Seven Men.* London, 1919.

———. *Things New and Old.* London, 1923.

———. *Zuleika Dobson.* London, 1911.

Bell, Quentin. *Virginia Woolf,* London, 1972.

Benkovitz, Miriam. *Ronald Firbank: A Biography.* London, 1970.

Benson, A. C. *Edwardian Excursions*, ed. David Newsome, London, 1981.

Bergonzi, Bernard. *Heroes' Twilight: A Study of the Literature of the Great War,* London, 1965.

———. *T. S. Eliot.* New York, 1972.

Birch, Alan and Macmillan, David. *The Sydney Scene.* Melbourne, 1962.

Birkin, Andrew. *J. M. Barrie and the Lost Boys.* London, 1979.

Blunden, Edmund. *Undertones of War.* London, 1928.

Bowen, Stella. *Drawn from Life.* London, 1984 (first published 1941).

Boyd, Martin (as Martin Mills). *Brangane: A Memoir.* London, 1926.

———. *Day of my Delight: an Anglo-Australian Memoir.* Melbourne, 1965.

———. *A Difficult Young Man.* Melbourne, 1965 (first published 1955).

——— (as Martin Mills). *Love Gods.* London, 1925.

———. *Lucinda Brayford.* Melbourne, 1969 (first published 1946).

———. *Outbreak of Love.* London, 1957.

———. *Retrospect.* Melbourne, 1920.

———. *A Single Flame.* London, 1939.

———. *When Blackbirds Sing.* Melbourne, 1962.

Brittain, Vera. *Testament of Youth*. London, 1978 (first published 1933).

Broadbent, James. *The Golden Decade of Australian Architecture: The Work of John Verge*. Sydney, 1978.

Brophy, Brigid. *Prancing Novelist*. London, 1973.

Camus, Albert. *The Plague*, trans. Stuart Gilbert. London, 1972 (first published Paris, 1947).

Carrington, Charles. *Soldier from the Wars Returning*. London, 1965.

———— (as Charles Edmonds). *A Subaltern's War*. London, 1929.

Cecil, David. *Max: A Biography*. Boston, 1965.

Charlesworth, Barbara. *Dark Passages: The Decadent Consciousness in Victorian Literature*. Madison, Wisconsin, 1965.

Chisholm, A. R. *Men were my Milestones*. Melbourne, 1958.

Clark, C. M. H. *A History of Australia*. Vols. 4, 5, Melbourne, 1978, 1981.

Clive, H. P. *Pierre Loüys. A Biography*. Oxford, 1978.

Crane, Stephen. *The Red Badge of Courage and Other Stories*. London, 1960 (first published 1895).

Croft-Cooke, Rupert. *Feasting with Panthers*. London, 1967.

Davenport, Guy. 'Persephone's Ezra'. In Eva Hesse, ed., *New Approaches to Ezra Pound*. Berkeley, California, 1969.

David, Mary Edgeworth. *Passages of Time*. St Lucia, Queensland, 1975.

Davies, Peter. *Colonel Lawrence and others on* Her Privates We [pamphlet]. London, 1930.

DeLaura, David. *Hebrew and Hellene in Victorian England*. Austin, Texas, 1969.

Desmond, Valerie. *The Awful Australian*. Melbourne, 1911.

Dobrée, Bonamy. *Modern Prose Style*. London, 1930.

————. 'T. S. Eliot a personal memoir'. In Allen Tate, ed., *T. S. Eliot*. London, 1967.

Dos Passos, John. *First Encounter*. New York, 1920.

Downes, William Howe. *John S. Sargent and his Work*. London, 1926.

Dyson, Will. *Artist among the Bankers*. London, 1933.

————. *Australia at War*. London, 1918.

————. *Cartoons*. London, 1913.

————. *Kultur Cartoons*. London, 1915.

Eliot, T. S. *The Letters of T. S. Eliot*, ed. Valerie Eliot. Vol. 1, 1898-1927. London, 1988.

————. *The Waste Land*. London, 1922.

Fairfax, J. G. *The Fifth Element*. London, 1937.

————. *The Gates of Sleep and Other Poems*. London, 1906.

————. *Poems*. London, 1908.

————. *The Troubled Pool and Other Poems*. London, 1911.

Falls, Cyril. *War Books*. London, 1930.

Firbank, Ronald. *The Complete Firbank*. (Introduction by Anthony Powell.) London, 1973.

Firkins, Peter. *The Australians in Nine Wars*. New York, 1972.

Fitzherbert, Margaret. *The Man who was Greenmantle: A Biography of Aubrey Herbert.* London, 1983.

Ford, Ford Madox. *Parade's End.* (Introduction by Robie Macauley.) London, 1982 (first published 1924–28).

Forster, E. M. *Goldsworthy Lowes Dickinson.* New York, 1962 (first published 1934).

———. *Howard's End.* London, 1910.

———. *The Life to Come and Other Stories.* London, 1972.

———. *The Longest Journey.* London, 1907.

Fox, Frank. *Australia: Painted by Percy F. S. Spence. Described by Frank Fox.* London, 1910.

Freeman, Hilda. *An Australian Girl in Germany.* Melbourne [1916].

Froude, J. A. *Oceana*, ed. G. Blainey. Sydney, 1985 (first published 1886).

Furphy, Joseph (as Tom Collins). *Such is Life.* Sydney, 1903.

Fussell, Paul. *The Great War and Modern Memory.* New York, 1975.

Galton, Arthur. *Acer in Hostem.* Windermere, England, 1913.

——— ed. *The Annals of Tacitus. The Reign of Tiberius.* London, 1890.

———. *The Appeal of the Church of England.* London, 1905.

———. *The Character and Times of Thomas Cromwell.* Birmingham, 1887.

———. *Church and State in France, 1300–1907.* London, 1907.

———. *English Prose from Mandeville to Thackeray.* London, 1888.

———. *The Message and Position of the Church of England.* London, 1899.

———. *Our Attitude towards English Roman Catholics and the Papal Court.* London, 1902.

———. *Protestantism of the Reformed and Catholic Church in England.* London, 1901.

———. *Rome and Romanizing: Some Experiences and a Warning.* London, 1900.

———. *A Thought for Each Day.* Birmingham, 1911.

———. *Two Essays upon Matthew Arnold.* London, 1897.

———. *Urbana Scripta: Studies of Five Living Poets.* London, 1885.

Garnett, David. *The Flowers of the Forest.* London, 1955.

Gaunt, William. *The Aesthetic Adventure.* London, 1945.

Gerster, Robin. *Big-Noting: The Heroic Theme in Australian War Writing.* Melbourne, 1987.

Goldring, Douglas. *The Last Pre-Raphaelites.* London, 1948.

Graves, Robert. *Goodbye to All That.* London, 1981 (first published 1929).

Green, Martin. *Children of the Sun: A Narrative of the Decadence in England after 1918.* London, 1977.

Grover, Philip, ed. *Ezra Pound. The London Years. 1908-1920.* New York, 1976.

Gurr, Andrew. *Writers in Exile: The Identity of Home in Modern Literature.* Brighton, England, 1981.

Harper, George Mills. *W. B. Yeats and W. F. Horton: The Record of an Occult Friendship.* London, 1980.

Hemingway, Ernest. *A Farewell to Arms.* London, 1929 (first published New York).

———— ed. *Men at War: The Best War Stories of All Time.* New York, 1979 (first published 1942).

Herbert, A. P. *The Secret Battle.* (Introduction by John Terraine.) Oxford, 1982 (first published 1919).

Herbert, Aubrey. *Mons, Anzac and Kut.* London, 1919.

Heyman, David C. *Ezra Pound: The Last Rower.* London, 1976.

Hobby Horse (London), vols 1–7 (January 1886–October 1892). New series, nos 1-3 (1893).

Hogue, Oliver. *Love Letters of an Anzac.* London, 1916.

————. *Trooper Bluegum at the Dardanelles.* London, 1916.

Holloway, David, ed. *Dark Somme Flowing: Australian Verse of the Great War, 1914-18.* Melbourne, 1987.

Homberger, Eric. 'Modernists and Edwardians'. In *Ezra Pound. The London Years*, ed. P. Grover. New York, 1976.

Hone, Joseph. *W. B. Yeats. 1865-1939.* London, 1962.

Horder, Mervyn, ed. *Ronald Firbank: Memoirs and Critiques.* London, 1977.

Houtin, Albert. *Alfred Loisy: Sa Vie, Son Oeuvre.* Paris, 1960.

————. *Une Vie de Pretre: Mon Experience 1867-1912.* Paris, 1926.

Hunt, John Dixon. *The Pre-Raphaelite Imagination. 1848–1900.* London, 1968.

Hussey, Maurice, ed. *Poetry of the First World War.* London, 1967.

Hutchins, Patricia. *Ezra Pound's Kensington.* London, 1965.

Hyde, H. Montgomery. *The Other Love.* London, 1970.

————. *Solitary in the Ranks: Lawrence of Arabia as Airman and Private Soldier.* New York, 1978.

Hynes, Samuel. *Edwardian Occasions.* New York, 1972.

————. *The Edwardian Turn of Mind.* Princeton, New Jersey, 1967.

Jackson, Holbrook. *The Eighteen Nineties.* New York, 1922.

Johnson, Lionel. *The Complete Poems of Lionel Johnson*, ed. Iain Fletcher. London, 1953.

————. *Some Winchester Letters.* (Introduction by Francis, Earl Russell.) London, 1919.

Jones, Alun R. *The Life and Opinions of T. E. Hulme.* London, 1960.

Joyce, James. *The Letters of James Joyce*, ed. Richard Ellman. London, 1966.

Jünger, Ernst. *The Storm of Steel*, trans. B. Creighton. London, 1930 (first published Hanover, 1920).

Kelly, Max, ed. *Nineteenth-century Sydney: Essays in Urban History.* Sydney, 1978.

————. *Paddock Full of Houses.* Sydney, 1978.

Kenner, Hugh. *The Pound Era.* London, 1972.

————. *Wyndham Lewis*. London, 1954.

Kershaw, Alister and Temple, P. J., eds. *Richard Aldington: An Intimate Portrait*. Carbondale, Illinois, 1965.

Keynes, John Maynard. *Two Memoirs*, ed. David Garnett. London, 1949.

Klein, Holger, ed. *The First World War in Fiction*. London, 1976.

Lago, Mary M. and Beckson, Karl, eds. *Max and Will: Max Beerbohm and Will Rothenstein, Their Friendship and Letters 1893-1945*. London, 1975.

Laird, J. T. *Other Banners*. Canberra, 1971.

Landor, Walter Savage. *The Complete Works*, ed. T. Earle Welby. London, 1927.

Languth, A. J. *Saki: A Life of Hector Hugh Munro*. Oxford, 1982.

Lawrence, A. W., ed. *Letters to T. E. Lawrence*. London, 1966.

Lawrence, T. E. *The Letters of T. E. Lawrence*, ed. David Garnett. New York, 1939.

————. *The Mint*. London, 1973 (first published New York, 1936).

————. *The Seven Pillars of Wisdom*. London, 1978 (privately printed 1926, first edition 1935).

————. *T. E. Lawrence to his Biographers*, ed. Robert Graves and Liddell Hart. London, 1963.

Le Gallienne, Richard. *The Romantic '90's*. London, 1925.

Levy, Paul. *G. E. Moore and the Cambridge Apostles*. Oxford, 1981.

Lewis, Wyndham. *Blasting and Bombardiering*. Los Angeles, 1967 (first published 1937).

————. *Letters*, ed. W. K. Rose. London, 1963.

Lind, Ruby. *The Drawings of Ruby Lind*. London, 1920.

Lindsay, Jack. *The Roaring Twenties*. London, 1960.

Loisy, Alfred. *The War and Religion*, trans. with Preface by Arthur Galton. Oxford, 1915.

Loüys, Pierre. *Aphrodite*. New York, 1933 (first published 1896).

McCarthy, Mary. *Occasional Prose*. London, 1985.

Macdonald, Lyn. *Somme*. London, 1983.

Mack, John E. *A Prince of our Disorder: The Life of T. E. Lawrence*. Boston, 1976.

Mack, Louise. *An Australian Girl in London*. London, 1902.

————. *A Woman's Experiences in the Great War*. London, 1915.

Mackenzie, Compton. *My Life and Times*. London, 1967.

McKinney, J. P. *The Crucible*. Sydney, 1935.

McMullin, Ross. *Will Dyson*. Sydney, 1984.

Mann, Leonard. *Flesh in Armour*. Melbourne, 1932.

Marsh, Edward. *A Number of People: A Book of Reminiscences*. London, 1939

Marwil, Jonathan. *Frederic Manning: An Unfinished Life*. Sydney, 1988.

Mee, Arthur. *Lincolnshire*. London, 1970.

Mérimée, Prosper. *Tales*. London, 1929.

Meyers, Jeffrey. *The Enemy: A Biography of Wyndham Lewis*. London, 1980.

———. *Homosexuality and Literature. 1890-1930*. London, 1977.

Moers, Ellen. *The Dandy: Brummel to Beerbohm*. London, 1960.

Monsman, Gerald. *Walter Pater*. Boston, 1977.

Moran, Herbert. *Viewless Winds*. London, 1939.

Mullins, Eustace. *That Difficult Individual, Ezra Pound*. New York, 1961.

Murphy, William. *Prodigal Father*. Ithaca, New York, 1978.

Murray, Gilbert. *An Unfinished Autobiography*. London, 1960.

Newbolt, Henry. *My World as in My Time*. London, 1932.

Nowell-Smith, Simon, ed. *Edwardian England*. London, 1964.

O'Farrell, Patrick, ed. *Documents in Australian Catholic History*. 2 vols. London, 1969.

Oliver, H. J. *Louis Stone*. Melbourne, 1968.

Palmer, Nettie. *Fourteen Years: Extracts from a Private Journal, 1925-1939*. Melbourne, 1948.

Palmer, Vance. *Intimate Portraits*, ed. H. P. Heseltine. Melbourne, 1969.

———. *The Legend of the Nineties*. Melbourne, 1954.

Partridge, Eric. 'Frank Honywood, Private' in *Three Personal Records of the War*. London, 1929.

——— (as Corrie Denison). *Glimpses*. London, 1928.

Pater, Walter. *Imaginary Portraits*. London, 1910.

———. *Letters*, ed. Lawrence Evans. Oxford, 1970.

———. *Marius the Epicurean*. London, 1885.

———. *Miscellaneous Studies*. London, 1910.

———. *Studies in the History of the Renaissance*. London, 1873.

Patmore, Bridget. *My Friends When Young*, ed. Derek Patmore. London, 1968.

Patrick, Arthur. *Lionel Johnson (1867-1902) Poète et Critique*. Paris, 1939.

Pearsall, Ronald. *Edwardian Life and Leisure*. Newton Abbott, Devon, 1973.

———. *The Worm in the Bud*. New York, 1969.

Pound, Ezra. *The A.B.C. of Reading*. London, 1934.

———. *Ezra Pound and Dorothy Shakespear: Their Letters 1909-1914*, ed. Omar Pound and A. Walton Litz. New York, 1985.

———. *Gaudier-Brzeska: A Memoir*. New York, 1970 (first published in *Blast* (London) July 1915).

———. *Guide to Kulchur*. London, 1966.

———. *The Letters of Ezra Pound 1907-1941*, ed. D. D. Paige, London, 1952.

———. *Literary Essays*, ed. T. S. Eliot. London, 1954.

———. *Pound-Joyce Letters. The Letters of Ezra Pound to James Joyce*, ed. Forrest Reid, London, 1967.

———. *Pound-Lewis: The Letters of Ezra Pound and Wyndham Lewis*, ed. Timothy Materer. New York, 1985.

———. *Selected Prose. 1909-1965*, ed. William Cookson. London, 1973.

———. *Some Letters of Ezra Pound*, ed. by Louis Dudek. Montreal, 1974.

———. *The Spirit of Romance*. New York, 1968 (first published 1910).

Pringle, John Douglas. *On Second Thoughts: Australian Essays*. Sydney, 1971.

Quinn, Vincent. *Hilda Doolittle (H.D.)*. New York, 1967.

Rachewiltz, Mary de. *Discretions*. London, 1971.

Ramson, W. S., ed. *The Australian Experience: Critical Essays on Australian Novels*. Canberra, 1974.

Read, Donald. *Edwardian England*. New Brunswick, New Jersey, 1982.

——— ed. *Edwardian England. 1901–1915*. London, 1972.

Read, Herbert. *The Innocent Eye*. New York, 1947.

Régnier, Henri de. *Les Jeux Rustiques et Divins*. Paris, 1926 (first published 1897).

Robinson, Janice. *H.D. The Life and Work of an American Poet*. Boston, 1982.

Ross, Robert H. *The Georgian Revolt: Rise and Fall of a Poetic Ideal. 1910-1922*. London, 1967.

Rothenstein, John. *Summer's Lease: An Autobiography*. London, 1965.

Rothenstein, William. *Men and Memories. 1900-1922*. Vol. 2. London, 1931-32.

———. *Portrait Drawings of William Rothenstein 1889-1925*, ed. John Rothenstein. London, 1926.

———. *Since Fifty. Men and Memories. 1922-1938*. Vol. 3. New York, 1940.

———. *Twenty-four Portraits*. London, 1920.

Rutherford, Andrew. *The Literature of War: Five Studies in Heroic Virtue*. London, 1978.

Sackville-West, Vita. *The Edwardians*. London, 1906.

Saki. *The Complete Works of Saki*. London, 1983.

Samuels, Ernest. *Bernard Berenson: The Making of a Connoisseur.* Cambridge, Massachusetts, 1978.

Santayana, George. *The Middle Span*. New York, 1945.

Sassoon, Siegfried. *Diaries 1915-1918*, ed. Rupert Hart-Davis. London, 1983.

———. *Memoirs of a Fox-hunting Man*. London, 1928.

———. *Memoirs of an Infantry Officer.* London, 1930.

———. *Siegfried's Journey. 1916-1920*. London, 1946.

Scott, Geoffrey. *The Architecture of Humanism*. London, 1929.

———. *A Box of Paints*. London, 1923.

———. *The Portrait of Zelide*. London, 1925.

Secrest, Meryle. *Being Bernard Berenson*. New York, 1980.

Selver, Paul. *Orage and the New Age Circle*. London, 1959.

Shorthouse, J. H. *The Life and Letters of J. H. Shorthouse*, ed. by his wife. London, 1905.

Sisson, C. H. *English Poetry 1900-1950: An Assessment.* London, 1971.

Skidelsky, Robert. *John Maynard Keynes.* Vol. 1. London, 1985.

Smith, C. N. 'The Very Plain Song of It'. In *The First World War in Fiction,* ed. Holger Klein. London, 1976.

Smith, Vivian. *Vance Palmer.* Melbourne, 1971.

Souter, Gavin. *Lion and Kangaroo: The Initiation of Australia, 1901-1919.* Sydney, 1976.

Speaight, Robert. *William Rothenstein.* London, 1962.

Spender, Stephen. *Eliot.* London, 1975.

Stanford, Derek, ed. *Pre-Raphaelite Writing.* London, 1973.

Stephen, Adrian Consett. *An Australian in the R.F.A.* Sydney, 1918.

Stern, J. P. *Ernst Jünger: A Writer of our Time.* Cambridge, 1953.

Strachey, John St Loe. *Adventure of Living.* London, 1922.

Strachey, Lytton. *Landmarks in French Literature.* London, 1912.

———. *Spectatorial Essays.* London, 1964.

Stock, Noel. *The Life of Ezra Pound.* New York, 1970.

———. *Poet in Exile.* Manchester, 1964.

Sweetser, Wesley. *Arthur Machen.* New York, 1964.

Symonds, John Addington. *Letters of John Addington Symonds,* ed. Herbert M. Schueller and R. Peters, Detroit, 1969.

———. *The Memoirs of John Addington Symonds,* ed. Phyllis Grosskurth. London, 1984.

Thompson, Paul. *The Edwardians.* London, 1975.

Thwaite, Ann. *Edmund Gosse: A Literary Landscape 1849-1928.* London, 1984.

Tomlinson, H. M.. *All Our Yesterdays.* London, 1930.

Twopeny, R. E. *Town Life in Australia.* London, 1883.

Ward, A. C. *The Nineteen-twenties.* London, 1930.

Ward, Russell. *The Australian Legend.* Melbourne, 1946.

The Webbs' Australian Diary, ed. A. G. Austin. Melbourne, 1965.

West, Rebecca. *1900.* London, 1982.

Wilde, Oscar. *The Letters of Oscar Wilde,* ed. Rupert Hart-Davis. London, 1962.

Williamson, Henry. *The Patriot's Progress.* London, 1930.

Wilson, Trevor. *The Myriad Faces of War.* Cambridge, England, 1986.

Wise, Bernhard. *The Commonwealth of Australia.* London, 1910.

Wohl, Robert. *The Generation of 1914.* Cambridge, Massachusetts, 1979.

Wood, W. de B. *History of the King's Shropshire Light Infantry in the Great War.* London, 1925.

Yeats, W. B. *Memoirs,* ed. Denis Donoghue. London, 1972.

Journal Articles.

Aiken, Conrad. Review of *Eidola. Dial,* vol. 65, 1918, p. 70.

Aldington, Richard. 'Australian Revaluations: An Introduction to Frederic

Manning'. *Australian Letters*, vol. 2, June 1959, pp. 26-30.

———. 'On Frederic Manning'. *Coterie* (London), no. 4, 1920, pp. 15-16.

———. 'Poetry from the Trenches'. *Dial*, vol. 62, 17 May 1917, pp. 426-47.

———. 'The Prose of Frederic Manning'. *Egoist*, vol. 1, 1 October 1914, pp. 374-6.

———. 'Remy de Gourmont'. *Little Review*, vol. 5, February-March 1919, pp. 32-4.

Army Quarterly. Review of *Her Privates We*, vol. 20, April 1930, pp. 177-8.

Bennett, Arnold. Review of *Her Privates We*. *Evening Standard*, 23 January 1930.

Bergonzi, Bernard. 'Before 1914'. *Critical Quarterly*, vol. 6, 1964, pp. 126-34.

Boyd, Martin. 'Dubious Cartography'. *Meanjin*, vol. 23, 1964, pp. 5-13.

———. 'Preoccupations and Intentions'. *Southerly*, vol. 2, 1968, pp. 83-90.

Clunies-Ross, Bruce. 'Frederic Manning and the Tragedy of War'. *Overland*, no. 75, 1979, pp. 45-9.

Cody, Richard. [Frederic Manning and 'Kore']. *Newsletter of the Friends of the Amherst College Library*, nos 5(2)-6(1), Fall 1977, [unpaged].

Collingwood, R. C. 'Two Books on Epicurus'. *Monthly Criterion*, vol. 6, October 1927, pp. 369-72.

de la Mare, Walter. Review of *Poems*. *Bookman*, vol. 38, 1910, p. 258.

Dobrée, Bonamy. 'Imaginary Conversations'. *Spectator*, 3 January 1931, p. 21.

———. Review of *Scenes and Portraits*. *Criterion*, vol. 10, 1931, pp. 733-6.

Eliot, T. S. Obituary of Frederic Manning. *Criterion*, vol. 14, April 1935, p. 436.

Fernandez, Ramon. 'The Experiences of Newman: Reply to Frederic Manning'. *Criterion*, vol. 4, October 1926, pp. 645-58.

Fussell, Paul. Review of *The Middle Parts of Fortune*. *New York Times Review of Books*, 23 October 1977, p. 26.

Galton, Arthur. 'An Examination of Certain Schools and Tendencies in Contemporary Literature'. *Hobby Horse*, vol. 4, 1889, pp. 98-108.

———. 'Assisi'. *Hobby Horse*, vol. 1, 1886.

———. 'Government House'. *National and English Review* (London), vol. 36, December 1900, pp. 537-44.

———. 'Matthew Arnold. April 15, 1888' [poem]. *Hobby Horse*, vol. 4, 1889, p. 70.

———. 'The Poetical Works of Matthew Arnold'. *Hobby Horse*, vol. 6, 1891.

———. Review of John Addington Symonds, *The History of the Renaissance in Italy*. *Hobby Horse*, vol. 2, 1887.

————. Review of Lady Wilde, *Ancient Legends of Ireland. Hobby Horse*, vol. 2, 1887.

————. 'Some Letters of Matthew Arnold'. *Hobby Horse*, vol. 5, 1890, pp. 47-55.

————. 'Some Modern Literature'. *Cosmos* (Sydney), vol. 1, September 1894, pp. 23-9.

————. 'Some thoughts about that "Movement", which it is the present fashion to describe too absolutely as "The Renaissance", and to admire inordinately'. *Hobby Horse*, vol. 5, 1890, pp. 15-27.

————. 'To the Century Guild' [poem]. *Hobby Horse*, vol. 1, 1886, p. 87.

————. 'Walter Pater: An Attempt at Appreciation'. *Nadirian* (Brisbane), vol. 1, 1894, pp. 52-7.

Gellert, Leon. 'Case of Private 19022'. *Sydney Morning Herald*, 13 March 1948.

Haq, Kaiser. 'Forgotten Fred: a Portrait of Frederic Manning'. *London Magazine*, vol. 23, December 1983-January 1984, pp. 54-78.

————. 'The Poetry of Frederic Manning'. *Journal of Commonwealth Literature*, vol. 20, 1985, pp. 1-16.

Hergenhan, L. T. 'Ezra Pound, Frederic Manning and James Griffyth Fairfax'. *Australian Literary Studies*, vol. 11, 1983-4, pp. 395-400.

————. 'Frederic Manning: A Neglected Australian Writer'. *Quadrant*, vol. 6, no. 4, 1962, pp. 5-18.

————. 'Novelist at War: Frederic Manning's *Her Privates We*'. *Quadrant*, vol. 14, July-August 1970, pp. 19-29.

————. 'Some Unpublished Letters from T. E. Lawrence to Frederic Manning'. *Southerly*, vol. 23, 1963, pp. 245-52.

————. 'Two Expatriates: Some Correspondence from Frederic Manning to James Griffyth Fairfax'. *Southerly* vol. 39, 1979, pp. 59-95.

Hulme, T. E. (as North Staffs). 'War Notes'. *New Age*, selected issues 2 September 1915-13 January 1916.

Kaeppel, Carl. 'Frederic Manning. Soldier, Scholar, Artist'. *Australian Quarterly*, vol. 26, June 1935, pp. 47-50.

————. 'Soldier and Artist'. *Sydney Morning Herald*, 8 January 1939.

Klein, Holger M. 'In the Midst of Beastliness: Concepts and Ideals in Manning's *Her Privates We*'. *Journal of Commonwealth Literature*, vol. 12, December 1977, pp. 136-52.

————. 'The Structure of Frederic Manning's War Novel.' *Australian Literary Studies*, vol. 6, 1973-74, pp. 404-17.

Laird, J. T. 'Australian Poetry of the First World War: A Survey'. *Australian Literary Studies*, vol. 4, 1969-70, pp. 241-50.

————. 'Australian Prose Literature of World War I: A Survey'. *Australian Literary Studies*, vol. 5, 1971–72, pp. 146-57.

————. 'A Check List of Australian Literature of World War I'. *Australian Literary Studies*, vol. 4, 1969-70, pp. 148-63. Revised vol. 12, 1985-86, pp. 275-87.

Lindsay, Jack. Review of *The Middle Parts of Fortune*. *Times Literary Supplement*, 9 April 1975, p. 423.

Macainsh, Noel. 'Baylebridge, Nietzsche, Shaw: Some Observations on the "New nationalism".' *Australian Literary Studies*, vol. 7, 1975-76, pp. 141-59.

Mann, Leonard. Review of *Her Privates We*. *Overland*, no. 31, March 1965, p. 47.

Marwil, Jonathan. 'Combative Companions'. *Helix*, nos 13-14, 1983, pp. 8-15.

———. 'Frederic Manning's Passionate Perfection'. *Sydney Morning Herald*, 25 November 1978.

Monroe, Harriet. 'Farewell to Two Poets'. *Poetry*, vol. 46, 1935, pp. 219-21.

———. Review of *Eidola*. *Poetry*, vol. 16, 1919, p. 281.

Morgan, Patrick. 'The Paradox of Australian Nationalism'. *Quadrant*, vol. 24, March 1980, pp. 7-10.

Morley, Christopher. Obituary of Frederic Manning. *Saturday Review of Literature*, 18 May 1935, p. 15.

Murray-Smith, Stephen. 'The Manning Revival'. *Australian Book Review*, vol. 3, 1964, p. 229.

Palmer, Nettie. 'Almost Ours'. *Bulletin*, 22 March 1933, The Red Page.

Parfitt, George. 'Frederic Manning and the Great War'. *Journal of Commonwealth Literature*, vol. 16, 1981, pp. 87-95.

Partridge, Eric. 'The War Comes into Its Own'. *The Window*, vol. 1, no. 1, 1930, pp. 72-104.

———. 'The War Continues'. *The Window*, vol. 1, no. 2, 1930, pp. 62-84.

Phillips, A. A. 'Barbara Baynton and the Dissidence of the Nineties'. *Overland*, no. 22, December 1961, pp. 15-20.

Pound, Ezra. Review of *The Vigil of Brunhild*. *Book News Monthly*, vol. 27, April 1909, pp. 620-1.

———. 'A List of Books'. *Little Review*, vol. 4, March 1918, p. 55.

Prichard, William. 'Telling Stories'. *Hudson Review*, vol. 31, Autumn 1978, p. 525.

Read, Herbert. 'Books of the Quarter'. *Criterion*, vol. 9, July 1930, pp. 763-9.

Rothenstein, William. Obituary of Frederic Manning. *The Times*, 28 February 1935, p. 17 (early editions only).

Smith, Graeme Kinross. 'Leonard Mann - a profile'. *Australian Literary Studies*, vol. 7, 1975-76, pp. 324-7.

Stromberg, Ronald. 'The Intellectuals and the Coming of War in 1914'. *Journal of European Studies*, vol. 3, 1973, pp. 109-22.

Taylor, Mark. 'Bourne again'. *Commonweal* (New York), vol. 106, 19 January 1979, pp. 26-7.

'Thinkers and Ironists' [Review of *Scenes and Portraits*]. *Edinburgh Review*, October 1909, pp. 442-6.

Wallace-Crabbe, Chris. 'Joseph Furphy: Realist'. *Quadrant*, vol. 5, no. 2, 1961, pp. 49-56.

White, Patrick. 'The Prodigal Son'. *Australian Letters*, vol. 1, no. 3, 1958, pp. 37-44.

Index